Purpose and Thought

Purpose and Thought
The Meaning of Pragmatism

John E. Smith

New Haven
Yale University Press 1978

Published in the United Kingdom and Commonwealth
by Hutchinson & Co (Publishers) Ltd
First published in the United States of America in 1978
by Yale University Press

Printed in Great Britain

Library of Congress Cataloging in Publication Data

Smith, John Edwin.
  Purpose and thought.

  Includes bibliographical references and index.
  1. Pragmatism. I. Title.
B832.S6 1978   144′.3   78–399
ISBN 0-300-02171-2

Contents

Acknowledgements

I am happy to have an opportunity to express my gratitude to two of my old friends and former teachers, James Gutmann and Herbert Schneider. The former conducted the first seminar in philosophy I attended when an undergraduate in Columbia College. I recall that we began with Plato's *Euthyphro* and the discussions we had about ethical issues left a vivid impression on my mind. The latter was responsible for introducing me to the study of the traditions of philosophy in America and especially the thought of Royce which, in turn, led me on to his contemporaries. I wish to thank my wife, Marilyn, who is a teacher of philosophy at the University of Hartford, for her enormous help in eliminating many of my double-jointed phrases and superfluous expressions thus making a clearer text. I am indebted to Mr Rob Deltete who is a graduate student in the History of Science programme at Yale for his painstaking reading of proofs and for saving me from a few errors on matters scientific. Lastly, I wish to thank Mrs Alan Slatter for her patience and diligence in typing the manuscript through two drafts.

John E. Smith

New Haven, Conn.
January 1978

Introduction

A new philosophical idea or theory, said William James, is received by its critics according to a pattern which can be recited in advance. First the novel conception is regarded as either unintelligible or outrageous or both; next it is said to be understandable, but obvious or trivial, and, finally, when the doctrine has become more familiar, those who initially opposed it claim that they discovered it first. This ironic summary has turned out to be a prophetic account of the odyssey of Pragmatism itself. The cluster of ideas known as Pragmatism was at the outset the subject of vigorous criticism at the hands of Russell, Moore, and, more profoundly, F. H. Bradley. Behind their criticism was the sense that the pragmatists made knowledge and truth thoroughly dependent on human needs and interests. Such subjectivism seemed to them monstrous and destructive of all critical thought. In the course of the succeeding decades the position came to be better understood, although, as it turned out, mainly for purposes of refutation. With the appearance of A. J. Ayer's *The Origins of Pragmatism* the discussion came full circle. According to Ayer, Pragmatism was 'thought to be a distinctly American product', whereas the truth is that it has 'fairly deep roots in the history of philosophy', and, if he was right, one of these roots reaches all the way back to Protagoras' doctrine that 'man is the measure of all things'.[1]

We need not pursue the comparison further; the important point is that the time is now ripe for a second look at the pragmatic movement, a reflective presentation aimed at producing a better understanding of what Pragmatism means both for advocates and critics. It is not necessary to suppose, as James frequently did, that all or most of the critical objections to Pragmatism were due to misunderstandings of what its advocates meant to say, but it would have to be admitted that much of the ensuing polemics expressed a greater concern to demolish than to understand. The pragmatists were partly to blame for the confusions engendered by their position. James, with his vivid imagination and arresting language, often used expressions which were either misleading or designed to confirm the prejudices of critics. His characterization of the true as 'the expedient in the way of knowing' at once conjures up connotations of 'calculating', 'self-indulgent' – in short, the determination of truth by appeal to individual interest and advantage – which stand clearly opposed to the impersonality, objectivity and timelessness classically attributed to truth. Peirce restated his views many times and frequently resorted to cryptic forms of expression which multiply the problems of interpretation. His celebrated pragmatic maxim with its reference to effects which 'might conceivably have practical bearings'[2] does not seem clear on a first reading and Peirce himself found it necessary to clarify it by explaining how much its meaning depends on 'conceivable' and cognate terms. Dewey did nothing to refute the thesis that the pragmatists must bear some responsibility for the fact that they were misunderstood and their doctrines caricatured. His tendency to spin an almost impenetrable web about an idea or distinction which calls instead for special clarification does not make him easy to read. His choice of the term 'doubtful', for example, to express the crucial concept of the 'problematic situation' led to that concept itself becoming doubtful in a sense not intended; critics like Russell and others never could see how a situation could be 'doubtful' except in the sense that it includes some thinker who is in doubt. This is precisely what Dewey did not mean, although it must be admitted that his choice of an intentional term to describe a 'situation' opened the door to confusion.[3]

The pragmatists, on the other hand, must not be asked to bear a disproportionate share of the blame for the misinterpretation of their views. Some of their main contentions were bound to be given that sort of unsympathetic treatment which hostility engenders, because the fact is that they were thinking against the stream. Their insistence on an intimate connection between action and thought ran counter to a long tradition in which all intellectual endeavour was seen as pure, theoretical knowing determined by a distinctly noetic ideal independent of the knower's activity and of the consequences following from acting in accordance with the knowledge gained. The idea of connecting thought with practical consequences and with the transforming of situations through an instrumental intelligence was taken to be a sure sign that thought had been deprived of its autonomy and that the essential message of Pragmatism could be summed up in the formula 'All thought is for the sake of action'. Or again, the pragmatists' emphasis on the role of purpose and will in thinking, and in the formation of belief, was set in opposition to long-standing logical ideals of objective and dispassionate thought with the result that Pragmatism was often identified with the doctrine that somehow the truth of a proposition is coincident with the fact that it is believed, or worse, that a proposition *becomes* true as a result of a passionate willing to believe that it *is* true. As will become clear, these interpretations are caricatures of Pragmatism which, as has been suggested, are partly the result of the unguarded way in which the pragmatists expressed themselves, and partly of the hostile frame of mind created by the sense that Pragmatism represented nothing more than a new subjectivism and relativism subversive of traditional patterns of thought. In order to redress the balance and achieve a fair and judicious perspective, it is by no means necessary to claim that the critics have all been mistaken and that the central theses of Pragmatism are beyond reproach. All that is needed is a persistent attempt to set forth those central theses as clearly as possible so that they can be reappraised in the light of current patterns of thought. In this way we may hope to avoid refutations of Pragmatism based on caricatures, or defences based on nothing more than the claim that the critics have misunderstood the position.

In attempting to set forth the meaning of Pragmatism, I should like to concentrate as far as possible on fundamental conceptions rather than on historical connections and developments. That there is some mystery surrounding the 'origins' of Pragmatism – largely because Peirce and James took turns at declaring each other to be the founder of some form of the position – is well known. Happily, a number of scholars have examined this problem with the greatest care; since I have nothing further to add to their conclusions, the reader is advised to consult their work. I shall concentrate on the following topics: the pragmatic theory of meaning and its relation to the 'practical', the theory of truth as expressed chiefly by Peirce and James, the meaning of experience developed by Dewey and by James in his 'radical empiricism', Pragmatism as a fundamental philosophical outlook, and some social, ethical and religious implications of this novel way of thinking. Along the way, I shall attempt to make clear the extent of the influence of natural science on the pragmatic philosophy.

Before proceeding further, there is something to be gained by considering briefly the reasons for reappraising Pragmatism at the present time. At least three reasons present themselves. To begin with, there is the fact that the nature of action and its relation to thinking and to knowing are major issues on the current scene. The political theory of Marxist writers, the involvement of social scientists in policy decisions and programmes of social engineering, and perplexing issues in biomedical ethics and ecology all testify to this fact. The relation between knowledge, belief and action was central in the writings of all the pragmatists. Secondly, at a number of critical points in modern technological culture, the question of the relation between natural science and human values has been given a sharp and urgent focus. That question was not only a basic concern of William James, but was *the* central problem of Dewey's entire philosophical work. Time and again, he returned to the predicament in which modern man has been placed as a result of the basic fact that the scientific outlook has radically transformed traditional moral and religious beliefs and values without providing any clear indication of what values and ideals are to be put in their place. Thirdly, Pragmatism is a philosophy of *experience,* a fact which at once links the position with the philosophy of existence, with phenomenology and, I would add, with the Wittgenstein who demanded that we return to the actual situation for a 'second look' and the Wittgenstein who proposed, as he said, 'possibilities of which you had not previously thought'. The appeal to what experience actually discloses, what James called 'the particular go of things', is at the centre of Pragmatism and that appeal serves as a powerful warning to would-be 'empiricists' for whom experience is less a disclosure of *what is* than an illustration of what *must be* if some philosophical programme is to be carried through successfully. Moreover, as will become clear, the meaning attached by the pragmatists to the term 'experience' is not to be identified with the account of experience to be found in the British empiricist tradition. Peirce and Dewey especially, and James to a lesser but still important extent, understood experience as richer and more complex than was possible within the confines of the traditional empiricism stemming from Hume, Mill and Russell.[4] Anyone who supposes that Pragmatism, in opposition to various forms of rationalism and absolute idealism, was chiefly an extension of the old empiricism, will be inclined to approach the position by seeking its answers to all the traditional 'epistemological' questions which formed the substance of that empiricism.[5] And to make that mistake is at the same time to overlook the fundamental sense in which the theory of knowledge, and especially the belief that it is the inescapable starting point of all philosophical thought, was being subjected to vigorous attack. Dewey at times even proposed to regard the traditional epistemological problems, not as perennial problems at all, but rather as historically conditioned questions that arose only as the result of assuming that experience is coextensive with the immediate knowing of ideas directly present to the mind. It is not that Dewey had no interest in the nature of knowing and knowledge; it is rather that he was unsympathetic to the 'epistemological' approach which for him meant starting with ideas which are 'internal' and then asking how we are to reach the 'external world'. In place of this approach, Dewey proposed a *methodological* solution to the problem of knowing, a solution thoroughly dependent on his reconstructed conception of experience.

The preceding point is of the utmost importance for any attempt at a reconsideration of Pragmatism at the present time. For the enterprise is not likely to be successful if it is undertaken solely against the background of the essentially epistemological questions which have been uppermost in the philosophical thinking of the past forty years. The reason is quite clear: Peirce and Dewey especially were reacting against the belief that the theory of knowledge as conceived by both traditional empiricism and rationalism forms a necessary starting point for philosophical thought. Therefore, in taking a second look at Pragmatism, it is necessary to return to original conceptions in relation to the problems which the pragmatists envisaged and sought to resolve. We must not suppose that their thought will be understood if we can succeed in discovering their answers to the questions posed by recent academic philosophy. The resources to be found in the pragmatic outlook for current thinking will become evident only when we succeed in recovering what the pragmatists had to say about their own questions and concerns. The succeeding chapters are meant to fulfil that aim.

ERRATA

p. 28, 3 lines from bottom 'possibilities' not 'possibilites'
p. 34, 4 lines from bottom 'trackless' not 'trackles'
p. 36, line 5 hyphen missing after 'our' at end of line
p. 40, line 14 some 12 blank spaces at end of line
p. 40, 8 lines from bottom 'falls' not 'fall'
p. 41, line 6 'seemed' not 's eemed'
p. 48, line 1 'or' not 'of'
p. 48, lines 16–17 from bottom should read 'on the other hand, paid far less attention to determining the validity of a world formula than he did to explaining the difference it would make if'
p. 56, 8 lines from bottom (*including* quoted lines) 'this' not 'his'
p. 61, line 19 'that' not 'than'
p. 93, line 26 'of' not 'on'
p. 111, line 30 'to' not 'o' and 'the' not 'he'
p. 111, line 31 'commonsense' not 'comonsense'
p. 121, 14 lines from bottom 'determinism' not 'determiminism'
p. 123, line 18 'theism' not 'thesim'
p. 137, line 8 'thirdness' not 'tiredness'
p. 175, lines 4–5 should read 'real but it is not the only way, and it is not appropriate to the being of God in Peirce's view to think in terms of the occupancy of a place among'

1 The pragmatic approach to meaning, belief and action: basic conceptions

It is difficult to imagine a discussion of Pragmatism which does not start with Peirce's 'How to Make Our Ideas Clear', a paper published exactly a century ago. Not only is this essay familiar to anyone who is acquainted with Pragmatism at all, but it also served as the backbone of James' California address in 1898, 'Philosophical Conceptions and Practical Results', in which he credited Peirce with being the father of the movement. Peirce himself regarded the essay as a basic statement of his views despite the fact that he later modified and clarified it and indeed went far beyond it in the development of his Pragmatism as a cosmic philosophy. Overworked as the category of the 'seminal' may be, 'How to Make Our Ideas Clear' certainly deserves to be so classified just because it was the seed from which has grown a comprehensive philosophical position and one that is still developing. The paper, moreover, provides a convenient focus for initiating discussion of Pragmatism because in emphasizing the attainment of clarity in thought it directs attention to the fact that the pragmatists regarded their position as a way of thinking as well as a set of insights about man and the world.

Peirce set out, not without characteristic touches of irony, with Descartes' two-fold distinction between clear and obscure ideas and between distinct and confused ideas. By clarity Peirce understood Descartes to mean a sort of direct apprehension or acquaintance with an idea such as would enable one to recognize it in varying circumstances and never mistake it for another idea. If, for example, one understands the meaning of the expression 'prime number' and is asked whether 32 is a prime number presumably one sees at once that the answer is 'no' because 32 is an even number larger than 2 and therefore is divisible by 2. Peirce, however, regarded this sort of acquaintance as no more than a subjective sense of having mastered an idea and one which could be mistaken. He took the fact that Descartes had introduced a second criterion – that of distinctness – as an indication that the first criterion is insufficient and stands in need of supplementation by a definition in abstract terms. Distinctness in Descartes' account amounts to the claim that there is nothing unclear about what is expressed in the definition of an idea. Peirce did not reject these criteria outright, but he was not satisfied with either of them taken in the sense in which Descartes understood them. Peirce had two objections in mind. He believed, first, that there is an important distinction between an idea 'seeming clear' and 'its really being so' and, second, as regards definitions, he insisted that nothing new is to be learned from analysing them. On the other hand, it would be unwise to overlook the fact that, despite his criticisms, Peirce did accept these two grades of clearness as essential for setting existing beliefs in order at the same time that he sought for a 'higher perspicuity' of thought which he called the third grade of clearness.

After 1890 Peirce carried the analysis still further in the quest for a fourth grade of clarity, a conception which seems to have been a critical response to James' development of the original pragmatic maxim into the thesis that 'the end of man is action'.[1] This move seems to be something of an overreaction on Peirce's part, for he already had enough to contend with in making clear his own pragmatic maxim which was supposed to reach the third grade of clarity. But the proposal of a still higher grade suggests not so much the idea of an increasing order of clarity but rather the sense that more important than grades of clarity is the problem of making clear what is meant by the appeal to action, practical consequences, etc., in achieving clarity of thought. Against James' thesis that the end of man is action, Peirce argued that action is unintelligible without an end or purpose and that neither can be set forth without appealing to something 'general' which is neither a fact nor a singular act. This line of thought is in accord with the original pragmatic maxim which emphasized the *upshot* of concepts and the idea of 'intellectual purport'. The essential point is that the practical facts to which the application of the pragmatic maxim leads must themselves be related to an ultimate good or what Peirce called the ideal of 'concrete reasonableness'.[2] This point is made explicitly in the following passage:

[the original pragmatic maxim for attaining the third grade of clearness] should always be put into practice with conscientious thoroughness, but that, when this has been done, and not before, a still higher grade of clearness of thought can be attained by remembering that the only ultimate good which the practical facts to which it directs attention can subserve is to further the development of concrete reasonableness ; so that the meaning of the concept does not lie in any individual reactions at all, but in the manner in which those reactions contribute to the development.[3]

Clarifying the pragmatic maxim as expressed in this essay can be more easily accomplished if we start by sorting out the two distinct lines of thought which Peirce introduced. On the one side there is the question of the function of thought as focused by such statements as 'the whole function of thought is to produce habits of action'[4] and, on the other, there is the maxim itself as a rule for attaining the third grade of clarity with respect to the 'intellectual purport' of concepts. The sense that Peirce was proposing to reduce all thought to action or that he was denying the validity of conceptual content not translated into acts has often prevented critics from understanding the maxim itself as a rational rule. One should, therefore, postpone consideration of the larger issue of the role of thought and concentrate on the clarification of the maxim. Following is the well-known original formulation:

Consider what effects, that might *conceivably* have practical bearings, we *conceive* the object of our *conception* to have. Then, our *conception* of these effects is the whole of our *conception* of the object.[5]

The entire point of this rule is that in conceiving of any *object* we are to conceive of the manner in which it would behave – effects having 'practical bearings' – in various conditions and circumstances. Notice that emphasis falls on the behaviour of the *object* and his claim is that the conception of that behaviour exhausts our conception of the object; there is no mention of any behaviour on the part of the conceiver although it is legitimate to regard the conceiving itself as an activity. In explaining his meaning further, Peirce pointed out that his repetition of the derivatives of *concipere* serves two purposes: first, to make clear that he was speaking of meaning in no other sense than that of 'intellectual purport', and secondly, to counteract the supposition that he meant to explain concepts 'by percepts, images, schemata, or by anything but concepts'.[6] Peirce, moreover, placed acts in the same category with percepts, images, etc., as far as the meaning of concepts is concerned precisely because acts in his view 'are more strictly singular than anything'; they can never constitute the 'adequate proper interpretation of any symbol'.[7] This statement should be sufficient to give pause to anyone tempted to suppose that Peirce identified the meaning of any thought with an act.

Peirce offered several illustrations of the pragmatic maxim aimed at showing how the third grade of clearness is actually reached. We are asked to consider 'what we mean by calling a thing *hard*'.[8] For an answer we must have recourse to the conceived effects of the objects in action and reaction with other things; a 'hard' object is one that will not be scratched by many other things and is capable of scratching objects 'softer' than itself. Peirce's move here may be described as a 'dynamizing' of predicates; instead of regarding an object as possessing a set of static or fixed characters often referred to as qualities – hard, dense, volatile, heavy – which are intuited or grasped in the fashion described by Descartes, we are to conceive the objects as *manifesting* these characters by producing effects in interaction with other things. If something is 'hard' it will behave, when put to the test, in ways different from a soft object and our conception of this behaviour is our conception of what it means for an object to be hard. Notice that Peirce is directing attention to what an object *would do* if it is characterized in a certain way; the process of testing is intimately bound up with the meaning of concepts and, since what would happen in such-and-such conditions makes a clear reference to an *outcome,* we have before us part of what the pragmatists meant when they spoke of 'fruits' and 'consequences'. A given liquid, for example, may be described as 'volatile'; what you conceive when you ascribe volatility to it is the rate at which it would actually evaporate under certain circumstances, a factor that can be determined only as the result of specific operations.

Peirce proposed a similar interpretation for the idea of weight. In both cases the appeal is to effects: 'to say that a body is heavy means simply that, in the absence of opposing force, it will fall.'[9] The meaning of the predicate in question is once again to be found in what an object would do in specific circumstances.

Peirce insisted that meaning must be sought in the relevant effects or consequences; in his discussion of the idea of force he criticized Kirchhoff for claiming that 'we understand precisely the effect of force, but what force itself is we do not understand'.[10] Peirce regarded this statement as self-contradictory on the ground that if we know what the effects of force are, 'we are acquainted with every fact which is implied in saying that a force exists, and there is nothing more to know'. Later on, however, he was to express dissatisfaction with his earlier view; he saw that he had involved himself in the error of 'nominalism'.[11] This error consists in identifying the 'intellectual purport' of the concept, and hence the reality in question, with the set of *singular effects* which exhibit that purport on some specific occasion. 'I must show,' he wrote (c. 1910), 'that the *will be's*, the actually *is's* and the *have been's* are not the sum of the reals. They only cover actuality.' In addition, the real includes the *would be's* and the *can be's;* the actual, he said, is subject to both the principle of contradiction and of excluded middle, and, while there is one sense in which the *would be's* and the *can be's* are also subject to both (i.e. a *would be* is the negation of a *can be*, and conversely) there is another sense in which a *would be* is not subject to the principle of excluded middle because both *would be x* and *would be not x* may be false. *Can be,* moreover, is regarded as not subject to the principle of contradiction, since if it is only true of anything that it *can be x,* then it *can be not x* as well. Peirce's case, to be sure, does not rest entirely on these few logical distinctions; his doctrine of thirdness, his Scotistic realism and his evolutionary metaphysic all point in the direction of supporting the thesis that 'the universe does contain both *would be's* and *can be's'.*[12] In revising his position of the 1870s he was concerned chiefly to point out that too much emphasis had been placed on what has been, what is and what will be, to the neglect of what can and would be.[13] The ontological bearing of these two modes must not be dissipated in epistemological interpretations. Peirce was not arguing for a phenomenalism aimed at the construing of some actual state of affairs solely in terms of what an *observer* 'would' see or experience if he were co-present with it. Peirce's insistence on the reality of the modes was meant to underline the objective traits, capacities and habits of the things which make up the natural world; his claim was that the nature of these things cannot be expressed adequately in terms of the wholly determinate, present, and actual occasions on which they manifest themselves.

From Peirce's repeated contrast between 'seminary' or school philosophy on the one hand, and 'laboratory' modes of thought on the other, it is clear that he was attempting to ground his rule for attaining the third grade of clarity in the experimental procedures of science.[14] And although he made provision for the contribution of ordinary experience through what he called 'critical commonsensism', there is no denying that science constituted his model for thought. Evidence for this point is furnished by Peirce's application of the pragmatic maxim in his account of the meaning of 'reality'. He regarded the idea of reality as one that is familiar in the first instance in the sense that everyone confidently distinguishes between a 'real' orange which contains juice and pulp and an 'artificial' orange made of wax. When, however, we come to the second grade of clarity which requires a definition in abstract terms, the matter is more difficult. He nevertheless proposed such a definition declaring the real to be 'that whose characters are independent of what anyone may think them to be'.[15] This essentially realistic position is one he consistently maintained, but it must be understood in the light of the idealistic feature introduced by Peirce's qualification of 'independent'. We shall return to the point presently, but first we must note Peirce's dissatisfaction with either familiarity or an abstract definition for making clear the idea of the real and the consequent need to appeal to the pragmatic rule. According to this rule, reality must consist 'in the peculiar sensible effects which things partaking of it produce'.[16] One effect of real things is to induce belief and the question then is: How is true belief (or belief in the real) distinguished from false belief (or belief in fiction)?[17] When the question of truth and falsity is introduced we need a method for settling opinion which is determined by fact and logical principles quite independent of the interests and predilections of any individual or any finite group of individuals. Peirce took it to be the basic presupposition, sometimes expressed as a 'cheerful hope', held by members of the scientific community that 'the process of investigation, if only pushed far enough, will give one certain solution to each question to which they apply it'.[18] The examples he drew from the history of science make it clear that he regarded this presupposition or 'hope' as supported by the progress of actual scientific investigation and the convergence of opinion resulting from numerous inquiries proceeding along different lines. Consequently, he characterized the real as the object represented by the convergent opinion. 'The opinion,' he claimed, 'which is fated[19] to be ultimately agreed to by all who investigate is what we mean by the truth, and the object represented in this opinion is the real.'[20] Peirce, ever circumspect with regard to his own conclusions, was well aware of the possible conflict between the correlation of the real with an *opinion* and his previous abstract definition of the real as 'independent' of what anyone may *think* it to be. Peirce's attempt to harmonize the two views is characteristic of his position as a whole: reality, he said, is independent, not of 'thought in general', but of the thought of any individual or finite collection of individuals; hence while what the real object is known as depends on the convergent opinion which is reached, that object itself does not depend on what any individual or finite collection of individuals thinks.[21] The view expressed can be seen as a form of objective idealism. If the real is in every respect independent of thought, then the real cannot be known, but that dependence of reality on thought which knowledge requires involves neither an individual finite knower nor an absolute mind as in the case of Berkeley or Hegel, but rather the convergent opinion of a community of investigators. To the objection that the convergent opinion or truth could be established as a convention by the members of this community, Peirce's reply was that this is not possible because the investigators as such are determined by experimental procedures and logical principles leading to results which they do not control and which are themselves under the constraint of what Peirce called the 'independent reals'. We see in this version of Pragmatism a replacement of the idealist identity of truth and reality in the Absolute by a social theory of reality and a theory of truth based on those opinions which come to be accepted by a community of scientific investigators, with every member under the constraint of the subject matter plus the same logical principles and experimental procedures.

Whatever confusions may be engendered by Peirce's numerous, and frequently different, statements of his Pragmatism, it is clear that the original pragmatic maxim was aimed primarily at the determination of the *meaning* of an idea, a proposition or a concept. In the course of elucidating the maxim and of applying it as a device for attaining the third grade of clearness, Peirce was led to introduce a cluster of other concepts – belief, doubt, action, practical consequences, intellectual purport, and truth – each of which must be clarified if we are to arrive at a comprehensive grasp of what Pragmaticism meant for him. The chief difficulty is that these concepts are all interrelated and, at times, Peirce seems to define one or more of them in terms of the others so that in attempting to elucidate them separately, we run some risk of distorting his view. On the other hand, he regarded the relevant concepts as distinct and some advantage is to be gained from considering them one at a time.

Central to the pragmatic maxim is the idea of effects which conceivably have 'practical bearings' and therefore it is essential to be clear about the meaning of 'practical consequences'.[22] To begin with, Peirce frequently stated that, with respect to any two conceptions, if it can be discovered that they involve different practical consequences the two conceptions must differ in meaning, or at least they cannot be said to have the same meaning. Thus we are told that 'we come down to what is tangible and conceivably practical, as the root of every real distinction of thought, no matter how subtle it may be; and there is no distinction of meaning so fine as to consist in anything but a possible difference of practice'.[23] The question now is: What does this 'practice' mean? I believe that Peirce was never wholly clear nor consistent in his answer to this question; much-depends on the extent to which we emphasize those passages in which a clear distinction is drawn between the context of science and experimental inquiry where the aim is the disclosure of fact, and the context of 'practice' where the aim is to 'wrestle' with facts for the purpose of controlling the situation and realizing human purposes in the world.

In 'Methods for Attaining Truth' Peirce drew the contrast sharply: science 'takes an entirely different attitude towards facts from that which practice takes'[24] and, whereas the former 'regards facts as merely the vehicle of eternal truth', for the latter 'they remain the obstacles which it has to turn, the enemy of which it is determined to get the better'.[25] Practice, said Peirce, 'needs something to go on', and the proposition which for science stands as an hypothesis is regarded from the standpoint of practice as 'inductively supported' and as an object of belief which is here defined as 'the willingness to risk a great deal upon a proposition'.[26] But, Peirce continued, 'this belief is no concern of science which has nothing at stake in any temporal venture'.[27] Science is here seen as a purely theoretical affair, unaffected by any human concerns other than the desire to learn the secrets of nature; practice, on the other hand, requires belief and the short-run assurance that we actually possess objective truth or the closest approximation to it we can attain. We have here Peirce's clear apprehension of the role played by the passage of time in human life and experience. Science, when unencumbered by the need to solve essentially engineering problems, has 'all the time in the world' to pursue its ends, whereas 'practice' requiring decision and action at a definite time is limited by some present state of affairs and must be content with whatever 'knowledge' we possess at that time. Practice cannot wait until everything is known; moreover, practice requires 'belief' that x is, as far as we know, the case, and cannot be based merely on *considering* or *entertaining* conceptual content as happens in theoretical inquiry. If Peirce had consistently maintained this neat arrangement, the meaning of practical consequences for his Pragmatism would be much easier to determine than it actually is. For, in science, practical consequences would be concerned exclusively with the arrangement of facts which means the particular behaviour we are to expect from an object or a system under certain conditions: 'if something is soluble, it would . . .'; 'if something is an acid, it would . . .', etc. And within scientific inquiry, there would be no need to introduce the sense of 'practical consequences' involved when we are engaged in building bridges, designing a system of public health care or making the individual decisions which are required by the fact that we are responsible moral beings. In all these cases, what is in question is our behaviour as agents who must decide here and now what to do; we need to know not only what particular line of conduct is enjoined by a given belief, but also what consequences our actions will have so that we shall know what we are responsible for.

The fact is that not all of Peirce's pronouncements about practice and practical bearings presuppose the clearcut distinction between theoretical and practical concerns which he drew when he was opposing logical analysis and science to 'vitally important topics'. On the contrary, the major thrust of the pragmatic outlook was to overcome the separation and to bring thought and practice into an intelligible relation to each other. Hence in the end it will not do to interpret Peirce solely on the basis of the science–practice dichotomy, however tempting it may be to do so.

It seems clear that Peirce wanted to determine the meaning of a proposition in accordance with its having some conceivable bearing on the conduct of life; yet he continued to express doubt as to whether the meaning of a belief can be said to be *exhausted* by these practical bearings. Consider first the following claim from 'What Pragmatism Is': [28]

You will find that whatever assertion you may make to [the typical experimentalist], he will either understand as meaning that if a given prescription for an experiment ever can be and ever is carried out in act, an experience of a given description will result, or else he will see no sense at all in what you say.

Here the meaning of the assertion is identified with a future *experience* because it is the *result* of an operation that requires time and is not immediate. This view has an affinity with classical empiricism except that it does not appeal to immediate sensing or perceiving, but rather to a consequent and interpreted perceiving which results from manipulatory operations aimed at disclosing how an object or system will behave.[29] Peirce generalized this view of meaning with the theory:

that a *conception*, that is, the rational purport of a word or other expression, lies exclusively in its conceivable bearing on the conduct of life; so that, since obviously nothing that might not result from experiment can have any direct bearing upon conduct, if one can define accurately all the conceivable experimental phenomena which the affirmation or denial of a concept could imply, one will have therein a complete definition of the concept, and *there is absolutely nothing more in it*.[30]

The question at once is: What is to be meant by the 'conduct of life' and 'bearing upon conduct'? Is 'conduct' to include *all* that I do and say, whether in the laboratory or not? Is it to include on equal footing my placing the litmus paper in the solution and seeing it turn blue, and my behaviour towards another person based on the belief that, for example, he is an end in himself and must never be treated merely as a means? Is all and any 'conduct' in the sense of an overt doing, achieving, synthesizing in thought, manipulating, etc., meant to figure in the meaning of an assertion, or did Peirce mean that there is some type of conduct appropriate for the laboratory which is relevant for the meaning of an assertion without that assertion itself – for example, 'the atomic number of oxygen is 16' – having any obviously identifiable bearing upon my conduct outside the laboratory? Peirce was aware of these difficulties and in a passage which does not seem to have received as much attention as it deserves he met the problem head-on. 'What,' he asked, 'is the *proof* that the possible practical consequences of a concept constitute the sum total of the concept?'[31] Peirce was not here questioning his basic thesis that belief means acting in accordance with the formula believed. Rather, his question here is: 'Whether this is *all* that belief is, whether belief is a mere nullity so far as it does not influence conduct'.[32] And in answering his own question, Peirce set some absolutely crucial limits to what is to count as 'conduct' from the pragmatic standpoint.

His proposal was to ask 'what possible effect can it have on conduct' if one believes that the diagonal of the square is incommensurable with the side? This relationship cannot be expressed as a rational quantity and therefore there exists a genuine distinction between that relationship and any other which can be expressed as a rational quantity. 'Yet,' said Peirce, 'it seems quite absurd to say that there is any objective practical difference between commensurable and incommensurable.'[33] And he went on to deny that the act of expressing a quantity as a rational fraction counts as a piece of conduct and therefore differs practically from the act appropriate in cases where the quantity cannot be so expressed. The substance of the attack is that a thinker 'must be shallow indeed if he does not see that to admit a species of practicality that consists in one's conduct about words and modes of expression is at once to break down all the bars against the nonsense that Pragmatism is designed to exclude'.[34] From this it would appear that differences in logical operations or in ways of manipulating signs are *not* to count as differences in practice, or as differences affecting practical outcomes.

Peirce's next comment is not only instructive in itself, but important as well for calling attention to one of the basic motives behind Pragmatism. What the pragmatist wants to be able to say is this: 'here is a definition and it does not differ at all from your confusedly apprehended conception because there is no *practical* difference'.[35] But, said Peirce, if a person claims that there is a practical difference which consists simply in the fact that he recognises one conception as his own and not the other, we cannot stifle this claim, but we must also point out that 'Pragmatism is completely volatilized if you admit that sort of practicality'.[36]

Practice and practical differences, it would appear from the foregoing, must involve overt and public differences in the behaviour of the objects referred to in a particular belief and in that of the person who is called upon to prepare a reaction. Differences in pen and pencil operations or in logical modes of expression do not, for Peirce, constitute practical differences; neither do some forms of intentional 'acts' such as 'saying' with respect to two expressions (which are otherwise without 'practical differences' in some admissible sense) that they are different, or in 'claiming' that the practical difference consists in the ability to 'recognize' one as 'mine' in contrast to another which is not. Whether consistently or not, the main drift of Peirce's appeal to practical differences in determining the meaning of expressions was precisely to change the court of appeal from that of intuitive apprehensions made by the individual mind to that of a community of experience shared and compared. The shift from the individual to the social, however, by no means coincides with the difference between theoretical and practical. For in Peirce's view there are real differences in situations involving judgement, assertion, belief which do not qualify as 'practical' differences.

A second point raised by Peirce's statement of what the pragmatist wants to be able to say concerns cases where two expressions seem to have the same meaning but actually differ, and those where two expressions are meant to differ but actually do not. He had great confidence in the appeal to practical consequences as a way of bringing disputes about meaning to a public court of appeal without falling back on intuitive apprehensions. Since it was this side of Pragmatism which James developed in his attempt to find a way of assessing the relative merits of different philosophical theories, an example is relevant at this point.

In approaching rival philosophical positions James was trying to settle disputes which he regarded as otherwise 'interminable' and at the same time to deflate certain concepts in rationalist theories which he believed could not survive the test of practical consequences. In his pragmatic examination of some classic philosophical problems, James singled out such concepts as substance, cosmic design and freedom in order to discover whether their meaning could be determined by appeal to practical consequences. From the examples cited it appears that to be a practical consequence is the same as having some bearing on the future course of experience. 'Pragmatically,' said James, the abstract term 'design' is 'a blank cartridge' because it 'carries no consequences, it does no execution'.[37] James was, of course, assuming that God's existence based on some argument from design is a merely speculative or theoretical affair since no practical consequence for an individual's future action follows from the concept of a purposefully arranged cosmos already accomplished in the past. There is here a radical contrast between maintaining that something is (or has been) the case without regard to consequent human behaviour, and the consideration of what someone must do or is likely to experience in the future if he believes an idea which can have practical consequences. The concept of free will, by contrast with the idea of design, appeared to James as just the sort of idea which has the needed consequences and therefore is of special significance to the pragmatist. 'Free will,' he said, 'pragmatically means *novelties in the world*, the right to expect that in its deepest elements as well as in its surface phenomena, the future may not identically repeat and imitate the past.'[38] Here the practical consequences in question clearly have to do with how we are to act and what we may expect the future to be like if we believe that freedom is a reality. It is important to notice that the ascription of freedom is not the assigning of some present and immediately possessed characteristic like the redness of the ball on the shelf; it is rather the claim that an action or event *would* take place or come to be experienced if one acted on the conviction that freedom is not an illusion. As has been suggested, James' version of Pragmatism stressed not finished fact that is over and done with, but rather the *finishable* features of the universe where the future becomes central and human effort is called into play to help effect an outcome that would otherwise be different or not be at all. For this reason James could find no significance in any articulation of the structure of existence where that structure makes no demand on the human will. His voluntarism, coupled with a basic scepticism about the possibility of discussing metaphysical issues in objective terms, led him to set aside as insignificant all cosmological and theological concepts which cannot be translated into some form of effort leading to a specifiable outcome or consequence. But, as has frequently been pointed out, a consequence in this case does not mean a logical consequence of the idea in question but rather a practical consequence, i.e. an act, which should follow if a person believes that idea.

The other line of thought running through Peirce's essay concerns the relations between thought, belief, doubt and action and the point of departure for this topic is the second of Peirce's foundational papers, 'The Fixation of Belief'.[39] Like Dewey, Peirce regarded 'the irritation of doubt' which he correlated with hesitancy and irresolution as the occasion where thought is called into play so that its function is to remove the doubt and establish settled belief in its place. Action enters the picture because belief is understood in terms of habits of action or dispositions to act in accordance with certain patterns which are themselves initially determined by thought. For Peirce 'the sole motive, idea and function of thought is to produce belief'[40] and while he did not deny that there are *dilettanti* who think for pleasure and do not relish the idea that their favourite questions may ever finally be resolved, he attached great seriousness to the process of thought that is aimed at the overcoming of doubt. 'Thought in action,' he wrote, 'has as its only possible motive the attainment of thought at rest'[41] by which he meant an actual asserting of the propositional content together with a habit or volition as a *final* upshot. Thought which is at 'rest', however, may be only temporary as when some doubt has been resolved in a belief which in turn is beset by another doubt so that there is a new starting point for thought. It is clear from what Peirce said that the process must be a continual one for belief is a *rule* for action and the *application* of that rule will invariably engender further doubt. At this critical juncture, misunderstanding is inevitable if it is supposed that Peirce was *identifying* belief and action. He spoke of belief as a *rule* for action and a rule always consists in what he called 'intellectual purport' which can be expressed only in concepts. The surest way to avoid confusion is to recall that, for Peirce, action is *singular* in character and belief as a thought or rule for action is necessarily *general;* it follows that thought and action, however they are related, can never be identical.

The function of thought in producing belief and the consequent reference to both habit and action can be clarified by attending to the key question: What is the nature of belief? At this early point in the development of his thought Peirce described belief as having three properties: first, it is something of which we are aware in the way of propositional content – 'I believe that the prisoner was falsely accused'; second, it appeases an antecedent doubt, which is to say that the belief is an outcome of a critical process aimed at resolving a difficulty which previously stood in the way of accepting the belief; third, and most significant, a belief involves 'the establishment in our nature of a rule of action or . . . a *habit*'.[42] Once again one must bear in mind that Peirce was not identifying belief with action but only with a rule and even if the rule was identified by him with a habit which is other than thought, still his conception of a habit always involves something general ('thirdness') and is therefore shot through with thought. 'The final upshot of thinking is the exercise of volition,' he said, 'and of this thought no longer forms a part.'[43] We may leave aside for the present the difference between the role of action in determining whether someone actually believes a given thought content and its role in determining the meaning of that belief itself. The distinction is by no means unimportant; running through much of the literature of Pragmatism is the idea that actually believing some propositional content is not the same as 'saying' that one believes it; willingness to act, and, in the case of James especially, the assumption of some risk and responsibility for action in relation to a belief, represent essential indices of actual believing.

More important here, however, is the relevance of different habits or modes of action for determining differences in belief. In specifying the mode of action as the criterion for determining when beliefs are the same or different, Peirce was attempting to avoid allowing that 'mere differences in the manner of consciousness'[44] of beliefs can serve to make them different beliefs. Curiously enough the examples which he gives, though they make manifest reference to differences of consciousness, do not refer directly to modes of action but rather to factual arrangements among objects and to the nature of objects themselves. Obviously, much depends on whether 'modes of action' is meant to include the *action* of thought itself. It is extremely difficult to find in Peirce a precise and consistent answer on this head. In so many places, action and practice are described as the 'upshot of thought', and the 'exercise of volition' is said to be such that 'thought no longer forms a part' of it.[45] On the other hand, it is frequently asserted that 'thought is an *action*',[46] and it is clear from much of what Peirce said about logical self-control that the development of *habits* of thought figured importantly in his Pragmaticism.[47] He asks us to consider the following figures:

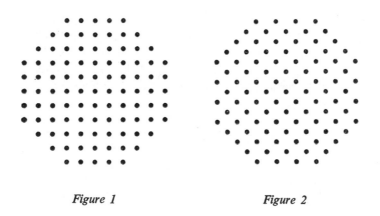

Figure 1 Figure 2

The objects, said Peirce, are arranged in exactly the same way in both figures, and to believe that they are arranged as in Figure 1, and that they are arranged as in Figure 2 is exactly the same belief, although it is possible that someone should assert one belief and deny the other. His claim was that to allow this possibility as a ground for the assertion that the beliefs are different is illegitimate. Two other examples are adduced: first, he said, we mistake the sensation produced by our own unclearness of thought for a feature of the object we are thinking about and thus suppose that there is something mysterious about this feature so that when the conception is finally presented in clear form we do not recognize it because the feeling of unintelligibility has vanished. From this example it is clear that Peirce was still pursuing his anti-Cartesian programme of directing attention away from consciousness and its manner of apprehending ideas and towards the object and the external arrangements in which it stands.

Another obstacle said to stand in the way of clear thought is the confusion of 'a mere difference in the grammatical construction of two words for a distinction between the ideas they express'.[48] It is interesting in this connection to note that Peirce referred to his own period as a 'pedantic age' in which more attention is paid to words than to things. As an example he referred to his own assertion that 'thought is an *action*, and, that it consists in a *relation*'.[49] There is, he claimed, no inconsistency involved because if one says that a person performs an action and not a relation he is merely calling attention to a 'grammatical vagueness' and not to a confusion in thought.

Peirce's basic remedy for avoiding the confusions which he believed were due to attending to the features and modes of consciousness[50] in the determination of meaning was an appeal to the *function* of thought in producing habits of action. Whatever is connected with a thought but is not relevant for this function forms no part of the thought itself. When Peirce's Pragmatism is understood as a way of attaining the third grade of clarity, the appeal to function becomes fundamental. In a note to be found in Peirce's interleaved copy of the *Century Dictionary* (c. 1902) he wrote: '*Pragmatism* is that method of reflection which is guided by constantly holding in view its purpose and the purpose of the ideas it analyses, whether these ends be of the nature and uses of action or of thought.'[51]

The drift of this position is clear: clarity of thought is a prospective affair in which one attends not to immediate consciousness and its content but to the ends or purposes at which the idea aims. Purpose appears in a double-barrelled form: there is, first the purpose or goal of the specific thought and the habits associated with it, and, second, there is the purpose of thought itself which is to produce habits of action. Purpose comes to function as a principle of selection or relevance, indicating what actually belongs to the meaning of a thought or what 'counts' as part of the thought in contrast with irrelevant associations which may attach to the thought simply because it is part of an individual consciousness involved in other aims and interests. This appeal to purpose and relevance in relation to thought is basic to Pragmatism in all its forms. If, for example, one were to define knowledge in the terms set forth by the Neo-Hegelians it would be necessary to envisage it as an all-encompassing system of logical determinations which is infinite not only because it is meant to express what is known by the Absolute, but infinite in the sense that from a purely theoretical standpoint there is no way to set a limit to the multiplication of details in any analytic process. Thus if I wished to express the spatial relations between *all* the parts of my pen and all the points on the sea-coast of China, without some purpose or selective principle in hand (e.g., that I do not count the specks of dust on my pen as parts of it) the process would have to continue without end. It was against the absolutist aim at a total or theoretical mirroring of *everything* in thought that Peirce, James, Dewey and even Royce with his 'absolute Pragmatism' argued for the need to find a way of arresting an otherwise endless advance – the bad infinite in Hegel's sense – and thus delineate a finite situation wherein it is possible to distinguish between what serves and what does not serve the purpose of reflective thought.

To understand the importance of this emphasis on the purpose or function of thought for the attainment of clarity in meaning, it is necessary to return to 'The Fixation of Belief' (1877) and Peirce's account of the relations between thought, belief, doubt, inquiry and action. Peirce, to be sure, later criticized this paper and its better-known companion piece for their 'nominalism' but both papers express what is basic for his Pragmatism; later criticism modified and clarified the original position without in the least setting it aside.

For Peirce all reflective thought starts with commonsense and begins not with some privileged idea or perception but rather, as he said, 'in *medias res*'. This means that everyone begins where he actually is and attempts to clarify the contents of a stock of beliefs already in hand. Wherever there is thought there is also the possibility of believing that such-and-such is the case or of doubting whether a given belief is in fact justified. Doubting and believing are seen as correlative so that Peirce's initial characterisation of doubt is given in terms of a contrast with belief. We know, as a rule, when we wish to ask a question as distinct from pronouncing a judgement, and there is, he argued, a decided difference between the *sensation* of doubting and that of believing. At the level of feeling or sensation, however, this difference does not constitute a 'practical' difference because no reference is made to habits of action. 'The feeling of believing,' Peirce said, 'is a more or less sure indication of there being established in our nature some habit which will determine our actions.'[52] Believing, for example, that human beings are never to be treated merely as a means is essentially connected with certain ways of behaving towards other persons which, as habits, are as much in our muscles as in our minds and are meant to exercise some control over the future. Doubting, on the other hand, carries with it no such effect since it arrests action and makes itself felt in the form of *hesitation*.[53] Though not as obviously bound up with action as belief, doubt is not to be entirely disconnected from action because it is a state which is uneasy and dissatisfied, a state from which we seek to free ourselves. Doubt is for Peirce the moving force which leads to the overcoming of itself and this overcoming is what is meant by inquiry, the third term between doubt and belief. With a doubt that is serious and not concerned merely with its own perpetuation as a form of professional scepticism there begins the struggle to attain belief from which alone action is possible. The triad of doubt, inquiry, belief forms the background of Peirce's well-known claim that 'the sole object of inquiry is the settlement of opinion'.[54] This claim has been the source of both opposition and confusion; Peirce was not unaware of the problems it raises.

To begin with, Peirce noted, it will be said that it is not mere opinion which is wanted, but a *true* opinion. Taken as an ideal, this demand is not one which Peirce rejected, but at the same time he could not accept it as a correct account of what actually happens in a larger number of cases. When firm belief is reached we are satisfied whether the belief be actually true or false because the doubt motivating inquiry has been appeased by 'a belief that we shall *think* to be true'.[55] Peirce was not asserting that the actual believing has anything to do with establishing the truth of the belief, but rather that in the absence of real doubt based on objective grounds for supposing that the belief might be false, inquiry does not continue; the belief reached is believed to be true. To the extent that no actual doubt is entertained, the belief remains firm.

It is not difficult to see that Peirce (and James as well in this respect) was accurately representing what actually takes place in the vast majority of situations involving doubt, belief and action in ordinary experience. Consider, for example, a person who discovers that several of his electrical appliances have suddenly ceased to function and supposes that a new fuse will overcome the difficulty. Being inexperienced, however, he tries to change the fuse without turning off the current and instead of remedying the situation he produces a display of electrical fireworks which leave a vivid impression on his mind. On a second try, he first turns off the main current, replaces the fuse and restores the current only to discover that all lights and appliances now fail to operate. In nine cases out of ten an individual in precisely that situation will believe at once that his first misguided effort was the cause of the ultimate failure and the more firmly this belief is held the less likely it is that he will entertain any doubt that would lead him to look for other possible explanations. 'I was so sure,' he will say, 'that what I did was responsible for the failure that it never occurred to me even to look for another cause.' The settled belief occupies the entire field of the mind and no others can gain admittance on the point. Suppose, however, it were later discovered that between his first and second efforts, a large transformer had broken down cutting off the electricity over a large area so that in the end his misguided effort had no effect at all on the outcome. What is the probability that an individual, actually experiencing the situation just described and having a vivid recollection of the electrical fireworks he had created, could *avoid believing* that his act was responsible and thus leave his thought open to the entertaining of such an unlikely possibility as actually was realized? After the fact, of course, it is quite easy to consider alternative explanations, but Peirce's point is that, in the actual situation, a firm belief will not only drive out rivals, it will stand in the way of even looking for them.

I do not find it illuminating, as apparently many do, to say that focusing on what people actually do in belief and action situations is merely 'psychological' in contrast to a 'logical' account which simply abstracts from the actual situation and considers the possibilities of belief and doubt in a purely theoretical context. In every occasion of experience, the 'rational' man must, to be sure, remain open to multiple possibilites of belief and action, but this openness itself has parameters determined by time, the urgency of the need to act, etc. For ordinary experience Peirce's main contention holds – when the settled belief taken for the truth is reached within the actual situation thought is at rest because there is no doubt to drive it further.

Having established the correlation of belief with the absence of actual doubt, Peirce concentrated on the nature of inquiry as the mediating factor between the two. He sought to find the most objective and reliable method of reaching opinions not only *thought* to be true, but opinions that have the best chance of actually being true because they represent the outcome of a public and self-correcting method. In citing what he called the methods of *tenacity, authority* and *agreeableness to reason* as ways of fixing belief, Peirce was again reflecting what he took to be the ways people actually reach and try to support their beliefs. He was aware, however, that a descriptive approach, though instructive, is not adequate; a critical or normative factor is needed. This factor appears in the form of an appeal to 'real things' and the ascertaining of the way things 'really are'. Not all methods for fixing belief are of equal validity because, as Peirce said, many people believe it is legitimate to determine belief by circumstances 'extraneous to the facts'[56] and this he rejected. The fact is that while Peirce was acutely aware of the grounds on which beliefs are frequently based, he aimed at setting forth the grounds on which they should be based. For the satisfaction of doubt, Peirce argued, 'it is necessary that a method should be found by which our beliefs may be determined by nothing human – by something upon which our thinking has no effect'.[57] For Peirce this is 'the method of science'.

No attempt need be made at this point to give a full account of Peirce's conception of scientific procedure for it extends over many papers and would involve discussion of such complex topics as induction, sampling, probability and abduction. More important at this juncture is to indicate in a general way the presuppositions of the method Peirce advocated and the grounds for his belief in its superiority over other methods for fixing belief. Science is said to rest on a fundamental hypothesis that there are 'real things' which affect the senses in accordance with regular laws that can be ascertained; a combination of knowledge of these laws, sufficient experience – by which Peirce meant the funded result of repeated encounters by many individuals – and reasoning will result in our reaching 'the one true conclusion'.[58] In a note added in 1893 Peirce cited an example which makes admirably clear how he understood the determination of opinion by experimental procedure. The first point is that changes of opinion come about 'by events beyond human control';[59] one can call this the 'realistic' dimension in Peirce's thought and he expressed it repeatedly in the idea that opinions are under constraint by what is not an opinion. 'All mankind,' he wrote, 'were so firmly of opinion that heavy bodies must fall faster than light ones, that any other view was scouted as absurd, eccentric, and probably insincere.'[60] How, then, is this opinion to be changed? Peirce's answer was that the 'laboratory men' must induce the proponents of commonsense opinion 'to look at their experiments' in order to discover that 'nature would not follow human opinion, however unanimous'.[61] The laboratory men, he said, learned the 'lesson in humility' because they saw 'that they had to abandon the pride of an opinion assumed absolutely final in any respect, and to use all their endeavors to yield as unresistingly as possible to the overwhelming tide of experience, which must master them at last'.[62] It is not only the particular opinion itself that is of significance, but the procedure whereby it is reached because this procedure furnishes the warrant for it. Referring back to the example of falling bodies, Peirce wrote, 'the trial of this method of experience in natural science for these three centuries . . . encourages us to hope that we are approaching nearer and nearer to an opinion which is not destined to be broken down.'[63] In this sense, experimental method justifies itself in virtue of the fact that its repeated and persistent application discloses the real and constrains us 'to listen to what nature seems to be telling us'.

If we consider the hypothesis on which the method of science is said to rest, and the relation of that method to the other ways of fixing belief, we can see how circumspect Peirce was in trying to avoid the simple circularity involved in invoking the hypothesis of 'reals' to support empirical method and at the same time using the method to support that hypothesis.[64] In attempting to resolve the problem, Peirce made four points which may be summarized as follows:

1. If empirical method cannot be said to prove that there are 'real things', it nevertheless does not lead to the contrary view; since the method and the conception on which it is based 'remain ever in harmony' no doubts about the method necessarily arise from following it. This is something which cannot be said about other methods.

2. Dissatisfaction in the face of two 'repugnant propositions' is the feeling which gives rise to any method for fixing belief; this feeling implies a vague admission that there is 'some *one* thing which a proposition should represent' or to which it should conform. The consequence is that no one can 'really' doubt that there are realities, since in that case doubt would not lead to the dissatisfaction just noted.

3. Everyone uses the scientific method in a large number of cases, and failure to do so occurs only when one does not know how to apply it.

4. Our experience of the method not only has not led us to doubt it, but its success in settling opinion actually explains why we doubt neither the method nor the hypothesis on which it rests.

It is important to notice that, with the exception of 2, each of these points presupposes an ongoing scientific enterprise and takes seriously into account what has actually been accomplished over the past three centuries in the way of gaining knowledge of the world through empirical inquiry. One can see in these four points both the appeal to success in attaining a goal as the justification of a way of knowing the world – an appeal associated with Pragmatism at all levels – and the appeal to realities that are to constrain opinion and overcome human waywardness and prejudice. It should be clear, therefore, that Peirce saw no such incompatibility between his Pragmatism and realism as was constantly alleged to exist by various schools of American realists.[65] Peirce took very seriously the point that whereas doubt may accrue to any particular proposition under investigation, the method of investigation itself as it is actually followed never leads necessarily to doubt about its effectiveness in fixing belief. The point at which the methods for fixing belief divide and the inadequacy of the other methods becomes manifest is when the question of self-criticism is raised. For Peirce empirical inquiry is the only method which 'presents any distinction of a right and a wrong way'.[66] The point is quite obvious as regards tenacity and authority, but less so in the case of *a priori* method; Peirce, as one can see, was undecided in his estimate of Hegel's philosophical method. It is not that he interpreted Hegel's philosophy as an attempt to construct the whole of reality in advance, as it were, on the basis of pure thought, but rather that he had a proper respect for the richness of his method of mediation and therefore he could not place it on the same level with the methods of tenacity and authority. With regard to beliefs based on tenacity, neither doubt nor error is possible because the method necessitates eliminating the influence of every alternative view to the one held fast by the believer. Authority, moreover, cannot be applied incorrectly because the only test allowed by the method itself is what the authority states. In both cases Peirce was surely right in seeing that the elimination of mediation at once disposes of the possibility of criticism.

He claimed that the same is true of the *a priori* method so closely associated with philosophical thought, but this case is not so obvious since it is not clear what Peirce meant by being 'agreeable to reason'. Nor is it easy to say whether he believed in a sharp distinction between what we find ourselves 'inclined to believe' and 'that which agrees with experience'. In short, his characterisation of the *a priori* method is not clear. In the long note added in 1893 to this section of his paper, Peirce confessed that 'many critics have told me that I misrepresent the *a priori* philosophers when I represent them as adopting whatever opinion there seems to be a natural inclination to adopt'.[67] It is highly significant that his account of this method is said to hold true for Descartes which would suggest that he was thinking of the use of a deductive method in philosophy. But Peirce's including within the scope of this method the thought of Plato and Hegel gives one pause. Neither proposed to interpret reality in any simple deductive fashion without regard for experience, nor is it obvious that either of their philosophies was developed under no other constraint than that imposed by what they were 'inclined to think'. Peirce acknowledged Hegel's attempt to develop the many tendencies and counter-tendencies of thought and arrived at the following view: 'Hegel thinks there is a regular system in the succession of these tendencies, in consequence of which, after drifting one way and the other for a long time, opinion will at last go right.'[68] Peirce seems to have thought, however, that even the *a priori* method involves an appeal to 'feelings and purposes', and this led him to question it. Referring to the method of science, Peirce wrote: 'the test of whether I am truly following the method is not an immediate appeal to my feelings and purposes, but, on the contrary, itself involves the application of the method.'[69] Here he expressed belief in the self-correcting character of empirical method as long as inquiry continues and is not subverted in any way. Once again the appeal is prospective to consequences and results rather than retrospective to foundations.

It is not clear to what extent Peirce understood the difference between the claim that empirical method is self-correcting with respect to its own previous conclusions and the claim that all questions can and indeed must be treated from a scientific standpoint. Those who have questioned whether the method of natural science is adequate for dealing with all intellectual issues have not meant to deny that empirical method is self-corrective with respect to conclusions already reached by the application of that method in the past. The problem is whether experimental method is appropriate to philosophical questions, including those posed by the philosophy of science and studies of empirical methodology. At times Peirce seems to have thought that philosophical inquiry represents an extension of empirical method and that science and philosophy are continuous. At others he was inclined to connect philosophy most closely with the indubitable beliefs of instinct and commonsense which are the result of pervasive experience over vast periods of time rather than the outcome of consciously controlled inquiry.[70]

Before turning to James' basic Pragmatism and his approach to meaning, action and belief, it will be helpful to indicate why it is that in the case of both Peirce and James, Pragmatism was initially characterized as a method for attaining clarity in meaning, but ultimately veered around to include a theory of truth. The first step was the appeal to action, practical consequences and results as a means of determining meaning as against previous intuitive theories, whether rationalist or empiricist. The next step is found in the claim that action implies belief and therefore that some means must be found for determining belief. To the extent, however, that belief implies doubt and the uncertainty that leads not to action but hesitation, it becomes necessary to find a way of overcoming doubt, a way, in short, of establishing belief on *critical* grounds so that a belief thus established will not be based merely on the *belief* that it is true, but rather on the *evidence* tending to support the claim that it is actually true, or, given the state of inquiry at a specific time, that it has a better chance of being true than any other alternative. Thus Pragmatism necessarily developed into a theory of truth, of knowledge, or, as Dewey would have said, 'warranted assertibility'. Confusion has most frequently appeared at the point where it is seen that *action* requires believing *that* the belief on which we are to act is true and it is also supposed that the truth of the belief consists in the fact of the believing itself. But this is not so, and even James, who allowed a greater latitude for 'the will to believe' than Peirce did, repeatedly insisted that belief must be determined by finished fact and he sided with Hume and against Descartes in holding that, in the presence of the determinate fact, a person is 'powerless' to believe otherwise. As will become clear, James' contention that an antecedent *belief* in the *possibility* of experiencing some fact or of achieving some goal can be one contributing factor *among others* in actualizing the possibility, does not concern present fact but rather some future state of affairs. In short, James' 'will to believe' has almost nothing to do with science except perhaps in the sense that no scientist would set out to answer a question unless he believed in the *possibility* of there being an answer.

The best resource for understanding James' basic Pragmatism is to be found in two papers, 'Philosophical Conceptions and Practical Results' (1898) and 'What Pragmatism Means' (1907). These papers express a concern which, while not unimportant for Peirce, was of greater moment for James, namely the finding of a way to resolve philosophical disputes over cosmic philosophical, moral, and religious issues. And if James did not believe that they could be resolved in their own speculative terms, he was determined to discover the practical import of possible answers to them in time for the beliefs entailed to make a difference in the conduct of life. The relevance, and indeed the inescapability, of philosophical belief for decision and action were never far from the centre of James' concern and they help to explain the opposition he envisaged between 'life' and 'logic'. It was not so much that life should be deprived of rationality, but rather that, for James, 'logic' signalled timeless thought and the theoretical standpoint, whereas 'life' meant the here and now of decision and action requiring that we seek to determine which particular thoughts, beliefs and items of knowledge 'count' with respect to dealing with the life situation at hand. It was his contention that 'intellectualism', with its aim of a theoretical comprehension of the whole, tends to blunt the relevance issue; for such an aim, *all* thought determinations are relevant because all are required if the totality is to be successfully represented.

The role of purpose in thought and the consequent appeal to relevance and selective emphasis are basic to Pragmatism; a few examples will serve to underline their importance. Consider the question of the degree of precision required for an idea to serve its purpose and the kind and amount of information necessary for accomplishing some specific aim. A host or

B

hostess inviting a guest to be seated on a 'divan' cannot be faulted for using the term to indicate what is in fact not a divan at all but a 'loveseat' as long as there is, in the immediate situation, no confusion of the piece of furniture intended with some other and different piece and the purpose of the host has been served. If the term used is sufficiently precise to direct the guest to the proper seat it would be superfluous and pedantic if someone were to ask for an analysis involving an absolutely clear distinction between a 'divan' and a 'love-seat'. On the other hand, a catalogue describing items of antique furniture to be sold at auction would be grossly inadequate if it failed to distinguish between the two types of furniture and simply referred to every piece capable of seating more than one person as a 'sofa'. The degree of precision in thought that is required depends on the purpose in hand; some situations can tolerate a degree of vagueness and ambiguity which would be disastrous in others. Suppose, further, that we are interested in setting forth a pattern of distinguishing features or characteristics such as would enable us to identify the birds of a region in the field and on the wing. A detailed ornithological manual based on the theoretical ideal of a total description of each type of bird derived from having one in the hand would not of itself serve the purpose. Of all that is known about these birds it is necessary to select just those items of information which would serve to identify them when seen perching or flying. On the whole, the size of the lower mandible in centimetres or the colour of the roof of the mouth, though an essential part of the scientific record, will be of no use to the bird-watcher trying to distinguish one bird from another in the field. What is needed to serve the purpose is a selection of characteristics which particular birds will exhibit under the appropriate circumstances; whatever cannot be so seen, accurate though it may be as part of the total scientific record, will not 'count' for achieving the aim in question. It was just this appeal to purpose as a selective principle for thought which James had in mind when he pointed to an encyclopedia – a model of a total knowledge of reality – and asked, 'When do I utter these truths?' The pragmatists were often over-optimistic in their belief that 'what makes a difference' will manifest itself in the exigencies of situations or that it can always be determined by consulting purposes, but this fact does not affect the importance of what they had in mind when they insisted on a principle of relevance in thought.

James' immediate aim in the address of 1898 was to indicate the best direction to follow in philosophy. He was fond of drawing on his experience of forests and hiking and he regarded philosophers as pathfinders who do not create anything beyond the marking of trails through the 'otherwise trackles forest of human experience' which enable us to use and enjoy its quality. Of the greatest importance for the development of Pragmatism was the fact that James cited Peirce's 'How to Make Our Ideas Clear' as the paper which provided him with the proper direction in which to go.

He offered a number of paraphrases of what he called 'Peirce's principle of practicalism'; these are revealing not only for an understanding of James' views but for their modifications of Peirce as well. In stating Peirce's principle 'more broadly', James changed the emphasis. What a truth means for us, said James, is 'the conduct it dictates and requires', but in stressing the fact that the response must be *particular* he ran counter to Peirce's insistence that meaning or intellectual purport must be general and embodied in habits no one of which can be identical with a particular response. The divergence is highly significant. James saw the pragmatic principle as peculiarly applicable to philosophical discussion and especially as a way of avoiding misunderstanding leading to the strife of systems. Peirce, while not unconcerned with such disputes, had as his primary aim the development of a general theory of conceptual meaning which would bring together consistently both his practicalism or the claim that there is an essential connection between meaning and patterns of behaving, and his Scotistic realism with its emphasis on the reality of the general and its exclusion of nominalism in all forms. In this regard, James should be seen not as having broadened Peirce's principle but rather as having narrowed it; the emphasis James placed on particularism is restrictive of Peirce's conception and confining the application of the pragmatic maxim to philosophical debates obscures the fact that Peirce intended it to express the entire range of meaning, scientific as well as philosophical.

James' interest in the pragmatic principle was closely connected with his concern to find a way of resolving philosophical controversies and, even more important, to show the relevance of philosophical and religious beliefs for decision and action in specific situations. His method was to take two opposed philosophical theses or positions and ask of each what 'conceivable practical consequence to anybody at any time or place'[71] would follow if the thesis or position were regarded as true. If there is no difference in these conceivable consequences as between the two propositions, then the supposed difference between them is, said James, merely 'specious' and 'verbal'. It is important to notice exactly what sort of thing is regarded by him as constituting a 'real' difference – a difference that 'makes' a difference – because there has been confusion on this head in the past. Mention is made of 'a difference of concrete fact' as well as 'of conduct consequent upon the fact' which suggests that he was not proposing to translate differences 'in abstract truth' solely into differences in conduct or behaviour. The determination, then, of what difference it will make if one world-formula rather than another and opposed world-formula is true, will involve not only what we are to do, but what the facts to be acknowledged are and how they are to be described. James assigned to philosophy the task of determining these differences, and he had a sanguine belief in the power of the pragmatic principle to reduce certain philosophical disputes to the purely verbal level. Whether, however, he was justified in this belief depends ultimately on the extent to which the relevant differences can be clearly and accurately specified.

The curious example that James proposed makes it clear that the actual functioning of the pragmatic principle is no simple matter and involves more than we had been led to expect. We are first to imagine our selves in a situation where the principle could not possibly be applied so that its function in situations where it can be applied will stand out more clearly. We are to suppose that the 'present moment is the absolutely last moment of the world, with bare nonentity beyond it, and no hereafter for either experience or conduct'.[72] In these circumstances, he claimed, 'there would be no sense whatever' in some of our most hotly contested religious and philosophical questions. Suppose the issue were whether matter is the producer of everything, or whether there is a God as well. James' contention is that the alternative is 'idle and unsignificant' if the world is finished and there is no more to come. It is clear that James had no thought whatever of viewing the alternative as an issue 'in itself', as it were, and concerned with what is the case. Such an outlook would presumably be to commit the 'intellectualist' fallacy. Instead he focused entirely on our personal reactions to the two alternatives, and while he admitted that on either hypothesis the experienced facts 'might be the same', he maintained that a coldness and deadness would come over us if we had to believe that the world was an accident and that the facts were informed by no purpose; on the supposition of God's reality, however, these same facts are said to become warm and full of significance. James' central claim at this point was that the different reactions just described are 'reasonable' for a prospective consciousness, but would be 'senseless and irrational' for a purely retrospective consciousness judging a world already past or finished.[73] The basis for this judgement seems to be that the retrospective consciousness viewing a world already gone is unable to attach any 'emotional interest' to the alternatives and therefore must regard the problem as 'purely intellectual'. Since there are difficulties involved in this appeal to the interest and concern of the individual in considering forecasts of consequences and courses of action, something is to be gained from considering several senses in which James could speak of differences and 'making a difference'. In many cases the 'difference' in experience which is to enable us to distinguish one philosophical position or concept from another is quite obvious and easily pointed out. Of this sort is the well-known example of the man circling the tree with the squirrel moving about the trunk in such a way that the man never sees the squirrel because the latter constantly keeps a diameter of the tree between itself and its would-be observer. The question then is: Does the man go round the squirrel? The answer is, of course, dependent on which of the two senses of 'go round' is intended; each sense can be clearly represented in a spatial diagram such that if by 'go round' is meant circling the tree and hence everything on it regardless of its position, the man does go round the squirrel, but if by 'go round' is meant that one is first to the south of an object, then to the east, the north, the west and back to the south again, then the man does not go round the squirrel. This distinction by means of which James proposed to resolve the problem is readily exhibited as two different arrangements of spatial positions. The difference in consequences has simply to do with the different sets of spatial positions which would obtain if one or the other meaning of 'go round' were assumed.

Another quite straightforward example concerns overt behaviour and the difference which the holding of a belief could make to the outcome of a situation. A few highwaymen, said James, can succeed in holding up a train despite the fact that they are heavily outnumbered by their intended victims because virtually no passenger will believe in advance that if he resists all the other passengers will follow suit and thus overwhelm their attackers. Here, one of the factors is the occurrence of a belief which could contribute to an outcome that would not come to pass at all without the belief, thus the belief 'makes a difference' not in the sense of creating a new fact out of whole cloth but *as a contributing factor* in determining a future consequence.

There is, however, another sense of 'make a difference' to which James frequently appealed and it is sufficiently familiar to have established itself in ordinary discourse. According to this sense, 'making a difference' has to do with the bearing or relevance of some fact, belief, event, etc., on a person's life and destiny.[74] Whether the earth will grow cold and no longer support life in fifty million years or ten million years 'makes no difference' to my present decision to choose poetry or medicine as a profession. The difference, though important from the standpoint of science, has no conceivable bearing on that decision. The distinction between this sense of making a difference and the 'differences' involved in the two preceding examples can be clearly stated.

The sense of 'difference' implied in the cases cited of difference in fact and of conduct consequent on such fact, contrasts with *sameness* or *identity*. The sense of 'difference' implied where our interest, purpose, destiny are involved contrasts with *indifference* in the sense of neutrality or of viewing a matter 'theoretically' so that emotional involvement is cancelled. Applying this latter sense of making a difference to the matter–God alternative above, one part at least of what James was saying is that it is only for the prospective consciousness 'whose world is partly yet to come' that the truth of the one alternative or the other will 'make a difference' to the conduct of his life and his destiny. For the retrospective consciousness with no future, the alternatives make no difference; the individual can generate no 'emotional interest'.

On the other hand, the original purpose of the matter–God example was to show the use and scope of the pragmatic principle in a situation in which the essential appeal to future consequences of any sort required by that principle would be ruled out. The question is: Did James want to show that in such circumstances there would be no way of distinguishing the *meaning* of the hypothesis A – there is God and matter does not suffice – from the *meaning* of the hypothesis B – there is only matter and it suffices? Or was he claiming that with the future eliminated, a person would have no 'emotional interest' in the alternative, since the matter would then become purely 'theoretical'? I confess that I find the point of the illustration far from clear. In a note referring to this article added by James in 1909,[75] he stated: 'Even if matter could do every outward thing that God does, the idea of it would not work as satisfactorily, because the chief call for a God on modern man's part is for a being who will inwardly recognize them and judge them sympathetically.' From this comment, it would appear, the two hypotheses do *not* have the same meaning, and the question then arises: from what source is the difference in meaning derived? It cannot arise from the 'facts' because, as James said, 'the actually experienced world is supposed to be the same in its details on either hypothesis';[76] the difference, therefore, can only reside in the manner in which an individual person views these facts, and, presumably, in some difference in conduct dictated by holding one alternative or the other. That this was in fact James' view becomes more clear when he turned to the prospective consciousness. 'Thus,' he wrote, 'if no future detail of experience or conduct is to be deduced from our hypothesis, the debate between materialism and theism becomes quite idle and insignificant.'[77] This 'insignificance', however, must not be supposed to result from any failure on the part of any individual to attach an emotional interest to the dispute; the debate is idle because the alternatives do not differ in meaning. For, as James said, apart from appeal to the future, 'matter and God in that event mean exactly the same thing'.[78] If this is so then the problem is to see how the appeal to the future introduces differences of meaning and of exactly what sort they are.

The principle of Pragmatism, according to James, leads us to consider whether the metaphysical alternatives involved have 'alternative practical outcomes, however delicate and distant these may be'.[79] And, he claimed, in every genuine debate over such alternatives, 'some practical issue, however remote, is really involved'.[80] The extent to which the future is essential for determining the practical issue in any given case becomes evident in James' reiteration of the previous claim that, as regards past facts – facts that are 'in', 'bagged', 'captured' – there is no difference whether we consider them as purposeless configurations of atoms or as due to the providence of God. This is a curious admission on the face of it, because it should be obvious that while James was claiming 'no difference' with respect to past facts, the alternatives in question represent a clear case of what Peirce meant by a 'conceivable' difference and, in fact, James would have to appeal to just this sense of difference if he were to know which alternative is which when he sought to determine what their respective 'practical consequences' might be.[81] As Whitehead pointed out in connection with all 'operational' conceptions of meaning, consequent operations can never be wholly identical with the meaning of an expression because *antecedent* conceptual meaning is required for locating the appropriate operations.

One must return to the question: What is, for James, the source of the difference in practical consequences when we consider alternative metaphysical views? The first part of an answer is obviously the adoption of the 'prospective' view, by which James meant the way an individual confronts the world and attempts to deal with the future both in thought and action. 'Theism and materialism,' he wrote, 'so indifferent when taken retrospectively, point when we take them prospectively to wholly different practical consequences, to opposite outlooks of experience.'[82] And he proceeded to outline what one who accepted the materialist hypothesis would be committed to believing with respect to the future of the cosmos, his own experience and ideals. The picture painted is the one made familiar in the late nineteenth century of a mechanical universe in which the 'lower' forces are the eternal ones so that in the end the work of evolution is undone and all the goods and heroic deeds of the past are swept up in a cosmic waste. Since it is often charged that James confused the logical consequences of a proposition or hypothesis with the consequences of *believing* the proposition or hypothesis, it is worth noting that there is no evidence of this confusion thus far in the argument of the 1898 paper. He was simply stating what one who held the materialist hypothesis would have to believe *about the universe and life in it* as the future unfolds if he is to remain consistent. And, on the other side of the ledger, the believer in God will be committed to the thesis that there is an ideal order which holds out the fulfilment of 'our remotest hopes'. In one phase of the argument, therefore, the entire emphasis falls on *what* a proponent of one or the other of the alternatives would be committed to in the way of belief.

At this point, however, James introduced another and quite different consideration, namely human needs and the possibility of their fulfilment. Instead of the two alternatives differing solely in their account of 'what's what' in regard to the future, their difference is now to be estimated with respect to their 'appeal' to the person called on to believe them and this means what each of the alternatives implies about the life and destiny of the person. The force of this new factor becomes apparent from the following statement:

Here then, in these different emotional and practical appeals, in these adjustments of our concrete attitudes of hope and expectation, and all the delicate consequences which their differences entail, lie the real meanings of materialism and theism – not in hair-splitting abstractions about matter's inner essence, or about the metaphysical attributes of God. Materialism means simply the denial that the moral order is eternal, and the cutting off of ultimate hopes; theism means the affirmation of an eternal moral order and the letting loose of hope.[83]

What new consideration has been added by this turn of the argument? The answer is quite simple, and it serves at the same time to make clear the connection between James' Pragmatism and a central feature of the contemporary philosophy of existence. James was asking a person viewing the alternatives to consider them in the light of what would have to be true *about his own life and destiny,* if one or the other alternative were true of the whole cosmic scheme. In this way he was attempting to keep the debate from appearing as a purely 'theoretical' discussion about the nature of things excluding consideration, by those who must choose, of what the alternatives imply in their own case. The shift is from 'something would be the case' to 'something would be the case for me', and this shift is *not* to be explained by invoking a distinction between the logical consequences of an hypothesis and the consequences of believing the hypothesis,[84] because, on the supposition that one or the other hypothesis is true, its implications would follow for *anyone* whether he believed the hypothesis or not. Violence can only be done to James' intent if one approaches him with too simple a dichotomy between 'logical' consequences in which belief does not figure, and believing which is supposed to turn everything into a 'psychological' affair.

The next turn of the argument is most instructive because it reveals what James was trying to do with the pragmatic principle in the context marked out by the theistic hypothesis. His aim was to connect theological concepts with experience, and in effect translate theology back into the religious substance from which it originally came. Like Kant who was not attempting to resolve his antinomies in objective, speculative terms but only to exhibit the predicament of reason and at the same time connect the antithetical assertions with human interests and purposes, James was not here actually arguing for the theistic hypothesis, but rather seeking to make clear the manner in which one must approach that hypothesis in adopting the pragmatic principle. As James interpreted it, the principle determines that the meaning of the idea of God resides in those differences 'which must be made in our experience if the conception be true'.[85] The concepts of theology must find whatever meaning they have in 'certain definite things that we can feel and do at particular moments of our lives, things which we could not feel and should not do were no God present and were the business of the universe carried on by material atoms instead'.[86] Emphasis here fall on *meaning* and James' attempt to find what he was later to call 'cash value' for the theological terms in the experience of the individual. As long as definite experiences are involved, 'God means something for us, and may be real'.[87]

Not unlike Schleiermacher and Jonathan Edwards, James sought to determine the experiential meaning which an individual can attach to the concepts making up the classical definitions of God – aseity, necessity, infinity, etc. For 'practical Americans', he said, these concepts awaken no 'sense of reality', by which he meant that no responsive active feelings are elicited by them and no particular conduct is called for.[88] Here one finds James' inveterate tendency to oppose theology and religion to each other in the sharpest possible way. Religion is seen as a 'living practical affair' and only those concepts of theology which have a 'practical' connection with life are allowed religious import. God's 'simplicity' to James s eemed to imply no experiential connection with human life, whereas the same is not true for 'omniscience' which can be taken to mean that God apprehends what remains hidden or obscured for man. The life of religion is in the experiences undergone 'of a wider spiritual life with which our superficial consciousness is continuous'.[89] The meaning to be attached to the word 'God' is just 'those passive and active experiences of your life'.[90] These experiences are 'the originals of the God-idea' and theology represents a conceptual translation of these originals which is secondary and derivative. One cannot but feel the force of the contrast between James and Peirce at this point. The latter argued for the reality of conceptual meaning and intellectual purport, whereas James, with his incipient nominalism, was always hesitant about allowing concepts to have any other than a representational meaning or a surrogate function.[91] Perhaps, however, this logical difference, important though it is, is not as important as James' practical intent which was to show the relevance, and the inescapability of theological and metaphysical controversies by translating the meaning of the alternatives into experiential differences of outlook, attitude and conduct. One more illustration of the application of the pragmatic principle must suffice – James' proposal for dealing with the problem of monism and pluralism.

What, James asked, do we mean when we call the universe or reality 'One'? The answer is to be sought by considering in what ways the oneness expresses itself in individual experience, and whether one acts differently towards a universe believed to be One than one would act towards a universe differently conceived. When we have to handle a thing, said James, we discover that we can pass from one part of it to another without letting go; with regard, however, to the passage from one mind to another, or from a mind to a physical thing, the transition is not continuous. From these 'practical tests' we are to conclude that the world manifests both oneness and plurality and therefore that neither monism nor pluralism as total doctrines can be correct. James, moreover, contended that if 'the maxim of Peirce' were applied, the debate could be settled because all parties would be forced to consider the issue, not in terms of a dialectic of concepts, but by having to deal with the facts disclosed when consequences are taken into account.

One may well ask, in view of the interpretation James placed on Peirce's principle and the specific examples of its use, to what extent his view differs from the empiricism associated with Locke and indeed from the tradition of British empiricism that stretches from Hume to Mill and later.

Even a partial answer to this question is of importance, especially for determining further the differences between Peirce and James, because Peirce was on the whole critical of classical empiricism and James, at least in the paper of 1898, seems to be following in its footsteps. It is, therefore, highly significant that James brought the paper to a close by suggesting that 'it is the English-speaking philosophers who first introduced the custom of interpreting the meaning of conceptions by asking what difference they make for life'.[92] And he went on to commend Locke and Berkeley for having asked, when confronted with such conceptions as personal identity and matter, 'What is it known as? In what facts does it result? What special differences would come into the world according, as it were, true or false?' James, moreover, approved of Hume's having treated causation in similar fashion. His only criticism of the British tradition is that its representatives did not go far enough in the very direction they marked out; they failed, said James, 'to track the practical results completely enough, to see how far they extend'.[93]

James' Pragmatism, then, included fundamental ideas of traditional empiricism and he was inclined to accept the nominalism in it as Peirce did not. On the other hand, it is not clear that the classical empiricists shared James' voluntarism and his concern to translate purported differences in the conceptual meaning of metaphysical alternatives into differences in conduct that would follow for an individual if he believed one alternative or the other. Despite his scathing attack upon Kant, James' programme of asking how I would have to act if I believed in freedom, for example, as distinct from the way I would act if I believed in determinism as a cosmic principle is completely prefigured in Section 3 of Kant's discussion of the antinomies. In asking for 'the interest of reason in these conflicts' Kant was asking what difference it *would* make to man's life and destiny if the thesis or the antithesis held true of the world. And this was precisely James' concern, but it is important to notice that for neither thinker is it possible for us to have *knowledge* of the prevailing alternative which is the reason for changing the court of appeal from theoretical knowing to that of practical reason.[94]

The second basic source for understanding James' version of Pragmatism is 'What Pragmatism Means' which is Lecture 2 of *Pragmatism,* first published in 1907. Here the pragmatic method is explicitly identified as a means of 'settling metaphysical disputes that otherwise might be interminable'.[95] The well-known case of the man and the squirrel cited earlier (p. 36) which at once introduces and illustrates this thesis may not seem like a prime example of a metaphysical debate, but it will serve to indicate what James had in mind. The solution proposed here has to do with what we 'practically' mean by 'going round'.[96] I believe the alternatives can be more simply stated than they were in the original version. If I think of two concentric circles representing the paths of the man and the squirrel respectively (such that the latter is wholly included in the former) then according to one sense of 'go round', the man *does* go round the squirrel because he goes round any and everything travelling the path of the inner circle, and this holds true even in the present instance where the squirrel's belly is always facing the man with the diameter of the tree in between. If, however, by 'go round' is meant that the man is first in front of the squirrel, then on his right, then behind, then on his left and finally in front of him again, the man *does not* go round the squirrel since the latter always has his belly turned to the man. James' point is that the dispute is ended once we see that it turns on the *meaning* of 'to go round', so that taken in one sense the answer to the original question is 'yes', and in another the answer is 'no'.

Although James continued to speak of the difference in question as 'practical', it is not entirely clear what this is to mean. In the above example it seems to mean no more than a precise construction of the actual situation and the proper arrangement of the facts so that one will operate with clear ideas and not be deceived by the confusion implicit in appealing to 'just plain honest English "round" '.[97] But when James went on to generalize from his example and to set forth the 'pragmatic method' we are told that in order to apply it to such questions as: Is the world one or many? fated or free? material or spiritual? – we need only 'to try to interpret each notion by tracing its respective practical consequences'.[98] 'What difference,' he asked, 'would it practically make to anyone if this notion rather than that notion were true?'[99] Two comments are in order at this point; first, are we to understand by 'practical consequences' the differences in the arrangement and construing of the facts as illustrated by the two senses of 'go round', or are we to attempt to estimate what 'difference' it would make to the life and destiny of an individual person if some thesis about the world he lives in were true? Second, there is no reference in the squirrel example to the 'true' sense of 'go round', but only to a distinction in meaning and the question as to what 'go round' *really* means does not arise. In citing Peirce's principle, James wrote as though it was meant primarily as a means of attaining clarity of thought about objects, and yet he was interested in the principle chiefly as a way of settling philosophical disputes by bringing them to a crucial test. Something more, it would appear, than clarity of meaning is involved; in addition there is the matter of which alternative is true. The aim is to discover, said James, what 'definite difference it will make to you and me, at definite instants of our life, if this world formula or that world formula be the true one'.[100] The question, of course, is whether the pragmatic method as James conceived it is supposed to help us discover whether a given alternative is true (or can be held with some warrant) or only what difference it would make if the alternative were true without further indication of whether it is true or not. In fairness to James it must be said that throughout his many writings the pragmatic method can be seen functioning with respect to both meaning and truth. There are cases where actual disputes are said to collapse through clarification of meaning and the discovery that nothing but differences in terminology are involved since the same facts are acknowledged by both parties. Then there are cases such as the extensive discussion of the problem of the one and the many[101] wherein James tried to indicate what the 'Oneness' of things is 'known as' by citing a number of practical consequences which entitle us to speak of the *unity* of things. In short, he was attempting to assess the validity of monism as a world formula by appealing to experience and at the same time to show the limits of that formula by pointing to disjunctions and the fact of disunity. His conclusion was that the world is truly described neither by a monism which reduces disjunctions to the status of appearance, nor by a sheer pluralism that excludes unity and continuity. Whether James thought that there is anything essentially 'pragmatic' about this fairly obvious conclusions is not clear. He described his view as simply 'empiricism' in philosophy. It is, however, doubtful whether all 'empiricists' would find themselves in agreement with some of the 'practical' parameters which James establishes for his Pragmatism.

One can find in 'What Pragmatism Means' several additional features of the position; these together with the central points made in *The Meaning of Truth* express the essentials of James' Pragmatism. James claimed first and foremost that Pragmatism is a *method* and an attitude which does not 'stand for any special results'[102] and that it is devoid of dogmas and doctrines. He illustrated this point by the image of the hotel corridor which connects many separate rooms. In one room someone is engaged in writing an idealist metaphysics, in another someone is investigating the properties of prime numbers, and in still another an attempt is being made to show the impossibility of metaphysics. All, however, must use the corridor if they are to pass in and out of their respective rooms. The corridor represents the method and what goes on in the individual rooms represents 'doctrines' as distinct from the method, although all presumably must use that method in order to do their work. The pragmatists were somewhat uncritical in their acceptance of this distinction; they often seemed to think that to specify a method does not involve presuppositions concerning what there is and what there must be if the method is to prove successful. James, to be sure, did say 'no doctrines save its method', thus suggesting that the method itself is not doctrine-free. The underlying problem is of the utmost importance because of the widespread belief to be found not only among philosophers but among scientists as well that there is a 'neutral' way of proceeding which is unencumbered by the biases inevitably expressed in 'doctrines'. This belief harbours a major threat to intellectual integrity because it leads to a refusal to acknowledge the doctrines implicit in all methods. An overemphasis on method, moreover, often has the effect of obscuring our responsibility for forming substantive opinions. Instead one retreats to the safety of the 'neutral' method which indicates no more than the way one *would* go about reaching a conclusion.

Even more serious consequences follow from an uncritical adherence to the 'supremacy of method'. Consider the superconfident claims of a psychologist like Skinner who contends that man is essentially a machine. This claim in fact reduces to the thesis that unless we conceive man in this way our scientific method will not work successfully. But it is a strange argument indeed that includes among its premises a thesis that is in question and then goes on to demand that unless this thesis is accepted our method of inquiry is vitiated. We must be wary of the latent dogmatism hidden in the belief that one can specify what sort of reality a given method *must* disclose. James and Peirce were more sensitive to this problem than Dewey, and they were more sympathetic to the concerns of philosophy and religion *vis à vis* the methodological imperialism frequently exhibited by scientists and naturalistic philosophers.

Pragmatism meant, for James, not only a method but a genetic theory of truth as well. This conception of truth has been the subject of much criticism and controversy, although the motives behind it have seldom been understood. The theory, in so far as it is distinctive, represents an attempt to do justice to two facts forced upon our attention largely by the development of modern science. These facts must be reckoned with by anyone seeking to develop a theory of truth. The first fact is that every truth claim is a function of some *process* of testing whereby the claim is established. It was this fact that led James to contrast a theory of the *nature* of truth as such with a description of singular processes through which particular 'truths' are reached. It is, however, not clear that the two need be set in opposition to each other. The pragmatists did move in the direction of replacing classical epistemological theories by methodology, but despite this fact they had their own *general theories* of the nature of truth and not only rules for showing how some particular proposition is verified.

The second fact has to do with the tentative and approximate character of scientific conclusions. In short, the pragmatists were attempting to come to terms with the *temporal* factor in inquiry, something more difficult to do in their day than in our own when the development of the history of science has dramatically shown the inescapability of the problem. For many traditional theories, knowledge was knowledge in a timeless mode; the true was regarded as 'true' in a sense that made it impervious to time and change. But, if so, what is one to do with the results of scientific inquiry – generally regarded as the paradigm of knowledge – which are said to be tentative in the sense of being based on this much evidence to date and to be approximate to the extent of the error involved in all experimental procedure? Even if, as was suggested above, it should be decided that the attempts of the pragmatists to account for knowledge and truth were not entirely successful, the fact remains that they were confronting the formidable problems that arise when one takes time and change seriously. If scepticism is to be avoided, knowledge, it would appear, must involve an identity and permanence that elevates it beyond the passing moment; on the other hand, however, inquiry is a temporal affair and its results are not independent of the contingencies that attach to every historical process. James, moreover, was determined to reflect in his theory 'the conditioned ways in which we *do* think'[103] and not only 'what we *ought* to think unconditionally'.[104] Consequently he often appears to have sacrificed that normative element which Peirce described as the opinion *destined* to be reached and the idealists expressed as the knowledge possessed by the Absolute. I do not believe that James did make this sacrifice; it is rather, as Dewey and others have pointed out, that he frequently expressed his ideas in an unguarded way and talked of truths as being 'made', of truth as a species of good, and of truth as the 'expedient' in the way of thinking, all of which gave the impression that truth is no more than a function of an individual's calculating what it is to his own advantage to believe.[105]

We need not pursue the topic further at this point because the theory of truth will be the principal subject of the succeeding chapter. There remain a few more points in 'What Pragmatism Means' which furnish important clues to James' version. James was foreshadowing Dewey in his claim that theories are 'instruments' for inquiry rather than answers with which we remain content. And this instrumental function figures not only in his conception of truth, but also in the description of the process by which new opinions come to be formed. Following Dewey and, as he believed, the pattern of scientific thought as well, James argued that at any moment of experience an individual has a stock of old opinions, any one of which may be called in question by a new experience, the discovery of a contradiction, the emergence of new facts, etc. The uneasiness accompanying this conflict or strain placed on previous opinion leads to an attempt at readjustment guided by the aim of saving as much of the old opinion as is compatible with acceptance of the novel fact or experience. The adjustment is made when 'some new idea comes up which he can graft upon the ancient stock with a minimum of disturbance of the latter, some idea that mediates between the stock and the new experience and runs them into one another most felicitously and expediently'.[106] New truth, said James, 'marries old opinion to new fact so as ever to show a minimum of jolt, a maximum of continuity'.[107] His claim was that a theory is held to be true just to the extent that it succeeds in solving what he calls the problem of 'maximum and minimum' with regard to change and continuity. This position assumes that we are dealing with what goes on in the thought process of an individual, and hence James could say that the 'truth' of a new opinion consists in the extent to which it 'gratifies the individual's desire to assimilate the novel in his experience to his beliefs in stock'.[108] Once again it is not difficult to see why many of James' contemporaries expressed concern about the individualism and the seeming subjectivism implied in making the truth of an assertion dependent essentially upon an individual's estimate or 'appreciation' of the function it performs in his ongoing mental history. Even if one accepts as a legitimate test of truth the success with which the new opinion performs the mediating function, it still seems necessary to have some intersubjective grounds on which an individual is to make a judgement concerning this success. Peirce, it is clear, was among those who had misgivings about this appeal to individual judgement and it was one of the factors which led him to coin the term 'Pragmaticism' as a name that would serve to indicate his own position. Peirce's thought was firmly rooted in the appeal to an intersubjectivity arising from a *community* of inquirers, and he had a deep suspicion of the particularism for which James had such fondness.

Before turning to a more detailed discussion of the issues raised by the pragmatic theory of truth – especially the question whether it is in fact a distinctive theory rather than a 'practical' version of some other theory – it would be well to turn to Dewey's attempt to clarify the concepts of 'meaning' and of 'practical' introduced in the growing literature of Pragmatism. In an essay entitled 'What Pragmatism Means by Practical'[109] Dewey sought to take stock of the position and to clear up some of the confusions that had arisen. Dewey quite correctly called attention to the fact that although James saw Pragmatism primarily as a method he did not pay sufficient attention to differences in the meaning of key concepts resulting from applying the method to diverse subjects. James considered under the same rubric particular philosophical controversies, the meaning of an object and of an idea, the notion of truth and the function of beliefs in the life of the individual. It was Dewey's contention that if Pragmatism is to be clearly and fairly represented an account must be given of both 'meaning' and 'practical' that will be appropriate for each case.

Dewey considered three sorts of subjects – objects, ideas, truths – in an effort to clarify the pragmatic position. In the case of objects taken as given the task is to arrive at a definition expressed in concepts. The meaning in this case is expressed in the definition and the reference to 'practical' means the responses, attitudes and acts which are appropriate when we have dealings with that object. Thus, for example, we associate with our conception of the object denoted by the term 'bull' its characteristic belligerent behaviour together with the apprehension, fear, flight to safety that would be our characteristic response in the presence of the animal. In the case of ideas, the situation, Dewey claimed, is reversed; the object is not given but rather the idea and the pragmatic approach dictates that the idea be 'set to work' in the stream of experience where it becomes an indication of the ways in which existence can be changed. Here the idea is seen as a 'draft drawn upon existing things' and as essentially an intention to act so as to arrange things in a certain way. To Dewey this implies that meaning is the denotative or existential reference of an idea while the *practical* aspect consists in the capacity of tendency of the idea in the form of an active intention to effect changes in prior existence.[110] The third case involves truths and there it is assumed that the meanings of the relevant ideas and objects have already been ascertained so that it remains only to determine the actual value or importance to be assigned to the truth in question. Here Dewey identified meaning with *value* and defined practical in terms of the desirable or undesirable character of certain ends in view.

There is a further point worth noticing in Dewey's commentary on James; it serves to point up the difference between Dewey's naturalistic outlook and the theistic position of James. Where philosophical world-formulas are involved, Dewey questioned whether the pragmatic method is supposed to discover or indicate in terms of consequences for life the value of some formula whose logical content is taken as already fixed, *or* whether it is supposed to criticize, revise and ultimately constitute the meaning of the formula. Dewey rightly perceived that James was often using the method in the first way whereas Dewey wanted to confine it to the second and this is precisely why he argued that it is unpragmatic for pragmatists to attempt to discover the value of a conception whose meaning was not pragmatically determined in the first place. This is not to say that James did not also employ the method in Dewey's second sense; it is clear, however, that in commending theism, for example, James understood what the formula 'promises' to the individual in traditional theistic terms and passed on to consider the value gained by believing it. Even allowing for the qualifications that would have to be made if *A Common Faith* were taken into account, Dewey's pragmatic naturalism would prevent him from allowing the theism James had in mind as a significant formula in any way warranted by the application of the pragmatic method. James, knowledge, it might appear that the pragmatists were merely adding world-formula than he did to explaining the difference it would make if it *were* true for anyone who believed and acted in accordance with it.[111]

On the subject of the concept of truth a word of warning will help avoid an impression that would actually be quite misleading. Since every discussion of Pragmatism must begin with problems of meaning, truth and knowledge, it might appear that the pragmatists were merely adding another chapter to what has proved to be the endless tale of epistemology in modern philosophy since Kant.[112] This is not so. On the one hand, Dewey attacked the 'epistemology industry' as concerned not with perennial problems, but with historically conditioned problems stemming from a misguided quest for certainty plus some questionable assumptions about the nature of experience. For Dewey methodology and the pattern of inquiry replaced the old theory of knowledge. On the other hand, Peirce attacked foundationalism in logic and his 'critical commonsensism' implies that philosophy cannot be based on the certainties put forth by traditional epistemology. In addition, the pragmatists were trying to develop a new conception of experience – a more 'empirical' one, as Dewey ironically put it – that would do justice to the active element and do away with the simple equation of experience with the passive reception of sense content immediately apprehended by the mind. And if these points are not sufficient for showing that the pragmatists did not regard philosophy as concerned exclusively with the nature of knowledge, one has but to recall their attack on the view that 'knowledge' marks out a privileged context. Knowing for them represents but one way of encountering what is; man has many relations to his environment other than that of being a theoretical knower. This and other points will be treated in more detail in the chapter on the theory of experience.

2 The theory of truth: basic conceptions

One can usually find, especially in books dealing chiefly with the theory of truth, a special section devoted to 'the pragmatic theory of truth',[1] and the assumption behind this division is that in addition to the well-known correspondence, coherence, idealistic, realistic, etc., theories of truth, there is one more theory, the pragmatic, which is supposed to be not only a unified theory but one which is distinct from all others and can be summed up in the formula that 'the true is what works'. Such a view is dependent, in part at least, on the belief that Pragmatism is a novel philosophical position whose proponents aimed at sweeping away previous philosophical traditions in order to establish a new and 'practical' outlook on the nature of things. Since a theory of truth has long been regarded as a fundamental philosophical topic, it is not difficult to understand why it came to be thought that there must be a unique pragmatic theory of truth intended at once to negate and supersede all previous theories. This assumption, of course, needs to be examined along with the closely connected supposition that 'Pragmatism' represents a sufficiently unified standpoint to contain but *one* conception of truth which can be identified as *the* pragmatic theory.

There are good reasons for believing that Pragmatism represents an indigenous American outlook on life and the world. Or, perhaps, to avoid any hint of jingoism, it would be more satisfactory to say that Pragmatism sums up beliefs and attitudes which have shaped the development of America as the many-sided phenomenon which it is – a people of peoples, a vast enterprise of industrial technology and the locus of a multi-levelled experiment in representative government. No one can read Peirce and James, Dewey and Mead and fail to appreciate their struggle to arrive at an understanding and interpretation of life and experience on the American scene. One senses at once the difference between their endeavours and the many attempts that were made to adapt philosophical ideas developed at other times and in other places for illuminating American life. This is not to say that American thought has not been heavily dependent, whether knowingly or not, on the insights of the Lockes, the Berkeleys, the Kants and the Hegels; it is rather that there is a very considerable difference between, for example, transplanting Hegel from Europe to America, as the so-called St Louis Hegelians sought to do, and reflecting on American life itself as a form of primary experience standing in need of philosophical analysis and interpretation. Pragmatism stands as one of the results of that original reflective endeavour, and the point of view developed has left its mark on every facet of American life.

If it is true that Pragmatism does embody this novel and distinctive character as a basic outlook, one may go on to ask the interesting philosophical question as to whether there is a distinctive pragmatic theory of truth, such as is often suggested in philosophy textbooks aimed at expounding familiar theories like correspondence, coherence, intitution, etc. Or is it perhaps the case that the pragmatists were reworking other theories, placing them in the context of inquiry and relating them to the demands of practical activity, without at the same time claiming that these theories are false or to be superseded? Such questions will remain in the background of the ensuing discussion to be considered after the basic conceptions have been set forth.

At the outset one would do well to accept the fact that, while Peirce, James and Dewey were at one in espousing a pragmatic approach to the determination of meaning, it is doubtful that all three understood the nature of truth and of knowledge in the same sense. In view of this fact it will be necessary to consider their ideas in turn and then attempt to point out the affiliations and divergences. In so doing, one must emphasize basic conceptions rather than attempt a genetic tracing of the many modifications in their views.[2]

It is characteristic of Peirce's position first to distinguish truth from reality, and then to relate the two to each other in an intelligible way.[3] Truth, he never tired of repeating, 'is that concordance of an abstract statement with the ideal limit towards which endless investigation would tend to bring scientific belief'.[4] What this concordance or correspondence means will be made clearer in what follows. Reality, on the other hand, is defined as 'that mode of being by virtue of which the real thing is as it is, irrespectively of what any mind or any definite collection of minds may represent it to be'.[5] Truth, as a character attaching to a proposition, therefore, is expressed as knowledge about a reality which maintains its independent tenure. Peirce, one should note, consistently refused to allow the collapse of the real into the true, even though in his view the two are intimately related. Truth is defined by him in terms of *correspondence*, the correspondence of a representation to its object.[6] The question is; What precisely does this correspondence mean, and in what circumstances can it be determined that the relationship holds between a representation and that of which it is a representation? Interested as he was in developing an abstract theory of truth, Peirce never lost sight of the need to relate the theory to actual processes through which truth is disclosed. Thought, to begin with, has the nature of a *sign* and involves necessarily the triadic structure of sign, object and interpretant. To arrive at the desired correspondence we must find the right *method* of thinking or of transforming signs, and truth is the final result to which following the method would lead us. That in the end to which the representation should conform is said to be something 'intelligible' or 'conceivable' and from this it might appear that Peirce was abandoning his realism in favour of some internal conformity between thought and itself. This, however, is not so; what Peirce was here maintaining is that in seeking truth we presuppose that the reality in question is intelligible, capable of being known and not an inaccessible thing-in-itself. The conceivability of the object, moreover, becomes essential if it is to be the object of the representation. Peirce was as insistent on this point as were Kant and Royce. There must be, he said, an *action* of the object on the sign if the sign is to be true, and without such action the object is not its object. The sign has to indicate its object, but in order to fulfil its function the sign must be compelled by the object.[7] In speaking of observation as a form of experience, Peirce said, 'It is the enforced element in the history of our lives. It is that which we are constrained to be conscious of by an occult force residing in an object which we contemplate.'[8] The object 'contemplated' must first have been indicated by the sign – 'What the sign virtually has to do in order to indicate its object . . . is just to seize its interpreter's eyes and forcibly turn them upon the object meant' – but that object is not the sign's object unless the sign is compelled by it. Though one might naturally stress the role of the sign or thought in qualifying its object in some mode or respect, Peirce was concerned to make room for the insistence of the object *vis à vis* the sign that represents it. There is here a clear demand that representations be in *conformity* with a reality intended, a demand that serves to distinguish Peirce's thought on this head from that of Dewey. The proposal to distinguish between *conform* and *transform* theories of truth is helpful at this point.[9]

The former position, as the term implies, appeals to the authoritative force of an antecedent reality and requires the adjustment of thought to that reality; the latter position rejects the antecedent reality, emphasizes the problematic or indeterminate character of the situation wherein thought is operative and aims at transforming that situation into a settled or determinate affair. That the transform approach is well illustrated by Dewey's logic is clear, but it is sometimes thought that transformism uniquely describes Pragmatism which is supposed to reject the condition of conformity. Peirce's thought, however, fails to fit the pattern because of his acceptance of correspondence and the consequent requirement that the true sign be in accord with an independent reality. James, it should be added, did not totally reject correspondence either; what he did claim is, first, that if correspondence is understood in the sense of 'copy', many of our ideas do not perform this function, and, second, that the 'static' relation of correspondence must be converted into an 'active commerce' between our mind and reality.

Going back to Peirce, we must understand his conception of truth as standing in continual correlation with his conception of reality. The true representation must conform to its proper object seen as independent of the representation. Since, however, truth is said to be a characteristic of a proposition or the thought that puts together the predicate and the object, the only meaning we can attach to the phrase that a thing 'has a character' is that 'something is *true* of it'.[10] The actual predication requires propositional form, and if the thing has the character predicated, the proposition is true. The character itself, however, is not dissolved into the truth of the proposition, but retains its tenure as a feature of the real.

The characterization of truth as such remains an abstract theory until it is recognized that truth is the goal of reasoning and the aim of inquiry. A full account of truth, therefore, cannot be separated from the process of inquiry through which it is or may be attained. Reference to the aim of this process of inquiry is what should be meant when it is said, whether of Peirce or of Pragmatism generally, that the test of truth enters essentially into the meaning of truth. On this view the theory of truth should serve as a guide or, what is the same, prescribe a method for determining the truth of a theory. Peirce was, of course, presupposing both the fact and the validity of the development of modern science, and much of what he said about truth residing in the opinion destined to be arrived at by the scientific community rests upon studies in the history of science which led him to the belief that the scientific approach has invariably led to that convergence of opinion which answers the questions initially prompting inquiry. The place of importance accorded method is clearly expressed in the following characterization of science:

... it does not consist so much in *knowing*, nor even in 'organized knowledge', as it does in diligent inquiry into truth for truth's sake, without any sort of axe to grind, nor for the sake of the delight of contemplating it, but from an impulse to penetrate into the reason of things.[11]

If truth is to attach to the representation expressing the outcome of inquiry and that inquiry itself is to exercise a normative or critical force with respect to the outcome, then it is essential that the logical structure of the process be set forth so that its probative function becomes evident. Peirce, as is well known, wrote extensively in the field of logic and the foundation of mathematics, and he is now acknowledged as a major contributor to the logic of relatives. None of his work, however, is more important for the theory of truth and knowledge than his account of the logical structure of scientific reasoning. All inquiry, he held, begins with questions and 'goes upon the assumption that there is a true answer to whatever questions may be under discussion, which answer cannot be rendered false by anything that the disputants may say or think about it; and further, that the denial of that true answer is false'.[12] Peirce regarded this as *the* assumption underlying all genuine truth-seeking and unless it is made, he was ready to claim that the inquirer is not serious. Inquiry involves three logical forms arranged in successive stages beginning with what is called *abduction*,[13] passing through processes of *deduction* and ending with the tests of *induction*. Abduction means the consideration of a mass of fact in such ways as to allow these facts to suggest a theory intended to explain them. Abduction represents the source of novelty in ideas and reaches out to the explanations of real things, but of itself it has no 'probative force', something which can be attained only through the further combination of deduction and experimental test. It must not be supposed, however, that because Peirce frequently related abduction to human instinct[14] and believed in an intimate connection or attunement between the 'natural light' of human thought and the structure of the universe, he regarded abduction as a purely immediate or intuitive affair. On the contrary, he referred to Kepler's feat in arriving at the true orbit of Mars as 'the greatest piece of Retroductive reasoning ever performed',[15] and it is clear from numerous examples that even when he described the proposal of hypotheses as 'guesses' he clearly meant 'sophisticated' guesses informed by fact and expressing provisional suppositions as to some general feature or relationship exhibited by them. Abduction has conditions, but these cannot be formalized for all cases; there is no 'logic' of discovery.

With a theory in hand, deduction comes into play for the purpose of deducing a variety of consequences such that, if certain acts or operations be performed, such-and-such experiences will be encountered. For example, taking it to be the case that sodium, nitrogen, carbon and boron cannot be decomposed chemically, we make the supposition that they are elements or 'simples', one of the consequences of which is that they will always behave differently, in at least one respect, from the way compounds such as sodium chloride will behave under definite conditions. For Peirce the deductive aspect of inquiry is necessary or certain but is applicable only to an ideal object. The function of deduction, then, is to inform us of what must follow if the theory is in force; it remains for induction or experimental testing to determine whether in fact the predicted consequences are realized. 'Induction,' said Peirce, 'gives us the only approach to certainty concerning the real that we can have',[16] and it is 'the only capable *imperator* of truth-seeking'.[17] It is clear that Peirce was, on the one hand, appealing to the actual successes of modern science as evidence for his view of truth as the outcome of inquiry, but, on the other, he was offering a logic of that 'success' in the form of the three types of reasoning with their respective functions and scope.

The foregoing abstract logical schema of inquiry and its aim of truth-seeking would remain quite incomplete were it not related to Peirce's idea of perseverance in inquiry and his belief in the force of truth and experience as determining a convergence of opinion in the form of an ultimate opinion to which inquiry is 'destined' to lead. In this regard the theory of science and of truth cannot, in Peirce's view, be elaborated without reference to a larger context embracing the nature of the real and its relation to the inquirer who seeks to grasp it in the form of truth. It would be a mistake to think of Peirce's theory as moving simply within the circle of the successes of science, wherein the validity of the reasoning is to rest on the large number of successes in particular inquiries, for this success itself needs to be explained. The self-corrective character of science and its superiority to the other methods of fixing belief were, to be sure, presupposed by Peirce, but he was also concerned to offer, in terms of his evolutionary cosmology, a theory of the nature of mind, matter and temporal pattern that would render intelligible the fact that man discovers some truth about the real through the light of reason. In other words, the successes of scientific inquiry are not left in their immediacy at the level of brute fact but must be understood as manifestations of patterns of development underlying the evolution of the entire universe. Thus Peirce, unlike Dewey, followed in the line of Kant and his concern to show how knowledge is 'possible', but his answer was more ontologically oriented than Kant's critical philosophy could allow. For Peirce, there are independent reals and the categories express the structure of these reals and not only the form of thought. The comparison with Dewey, however is instructive, because Dewey invariably took the 'How is knowledge possible?' question to mean the quest for an absolute guarantee involving our knowing for certain when we know. Dewey, moreover, insisted that answers to questions about the nature of knowledge should themselves function in the process of reaching warranted assertions, i.e. they belong to methodology. Peirce, on the other hand, was more speculative in his approach; knowledge, no less than anything else, must be explained in terms of an intelligible scheme of things.

In his account of the logic of science[18] Peirce claimed that different sciences are concerned with different kinds of truth, and he enumerated mathematical truth, ethical truth and the truth about the actually existing state of the universe as examples. These conceptions, he said, have a basic feature in common, a feature he regarded as 'very marked and clear'. It is stated as both a hope and an aim of all inquirers; the passage bears quoting in full.

We all hope that the different scientific inquiries in which we are severally engaged are going ultimately to lead to some definitely established conclusion, which conclusion we endeavor to anticipate in some measure. Agreement with that ultimate proposition that we look forward to, – agreement with that, whatever it may turn out to be, is the scientific truth.[19]

To avoid confusion here, two things must be kept in view. First, the 'agreement' in question does not mean simply that all serious inquirers will 'agree' to accept the opinion expressed in the ultimate proposition. That sort of 'agreement' is presupposed in any case. Secondly, what is meant is that with respect to every intelligible question there is grounded, *in the nature of the real objects* referred to, a definite answer to be found and when the ultimate answer is expressed in the ultimate proposition as the truth, that proposition will be in agreement with reality. On Peirce's view this reference to reality is necessary to show that the opinions of inquirers stand under an independent constraint that goes beyond the constraint which they impose upon themselves in logical self-control. Were it not so, his view could be reduced to the thesis that truth is simply identical with what a community of inquirers 'agree' to accept, a thesis which clearly does not eliminate the perpetration of an organized 'scientific' hoax. Therefore, when one says that Peirce's proposal is to translate truth and objectivity into intersubjective agreement, this is true only when asserted in conjunction with the independent constraint exercised by the real.[20]

In a section of the *Logic* of 1873 Peirce made a special point of analysing the conception of external realities and the force they exert in order to relate that conception to his doctrine that investigation leads, in time, to a definite conclusion. There Peirce argued that it is a pervasive fact about the nature of controlled observation that, although singular observations may differ among themselves, a convergent or identical result is obtained. The question is: How is this fact about observation to be explained? Peirce's proposal was the conception (or hypothesis) of external realities,[21] which implies that the observations are the result of the 'action' upon the mind of external things, while the diversity in observation is due to the plurality of relations in which we stand to what is observed. Critical judgement attributes the identical result of observation to the 'identity of the things observed', and at the same time separates this constant element from the differences in observation which are put down to the differing and varying elements occasioned by our varying relations to the thing in question. Peirce's claim was that the supposition of external things exerting a constant influence on observers 'removes the strangeness' of the fact that observations, though different, come finally to yield an identical result. The appeal, however, to a *causal* relationship as explanatory of truth in the form of the definite conclusion in which inquiry terminates, is not an appeal that ever satisfied Peirce.[22] He recognized the force or insistence of fact – what he called 'secondness' manifest in action and reaction – and criticized Hegel for failing to take sufficient notice of his insistence in his inexorable pursuit of mediation (Peirce's 'thirdness'). Though acknowledging the causal role of external realities in the observational phase of inquiry, however, Peirce was not willing to assimilate the truth that attaches to the outcome of inquiry to the causality implicit in the dyad.[23] His own statement is clear and explicit:

. . . is not that fact that investigation leads to a definite conclusion really of so different a character from the ordinary events in the world to which we apply the conception of causation that such an assimiliation and classification of it really puts it in a light which, though not absolutely false, fails nevertheless to bring into due prominence the real peculiarity of its nature? That observation and reasoning produce a settled belief which we call the truth seems a principle to be placed at the head of all special truths which are only the particular beliefs to which observation and reasoning in such cases lead.[24]

From such a statement it is clear that, for Peirce, truth is not to be regarded as merely a collective name for many truths, nor is it a term denoting singular verifications, nor again is it to be wholly understood in terms of the causal relation involved in dyads. Truth is the critical and normative character attaching to the outcome of inquiry that has taken place in accordance with logical and experimental canons. The disclosure of truth on any singular occasion is very far from exhausting its meaning because the conditions of such disclosure are *general* and involve the relations between the real, the structure of inquiry and the activity of the human mind. Peirce's account of science and truth in the end is neither a genetic account of belief, nor the logical syntax of scientific language nor even the process of verification. It is instead a proposal pointing to the 'attunement' between human reason and the independent reals which ultimately determine the answers to well-formed questions about them. The primordial abduction made in the pursuit of truth is that the facts in question admit of 'rationalization' by human knowers. The next consideration is that the possible explanations 'may be strictly innumerable' and, therefore, some other factor must be operative for the 'shortening' of the process of selection. Peirce had much to say about the role of 'economy' in experimental procedure which not only manifests his reliance on the actual development of science as opposed to accounts of its supposed 'timeless' logical structure, but shows his anticipation of the current appeal to the history of science as well.

In numerous places[25] Peirce discussed the role of instinct in the *selection* of hypotheses which initiate inquiry, and he was prepared to express this role in the form of another hypothesis underlying abduction or the first phase of inquiry. 'It is a primary hypothesis underlying all abduction,' he wrote, 'that the human mind is akin to the truth in the sense that in a finite number of guesses it will light upon the correct hypothesis.'[26] It was Peirce's contention that this abduction is itself inductively supported by evidence from the history and development of scientific inquiry. One must not be misled by Peirce's use of the term 'guess' because he was not referring to 'random' guesses or what has been called 'sheer guessing' – assuming that 'sheer guessing' is possible in any situation sufficiently determinate to indicate *what* one is guessing about – but rather to guesses made in conditions that greatly narrow the rational possibilities. Suppose, for example, one were asked to guess the 'fine structure constant' without any knowledge whatever about the meaning of the expression except that the answer is a *number* of some sort, rather than, let us say, a colour or the name of a chemical compound. That one item, however, vastly reduces the possibilities. Peirce's point is that if, for every surprising phenomenon it were necessary to run the gamut of such possibilities as that the behaviour of the empress five hours previously or the positions of the planets determined the fact, no progress in science would have been made, or at least none of the proportions represented by the actual development of science in the last three centuries. But, he argued, the actual situation is quite otherwise:

That we have made solid gains in knowledge is indisputable; and moreover, the history of science proves that when the phenomena were properly analysed, upon fundamental points, at least, it has seldom been necessary to try more than two or three hypotheses made by clear genius before the right one was found.[27]

None of this, of course, is meant to imply that the instinctive, as distinct from the reasoning, factor in knowing plays a major role outside of abduction. The underlying thesis of Peirce concerns the relation between the human mind and the reality it seeks to know, and the argument which follows his own pattern for inquiry embraces an inductively supported abduction about the evolution of science. One of the best accounts of the foundations of inquiry was given by Peirce in his remarkable article 'A Neglected Argument for the Reality of God'.[28] There he rejected the theory that the fact of scientific development can be explained by invoking chance because

there is a reason, an interpretation, a logic, in the course of scientific advance, and this indisputably proves to him who has perceptions of rational or significant relations, that man's mind must have been attuned to the truth of things in order to discover what he has discovered.[29]

The significance of the science of evolution for Pragmatism has been thoroughly explored,[30] but it seems that not enough attention has been paid to the significance Peirce attached to the evolution of science itself. Both Peirce and Dewey relied heavily on the *fact* of science and its development in arriving at their philosophical conclusions. Peirce's theory of knowledge and truth is, as should be clear, an abduction from the history of science, and Dewey's fundamental claims about the essential connection between thought and action are based on the fact that science is a *working togetherness* of theory and the manipulation of natural objects and forces in controlled experimentation.[31] In both cases, the significance of science for Pragmatism consists not so much in pointing to its authority as a method of knowing but rather that the pragmatists sought to find a theory that would explain or make intelligible the fact of scientific advance.

The foregoing account shows that Peirce had a normative conception of truth rooted in an essentially realistic conception of things. Before proceeding to James' understanding of truth, a brief comment is in order concerning Peirce's critical attitude towards the idea that truth is bound up with what is 'satisfactory'. In the 'Basis of Pragmatism' (1906) Peirce commented on the thesis that 'the true is simply the satisfactory' with the rejoinder: 'To say "satisfactory" is not to complete any predicate whatever. Satisfactory to what end?'[32] Therefore, Peirce argued, unless the equation of 'true' and 'satisfactory' means no more than the proposed synonymy of the two words, it is necessary to specify further what is meant by saying that the true is the 'satisfactory in cognition'. Peirce rejected the possibility that 'satisfactory' is to mean 'whatever excites a certain peculiar feeling of satisfaction'[33] as a form of 'hedonism'. With his own idea that truth is the aim of inquiry in the background, Peirce insisted that to speak of an action or the result of action as 'satisfactory' requires that it is in conformity with an aim which must be specified in advance. In the absence of such an aim, satisfactoriness cannot be determined. It is clear that Peirce was here trying to avoid any appeal to individual feeling as a criterion and at the same time to subject the determination of what is 'satisfactory' in the way of cognition to the aim of inquiry which is the *truth*. In this way Peirce was able to retain the prospective emphasis of his Pragmaticism according to which truth consists in congruence with or conformity to an end, and at the same time ensure that the determination of when this conformity holds is an objective affair subject to the constraining rules of inquiry.

One of the reasons why James' thought proves to be more difficult to comprehend than one might have supposed is that he constantly strove to give to the reader a sense of how easy everything would be if he would only consult his own experience and avoid being deceived by 'abstract', 'intellectualist' jargon. One is likely to be carried along on the crest of ordinary experience only to find that this experience itself is not so familiar after all, and that the 'jargon' of philosophers is the result not so much of an esoteric tendency but of the shortcomings of familiar and even colloquial language to make clear what is involved in the situations wherein such language is used. There is, to be sure, much truth in the drive back to primary experience, and, like Wittgenstein, James was adept at making the move, but his use of ordinary expressions to express philosophical ideas which, despite their relevance to ordinary life, are not themselves ordinary, holds out possibilities for misunderstanding.[34] One need only cite the use of such terms as 'success', 'practical', 'cash value', and 'expedient' in order to make the point.

With this warning in mind, one may proceed more confidently in the attempt to understand what James meant by the concept of truth. To begin with, he insisted on the centrality of this concept and claimed that establishing a pragmatic theory of truth is essential as a foundation for the doctrine of 'radical empiricism' which occupied him in his last years. The connection between the two is obviously important because, as *The*

Meaning of Truth makes clear, James developed his concept of truth along the lines of his radical empiricism. The latter, he tells us, can be summed up in terms of a postulate, a fact and a generalized conclusion. The *postulate* is that all that can be debatable among philosophers shall be 'things definable in terms drawn from experience'. The *fact* is that the conjunctive relations between things ('and', logically, and 'with', existentially) are as much a matter of particular experience as the things themselves and the more highly emphasized analytic or disjunctive relations. The *generalized conclusion,* actually James' most distinctive metaphysical thesis, is that the universe contains its own continuous structure and is therefore not in need of 'trans-empirical connective support' stemming from beyond in the form of Absolutes and transcendental egos.[35] In accordance with this doctrine the meaning of truth would have to be expressed as a sort of continuous process wherein one passes from some particular idea or judgement to the object or state of affairs about which that idea or judgement makes a claim. For James, truth like everything else is to be understood in terms of what it is 'known as', which means the tracing out of what actually happens when a claim to truth is verified. If one were to single out the view which was the primary target of James' criticism, it would be the thesis that there are timeless meanings expressed as 'propositions' which stand in an equally timeless relation of correspondence to their objects, quite apart from any singular occasion when an existing person believes or asserts such a proposition and engages himself in the process of discovering whether it is true or not. The point is not that James rejected correspondence or agreement as definitive of truth – although he was aware of the extent to which not all of our ideas can 'copy' reality – but rather that his humanism and his conviction that a truth must 'make a difference' led him to reinterpret this agreement, replacing the 'static' relation between idea and object with a dynamic structured process whereby the individual holding the idea is brought into relation with whatever it is that the idea refers to. Being thus related, moreover, is not mere conjuction or juxtaposition of an individual and an object but rather the coming into the presence of the object or state of affairs as the direct result of being led there by following the clues furnished by the idea as to what would verify it. In short, James was building into the idea of truth the process that must be initiated and carried through if one is to discover on any singular occasion whether one has *a* truth or not. By 'workings' and 'consequences' James meant precisely the process of verifying, and by 'success' he meant the situation wherein the claim or expectation expressed in the idea or judgement is fulfilled in the object. He insisted, moreover, 'that the existence of the object, whenever the idea asserts it "truly", is the only reason, in innumerable cases, why the idea does work successfully'.[36] The reason for the qualification introduced by 'in innumerable cases' is important and attention to it will help to avoid the confusion that invariably enters at this point. One might have expected

James to say 'in all cases' and indeed were he interested exclusively in external or completed fact – the gold in yonder mountain is there or not quite independently of any belief about it – he would not have added the qualification. James was, however, interested in future states of affairs involving human purposes, resolves and actions where what will later be called a fact, has either not yet taken place or is in the making (leaping across a chasm or trusting a friend) and where, as he maintained, belief in the *possibility* of the outcome's having a certain character is, or may be, a factor in producing the result. In these cases involving a future outcome where the 'object' does not have, as the gold does, an independent tenure in advance of all human will and effort, one cannot simply refer to the existence of the object as the sole reason why the idea works 'successfully'. Wild has referred to these cases as 'existential beliefs' that concern ourselves and are self-verifying or self-falsifying depending on the outcome. If I act on the belief that I *can* leap the chasm and antecedent belief in the possibility of success affects my effort in a positive way, then I have contributed *in some measure* to the outcome if it is successful. James' point is not that one is entitled to the simplistic claim that the leap was successful *because* of the antecedent belief in its possibility, but rather than acting on that belief helped to contribute to an outcome that, without it, would have turned out differently. If this is so, the belief is 'true' about some aspects at least of the total situation in which it figured.

What James did not sufficiently distinguish, to the consternation of supporters and critics alike, is the difference between acting on a belief when the aim is to *discover* what's what about finished fact taken to be quite independent of an individual's purposes, interests, etc., and acting on a belief when the aim is to *produce* or bring about some future state of affairs not obviously independent of the resolve and effort of an individual. This difference is not accurately expressed through the oft-repeated contrast between the logical consequences of the idea or judgement, and the consequence of believing. Both cases represent the consequences of believing, but the aims are different. In the first case, the aim is to test – in accordance with the theoretical purpose which James fully accepted as *one* purpose among others – a claim about finished fact, and in the second the aim is to contribute to the shaping of an event which, without my resolve and effort, would not occur or, if it did occur, would occur differently. James, not unlike Dewey at certain points, was always close to conflating knowing, making and doing (the classical Aristotelian distinction) largely because of his stress on the fact that knowing involves doing and his concern to show the relevance of knowing for both making and doing.

James shared with the phenomenologists the assumption that questions concerning the meaning and nature of things can be resolved by accurate description of the situations and processes in and through which these things manifest themselves. Thus James could say, on page 1 of 'The

Function of Cognition' that his inquiry is not into the 'how it comes' but into the 'what it is', and at the same time refer to his analysis as 'a chapter in descriptive psychology'. The distinction drawn cannot be regarded as clearcut, since James' account of cognition draws heavily on 'what actually happens' when cognition occurs and how the intermediaries in experience work to do away with any ultimate gap between an idea and the object it is supposed to know.[37] And indeed were this not so, it would be difficult to explain why James was repeatedly forced to meet the charge of those who claimed that the 'workings' – are these not the 'how it comes'? – may *accompany* truth but they do not *constitute* it. However this particular issue may be resolved, James could hardly rule out consideration of 'how it comes' in his discussion of truth because of his emphasis on the process involved in verifying. 'Truth *happens* to an idea,' he said. 'It *becomes* true, is *made* true by events.'[38] All of which is to say that, on his view, truth cannot be understood apart from the sequence of events – mental or physical – required for determining when an idea has been verified.

Like Peirce, James understood truth as a relation between an idea (statement, belief) and an object, and he stood ready to accept the view that this relation is one of agreement in the case of truth and disagreement in the case of falsity.[39] He was quite insistent that in all cases a 'real' object is involved existing independently of the ideas and feelings ingredient in the process of cognition. On the other hand, one must not overlook the fact that James repeatedly placed primary emphasis on the idea, its function in the living experience of the knower, and especially its directive force in focusing the attention and action of the one who has it. By contrast, he thought of the 'intellectualists' as favouring the reality of the object and its being 'just there' as something demanding conformity to itself apart from all ideas and would-be knowers. While James did not go as far as Dewey in identifying an idea as an instrument or weapon, he did express dissatisfaction with the doctrine that the function of the idea is merely to duplicate the object and thus give rise to a reproduction in thought of a world once given in fact.

It has frequently been pointed out that James was unique among the pragmatists in assigning to the sensible element in knowledge a cognitive force of its own. This is true and it constitutes his point of closest contact with classical empiricism and its reliance on sense as an ultimate criterion. Had James not, after all, described his thought as exhibiting a mosaic character like that of Hume, and did he not claim that Hume was on the right track in tracing all ideas back to their sensible origins, except that he had not gone far enough in his quest and consequently missed the connections and continuities because of his belief that the disjoined and the distinct are primordial and more 'real'? Peirce and Dewey, on the other hand, regarded sense experience as but one element in an ongoing process of inquiry and neither allowed that there is any knowledge based on sense alone. Moreover, they not only accorded to conceptual transformation a more significant role than did James, but they also refused to see in the concept nothing more than a token – a 'bank note', in James' phrase – whose validity is identical with its being actually exchanged for 'cash'.

At the root of James' theory of cognition and of truth stands the distinction between *acquaintance* and *knowledge about*, a distinction which proved to be just about as large a bone of philosophical contention during the first three decades of this century as can be imagined. Dispute revolved about at least three issues. First, there was the question whether it is legitimate to claim that there is 'knowledge' by acquaintance; second, there was the issue as to whether acquaintance forms an ultimate criterion for knowledge about, as is suggested by James' claim that knowledge about must always be traceable to acquaintance as its foundation, and, finally, it was asked whether it is correct to characterize acquaintance solely in terms of the *percept* taken as the sensible component in contrast to knowledge about, which is regarded as wholly *conceptual* in nature. With whatever wisdom comes from hindsight it is now possible to take a more measured look at these issues, and especially to determine the extent of verbal confusion involved.

James' initial distinction between acquaintance and knowledge about was derived, as he clearly acknowledged, from John Grote. James was unambiguous in identifying acquaintance or familiarity with the object through co-presence, handling it, etc., with sensation and the percept, while knowledge about is said to be conceptual or symbolic in form. And it is clear that, if one asks what answers to the 'about' in this conceptual knowledge, the proper response is that knowledge about is *about* the realities that are matters of acquaintance. As it stands, this doctrine might occasion no special difficulty were it not for the fact that James took the percept to be a distinctive component and one endowed with a cognitive capacity of its own which seems to have no essential involvement with or dependence on a conceptual feeling or thought. On this view, the percept p is said to cognize q if two conditions are fulfilled: p must in the first place resemble q, and, in the second place, p must directly or indirectly 'operate on' q. The first condition alone does not suffice, said James, because there are innumerable resemblances that do not involve cognition. More important for establishing that p refers to and is cognizant of q is that p must have some *effect* on q. Despite the length of James' discussion, the central point does not stand out as clearly as one could wish. His claim is that I can be sure that you mean the same world I mean if you effect it '*just as I should* if I were in your place'.[40] 'I think,' he wrote, 'you have the notion of fire in general, because I see you act towards this fire in my room just as I act towards it . . .'[41] In the end, he concluded, we all know, think and talk about the same world, '*because we believe our* PERCEPTS *are possessed by us in common*'.[42] And the basis of this belief is that our percepts seem to be changed as a regular *consequence* of changes in the percepts of someone else.

More important, however, than James' theory of the cognitive function of percepts as such is his further claim that a concept has its cognitive role solely in virtue of the fact that it terminates in a percept that operates on or resembles its reality. Percepts – sometimes called by James sensations, though he clearly distinguished the two in *The Principles of Psychology* – represent both the *terminus a quo* and the *terminus ad quem* of all thought. In short, the 'knowledges by acquaintance' represented by percepts 'are the only realities we ever directly know'[43] and all supposed 'knowledge about' must end in these percepts. Concepts, it would appear, have no distinctive cognitive office of their own, but are to serve merely as maps and plans whereby one is brought face to face with the percepts that represent the cash value of these conceptual bank notes.[44] The empiricist thrust of his position is clear, as is also the motive behind it: thought must be repeatedly checked and controlled by the subject matter to which it refers or is 'about' and, as James' critique of Bradley shows, his distrust of 'abstractions' stemmed from the belief that if thought is allowed to have its own self-contained aim its flight will proceed entirely on the level of ideas without those 'perching places' in experience which serve to determine whether there is any 'cash' for the 'bank notes' with which thought trades. Despite the too-simple conception of an 'exchange' between percept and concept implied in this account, James was justified in his demand that primary experience not be allowed to fall from sight, and that it should remain as a constraining force *vis à vis* conceptual elaboration. But one may well question the dichotomy set up by the identification of primary experience with percept and 'knowledge by acquaintance' as over against 'knowledge about' which is exclusively conceptual. It does not, moreover, suffice to say that acquaintance and knowledge about form two coordinate domains. For it is clear, as Royce and others pointed out in James' time, that both perceptual and conceptual elements are on *each* side of the dichotomy. What James meant by 'acquaintance' cannot be realized without invoking concepts and what he meant by 'knowledge about' clearly cannot be regarded as devoid of all perceptual content. The two, therefore, cannot be adequately described in terms of a perceptual–conceptual dichotomy. This, it will be recalled, was the third of the issues previously mentioned in connection with acquaintance and knowledge about; the other two concern, first, the legitimacy of claiming that there is 'knowledge' by acquaintance, and, second, whether acquaintance can be the full and final criterion for judging knowledge about.

As regards the claim that acquaintance is knowledge, one aspect of the controversy is purely verbal. If the term 'knowledge' is reserved exclusively for the *outcome* of consciously instituted and critically controlled inquiry as expressed in propositional form, then there is no 'knowledge' by acquaintance. The reason is simply that acquaintance involves a direct encounter with whatever is the object of attention, and while that may also include 'knowing how' to use or handle it, there is no reference to any sort of inquiry. James did not in fact always mean this much by 'acquaintance' and he frequently thought of it as confined to the presence of an object to someone who experiences it; the important point is that in acquaintance there is no deliberate inquiry involved of the sort which Peirce and Dewey described as the hallmark of science. Acquaintance situations, on the contrary, belong for the most part to ongoing *experience* and represent occasions when it is quite inappropriate to speak of an *experiment* taking place. It seems clear, therefore, that however we characterize acquaintance, it is not knowledge if the latter term is rigorously confined to the critical results of purposely instituted experiment.

So much for the verbal aspect of the issue. What, however, is to be said about the more substantial problem of how to characterize the acquaintance situation itself? For even those who deny that it yields knowledge have not generally gone on to claim that acquaintance means nothing at all. Dewey sought to deal with the problem by distinguishing between 'having' and 'knowing': the former represents encounters with the world and experiences undergone or 'suffered' without there being any need to 'know' them, while the latter is identified exclusively with the warranted assertions resulting from controlled inquiry. This view has some merit, but it has the disadvantage of turning all direct experience into something basically 'aesthetic' – to be 'had' and not 'known' – and it fails to do justice to all that human beings discover about themselves and the world as a result of a lived experience for which there is no substitute. Acquaintance in the form of sensation or direct presence may be, as James said, 'speechless', but it cannot be 'I know not what' nor can it be a bare 'that' awaiting a 'what' at the hand of 'knowledge about'. The reason is that there is no bare 'that' devoid of some connotation, and as for the speechlessness, that may be due to nothing more substantial than the fact that 'speech' has been illegitimately handed over entirely to knowledge about. Acquaintance on this account may be 'speechless' but it cannot be dumb!

No one can consistently deny, except perhaps in the interest of a theory specifically developed to exclude ordinary experience, that much of what everyone thinks about, talks about and acts upon, comes to our attention or finds its way within our 'ken' through the medium of acquaintance of some sort or other. Friendship, love, vengeance, forgiveness – the best examples because they involve primary relations between persons – would be mere words[45] to anyone who had not actually stood in those relations or at the least participated in them vicariously through the medium of imaginative literature. The question is: Can one live through, suffer, undergo the experience of vengeance or forgiveness and yet 'know' nothing of what they mean? This seems quite absurd on the face of it, and yet it is precisely what is implied by the view that knowledge properly so-called can be nothing but the outcome of controlled inquiry. And to make the matter worse, one has but to consider that many such instances of primary experience would be transformed or even destroyed if an attempt were made to introduce 'inquiry' into the situations in which these experiences are realized. It is as if one said, 'I wasn't really forgiving you, I was only practising forgiveness in order to verify an hypothesis about human behaviour in forgiveness situations.' The point is not to deny the value of theoretical inquiry, but rather to point out that most acquaintance situations, especially those involving relations between persons, are not situations of purposive, controlled inquiry even though one may come to know something about a person or thing through acquaintance. One does indeed understand, discover, know, through acquaintance, but two decisive limitations must always be taken into account in connection with such knowledge: first, it is *vague,* having no more precision than is generally required in ordinary ongoing experience, and, second, it is subject to *error* because it is shot through with habitual interpretation and inference which in the actual situation invariably go unchecked.

It seems quite likely that knowledge by acquaintance will be more readily admitted in the case of interpersonal experience than in that involving physical objects, events and complex relations between them. There is, however, no indication that James intended to restrict such knowledge to the former category. There are, in fact, indications that James thought of *all* knowledge about as having acquaintance for its ultimate referent. The question is: Can this relationship be expressed in an unambiguous way? On some occasions James clearly regarded acquaintance as furnishing the reality or 'cash' answering to what 'knowledge about' is about. Thus, I may have the idea of a large island off the Asian mainland named Japan, and about that island I may claim to know that there is on it a beautiful and fabled mountain located between Tokyo and Kyoto and known as Fuji. To the extent that I am not acquainted with either the island or the mountain, i.e. I have not landed on the island or seen the mountain, my idea and purported knowledge represent trading on credit with conceptual 'bank notes' which, though they may be *cashable* through actual acquaintance, have not in fact been cashed by me. But even in this case, I would have to understand that what my idea and knowledge are *about* is the island and the mountain with which I would be acquainted if I were in their presence. This role of acquaintance in introducing realities and actual subject matter into the knowledge context is unobjectionable and appears quite continuous with traditional empiricism and its demand that the knower should be, or be capable of being, in *the presence* of the object which he purports to know. There is, however, in James' account a second and somewhat more ambitious role assigned to acquaintance: it appears not only as a secure *foundation* for knowledge about, but it serves as well as its *test* in the sense that in the absence of having a specific counterpart in the manifold of acquaintance, a given idea or conceptual expression is a 'mere' idea, a bank note that is bankrupt. To the extent that acquaintance is assimilated to percepts and knowledge about to concepts, the necessary consequence is that *sense* is the ultimate criterion of truth and conceptual thought is no more than a surrogate or a means for coming into the presence of the sensible reality.

The analysis given by James in 'The Tigers in India'[46] clearly supports this interpretation, except that there James spoke of 'immediately' or 'intuitively' knowing things as synonymous with 'acquaintance' and he identified conceptual knowing as 'representative' by contrast. To say that we now, located in, say, America, know the tigers in India conceptually is to say that our thought 'points to' the tigers, and this 'pointing' is 'known simply and solely as a procession of mental associates and motor consequences that follow on the thought, and that would lead harmoniously, if followed out, into some ideal or real context, or even into the immediate presence, of the tigers'.[47] There is, according to James, no 'self-transcendency' in our 'mental images' (concepts?) so that their 'pointing to' the tigers is a purely intra-experiential relation as long as there is a connecting world – presumably of thoughts and actions as well as space and time – through which we can pass from thought to thing. Conceptual knowing here and now of the absent thing, then, is the same as *being led to it* through the intermediaries. By contrast, acquaintance is knowing face to face without intermediaries, and it is clear that James regarded the 'ultimate data' of acquaintance as precisely what one is led to when one follows the pointings of conceptual or representative thought in order to come into the presence of the object indicated.

It is difficult to be clear about James' meaning here. On the one hand he was wary about the 'self-transcendency' of ideas and as against that he urged some 'intra-experiential' pointing or 'leading' function for the idea, the meaning of which is to be the actual leading or the actually being led to the object 'meant'. The difficulty, however, is that the object to be led to must be absent, but it must also be 'meant' *while it is absent* and that 'meaning' or 'intending' cannot be *identical* with some actual process of passing through intermediaries to reach the intended object. Reaching that object, moreover, cannot be a matter of mere conjunction; the object must be the object that was 'meant' and it must have been reached as the purposive result of using the idea as a map or recipe for reaching the object meant. A person standing next to or leaning against Memorial Hall could not be said to be *knowing* it in the sense in which this would be true of a person who had been led to just that object by having used the idea of Memorial Hall as a map for reaching the object meant. Hence, even if the 'meaning' or 'pointing' were translated into the successful process of arriving at the object, the 'purposive' or 'intentional' aspect of the process would remain, i.e. we would have to know that the object reached was the one 'meant' and that it was reached via the purposive use of the idea.

Again, there is nothing essentially novel from the classical empiricist standpoint in this account. The concept means and is judged by the sensible data yielded by the presence of the object, and it has no cognitive office other than to lead to that object. The leading, however, is not an 'intentional' function, but an *operation* of passing through intermediaries from thought to thing so that reference becomes *identical* with the process whereby it is determined whether there is anything to which the concept refers. For all of James' charges that rationalistic idealists confuse truth with reality, it is difficult to see why the same charge could not be made against his or any position which makes the validity of the concept a function of its successfully leading us into the presence of the object. The 'cash', it would appear, *is* the *truth* of the 'bank notes'.

No extended discussion of the third issue mentioned previously – the propriety of describing direct presence or acquaintance exclusively in terms of percept – is necessary. The fact is that there is no denying the validity of Kant's central thesis that all experience requires a togetherness of perceptual and conceptual elements and that the perceptual or sensible component considered by itself is but an abstract element. Acquaintance cannot be understood in terms of pure percept because there is no such thing; acquaintance and familiarity with the object is shot through with both concept and inference, and conversely, at the level of conceptual apprehension it would be difficult to find expressions totally devoid of some perceptual content.[48] One is tempted to say that the percept–concept dichotomy which James presupposed simply will not 'work'; it is especially inadequate at the point where it necessitates the identification of acquaintance with the percept as if percepts were possible without either concepts or language.[49]

One would, however, do James a great injustice not to point out the crucial fact that the meaning which 'percept' bears in his epistemological discussion is abstract in the highest degree. In focusing on the nature of knowledge and truth, James understood the percept essentially in terms of the sensible singulars of acquaintance – the 'cash' or states of affairs to which concepts refer or express knowledge about – which stand over against general ideas. Such a view of the percept, however, is not as rich and complex as the account of perception given by James in his own *Principles*.[50] Numerous questions about the nature of the percept raised by his characterization of acquaintance through the percept when he was discussing the nature of truth are answered by his experiential treatment of perception in the context of descriptive psychology. I do not mean to suggest that perception is understood in the *Principles* in a sense totally different from the meaning assigned to it in *The Meaning of Truth*, but rather to call attention to the abstractness of the epistemological discussion so that the full dimensions of his phenomenological account will not be ignored.[51]

In attempting to summarize James' presentation of the pragmatic conception of truth, it will be helpful to attend first to his own summary,[52] and, second, to his 'final word' on the topic as set forth in 'The Pragmatist Account of Truth and its Misunderstanders'.[53] In the summary James was at pains to point out six features emphasized in the earlier account, by which is meant chiefly 'The Function of Cognition' (1884), and four points on which he later regarded that account as defective. In the paper of 1884, James claimed that he clearly asserted the following: (a) the reality as external to the true idea; (b) the reader's belief as the warrant for the existence of this reality; (c) the experienceable environment as the medium connecting knower and known in the *cognitive relation*; (d) the notion of *pointing* through this medium as a condition of our being said to know the reality pointed to; (e) the ideas of *resembling* and *affecting* the object as indications that the idea points to that object and no other; (f) the elimination of the 'epistemological gulf' between idea and object and the locating of the truth-relation wholly within experience. Reconsidering these points later at the time of the publication of *The Meaning of Truth* (1909), James pointed out the following 'defects' in it: first, an undue emphasis on resemblance, and also on the capacity of the idea to operate on its object; secondly, insufficient clarification and development of the conception of the 'workability' of the idea as equivalent to that 'satisfactory adaptation' of idea to object which constitutes the truth relation,[54] and, finally, the inadequacy of regarding percepts as the only realm of reality, and the need to add concepts as a 'co-ordinate realm'. The curious fact about this last point is that James did not re-examine the initial percept–concept distinction, but, upon recognizing the inadequacy of reducing all knowledge to the percept,[55] he thought to make up the deficiency merely by 'adding' concepts. As Royce pointed out, James never got away from the idea that concepts can be handled simply by 'exchanging' them for percepts.

It is interesting in the extreme that James, sensitive though he was to criticism and to the views of others, only belatedly thought to attribute the persistent misunderstanding of his position on the part of others to his own choice of language and form of expression. It is indeed a quite unusual source of confusion that has no basis whatever in the texts themselves. But James seems to have thought that the concreteness and perhaps even the obviousness of what he was saying would either command immediate assent, or be totally lost on those thoroughly steeped in the 'intellectualism' of professional philosophy. In either case, James invariably placed the main responsibility for misunderstanding on others. Not that he was entirely without justification; on the contrary, there is much evidence furnished by the response of critics to suggest that not many had a strong desire to make their ideas about Pragmatism clear. And yet, as James himself recognized, his language was sometimes 'slipshod' and 'elliptical',[56] and, as he further recognized, such language is entirely inappropriate for expressing unfamiliar ideas and for communicating them successfully. Where understanding and sympathy in outlook prevail, hints and clues as to one's meaning are readily picked up, supplemented and surrounded with the context necessary for completing their meaning. But one cannot expect an unsympathetic and perhaps even hostile reader to furnish the supplement needed for grasping what has been only partially or carelessly expressed. These considerations, to be sure, belong essentially to the rhetoric rather than the logic of the situation, but much confusion about James' ideas could have been avoided if he had paid more attention to the reasons why they were so repeatedly misunderstood.

Turning now to James' attempt to deal with what he took to be the main misunderstandings involved in the pragmatist conception of truth, it is in the best interests of philosophy, as distinct from polemics, to concentrate on his positive assertions as indicative of what he had essentially meant to convey about the meaning of truth. This emphasis does not imply total acceptance or assent, since the question of the legitimacy and consistency of James' position properly understood remains as a desideratum, but if one wants to be as clear as possible about his meaning, attention should be directed to what he ultimately wanted to assert rather than to what others thought he meant. Four points command special attention: the 'realism' James claimed for his Pragmatism; the importance of his maintaining, as against the idealists, a distinction between truth and reality; the stress on action as a secondary outcome of an idea; and his attempt to respond to the argument against Pragmatism from the standpoint of self-reference, i.e. the charge that Pragmatism cannot consistently assert the truth of its theory of truth without appealing to another and non-pragmatic conception of truth. In considering these four points it will be necessary as well to seek further clarification of the idea of 'satisfaction', a term which proved to be a constant source of resistance on the part of critics, including Peirce who wanted to know the aim or end involved.

In replying to those who claim that pragmatists cannot believe in 'ejects' (i.e. the term then used for the feelings or consciousness of another), James insisted on precisely the opposite. His argument was that the pragmatist is not content merely with belief in the outward manifestation of consciousness to the exclusion of belief in the reality of the consciousness manifested. The example of the 'automatic sweetheart' is intended to make this point. If one constructed a 'soulless body' indistinguishable from an 'animated maiden' and capable of laughing, blushing, talking, etc., no one, he claimed, would regard her as a full equivalent, and the reason is that the value of the outward expression derives from belief that it is the expression of the accompanying consciousness. In James' language, belief in the outward manifestation alone will not 'work', because as human beings we crave 'inward sympathy and recognition, love and admiration',[67] and all of this would be lacking without a firm belief in the reality of the consciousness expressed through the overt activity.[58] His appeal here is clearly to the conviction that, in an actual living situation and quite apart from textbook examples, no one would take seriously the hypothesis that the automatic sweetheart is the equivalent of the conscious person.

In the above example, belief in the reality of ejects is bound up with a human need and its fulfilment; further on in James' consideration of the charge that no pragmatist can be a realist in epistemology, he made a stronger claim for his realism as the positing of reality *ab initio.* 'Ideas,' he held, 'are so much flat psychological surface unless some mirrored matter give them cognitive lustre.'[59] Without a reality for an idea to be true about, there can be no truth at all. And, James admitted, 'if the reality assumed were cancelled from the pragmatist's universe of discourse, he would straightway give the name of falsehoods to the beliefs remaining, in spite of all their satisfactoriness'.[60] If this is so, it is not easy to understand what the appeal to 'satisfactoriness' or 'satisfaction' means or accomplishes. James held that satisfactions are 'indispensable' for truth building, but not 'sufficient'. One must assume, then, that satisfactions play some essential role in the process of verification, and there are passages in which reference to them is meant to distinguish the concrete approach to truth of the pragmatist from those 'intellectualists' who are content with the 'vague' (general?) statement that ideas must 'correspond' with reality. Referring to the pragmatist, James said, 'He finds first that the ideas must point to or lead towards *that* reality and no other, and then that the pointings and leadings must yield satisfaction as their result.'[61] From this it would appear that a 'satisfaction' is nothing more mysterious than the outcome of some test in which an expectation has been *fulfilled.* If one has the idea 'the liquid in the beaker is an acid', and has grounds for believing that there is a certain kind of paper which, when placed in that liquid, will turn red if the liquid is in fact acid, and then actually carries out the test, the discovery that the initial idea 'agrees' with its object must be regarded as a 'satisfaction'. It is, however, not clear why James continued to use this term especially when, in arguing that to call a satisfaction 'indispensable' is not to say that it is 'sufficient', he insisted, 'I have everywhere called them [satisfactions] insufficient, unless reality be also incidentally led to.'[62] But surely it is the reality led to that constitutes the satisfaction, and it is curious that meeting the reality should be described as something happening 'incidentally' (though it is possible that James meant simply 'in due course' or 'in the process') as if it were not *the* explicit aim of the test.

It is difficult not to agree with Peirce and others who have found James' appeal to 'satisfactions' and the 'satisfactory' confusing. One can, on the other hand, appreciate the chief motive behind his refusal to abandon the language which caused him so much grief. James was, above all, concerned to keep the individual in view and therefore uppermost in his mind were not the general concepts 'idea' or 'reality' but *this* idea actually entertained by *this* individual now situated and moving about in *this* portion of the universe, acting in accordance with the idea and discovering for himself whether it is true or not. And he seems to have believed that acquiescing in an 'abstract' theory of truth – by which he meant the *general* thesis about correspondence as opposed to *specific* processes of verification – would necessarily exclude the individual and his idea. The point is that, for James, the idea is always at 'work' in someone's stream of thought and is therefore a significant factor in his biography; above all he wanted to emphasize the relation between the career of the idea and the total career of the person who has it. In the end it was James' humanism and his bent towards nominalism that led him to erect barriers between conceiving truth in universal terms and conceiving it in terms of individual satisfactions. When pressed, however, James' realism always reasserted itself in the form of an insistence on belief in both prior realities and their essential role in the theory of truth.

Closely connected with the foregoing is the emphasis James placed on the need for a distinction between truth and reality. The argument advanced is somewhat puzzling in that it includes a disclaimer with regard to verification which is by no means consistent with what he had said elsewhere about the superiority of his concrete approach whereby 'agreement' or 'correspondence' is actually shown to hold *in individuo*. He charged the anti-pragmatist with supposing that 'in undertaking to give him an account of what truth formally means, we [pragmatists] are assuming at the same time to provide a warrant for it, trying to define the occasions when he can be sure of materially possessing it'.[63] This charge is curious indeed in view of James' repeated criticism that, in contrast with those who are satisfied with some vague talk about 'correspondence', 'the pragmatist insists on being more concrete, and asks what such "agreement" may mean in detail'.[64] The demand for a specification of the meaning of correspondence does not, to be sure, involve the claim to know for *certain* when the relation actually obtains, but, on the other hand, the inclusion within the concept of truth of the process whereby the 'leadings' and 'workings' of ideas are to issue in satisfactions and to actually reaching the object meant, can scarcely mean anything else than providing a *warrant* for a truth claim in a specific case. Critics, James contended, misunderstand Pragmatism because they confuse truth and reality and thus fail to see that for pragmatists truth hinges on an 'independent' reality which just *is* and by itself is not 'true'. What is 'true' is instead a belief about a reality, and, according to James, all that Pragmatism claims is that if there is to be truth 'both realities and beliefs about them must conspire to make it'.[65] Then, as if to reduce his claim even further, James maintained that Pragmatism never pretends to determine (a) whether there be any such thing as truth, or (b) how anyone can be sure that his beliefs possess it. Whether such conclusions would be reached by anyone who had read all James' pronouncements on the topic is highly questionable. More important, however, for understanding James' position is his resolute adherence to realism and independent realities and his refusal, in company with Peirce, to accept the identity of truth and reality. In this regard, despite the force of his moral 'idealism', James should *not* be dubbed a philosophical idealist.

The third important consideration stemming from James' response to the misunderstanders of the pragmatic theory of truth, is his attempt to place the role of action in a new perspective. Replying to what he took to be the mistaken thesis that 'Pragmatism is primarily an appeal to action',[66] James admitted that the term 'Pragmatism' and its connotation of action may have been an unfortunate choice, and that talk about ideas 'working well' could easily be taken to mean 'their immediate workings in the physical environment' where the emphasis would fall on the gaining of all sorts of 'practical' advantages. James rejected this line of thought and claimed instead that, for Pragmatism, ideas 'work indefinitely inside of the mental world also',[67] and that in fact Pragmatism begins with 'the refined theoretic question' about the function known as truth which, once answered, then leads to secondary, practical corollaries. On this interpretation, previous realities are not the only independent variables; ideas, as well, assume this status, and become 'complemental factors of reality',[68] such that 'they partly predetermine the existent', and without them 'reality as a whole appears incompletely definable'.[69] James' complaint was that critics ignore this acknowledgement by the pragmatists of the prior reality of ideas and of their function in the gaining of truth, and 'make the relation to action, which is our secondary achievement, primary'.[70] There is no doubt that James took ideas seriously, as is evidenced by his claim that every man has a philosophy 'under his hat', and that no one can avoid having some belief about every aspect of experience including the imponderables of moral and religious questions. What is not so clear, however, is that James was willing to grant to the concept a distinctive, theoretic function, as Peirce did, or whether he did not in the end see ideas as no more than 'plans of action' intended to lead to the perceptual 'cash' which alone constitutes their essential meaning. Moreover, the stress he laid on determining the differences in the meaning of ideas by appealing to the different courses of action or conduct to which one would be committed if he believed one or another idea to be true, led many to think of action as having for him just the primacy he later denied.

With regard to the self-referential attack on the pragmatic conception of truth, James had a characteristic and even ingenious reply at least to one version of the criticism. He did not mention the fact, but it was Royce who pressed this attack most vigorously, maintaining that the *truth* of the pragmatic theory of truth cannot be upheld in its own terms. Royce's contention was that the truth claim which the pragmatist must make for the theory cannot be supported on the basis of the leadings, workings and satisfactions which define James' conception of truth.[71] James' rebuttal takes the form of considering the force of the self-referential argument in relation to scepticism in general. James rightly saw that the rationalist refutation of scepticism requires that the sceptic *express* the sceptical thesis in propositional form and assert it as a general truth, something the sceptic refuses to do precisely because, as James said, 'The live mental attitude of refusing to conclude is involved'[72] and this is a habit rather than a proposition. Consequently, scepticism *embodied* cannot be annihilated by 'instantaneous logical refutations', and the most that the rationalist critic has for consolation is the fact that the sceptic cannot consistently *believe* that scepticism as a philosophical *theory* is true. Since, however, the sceptic does not believe in the timeless truth that would refute him were he to formulate his position, he feels free to 'hang back', and, said James with characteristic candour, 'he often impresses us by his intellectual superiority'.[73]

It is obvious that James was seeking to set up an analogy between the position of the sceptic and the pragmatic theory of truth. His claim is that the pragmatist's utterance with regard to truth, far from being inconsistent, actually exemplifies its own content. Truth, he held, is an attribute of beliefs which are 'attitudes that follow satisfactions';[74] the ideas involved are hypotheses that challenge belief to take a stand. The pragmatist idea of truth *is itself a challenging hypothesis* which the pragmatist finds 'ultra-satisfactory' and he sets it forth for the consideration of others to come to a decision about it in terms of its own satisfactoriness. In short, James believed that the pragmatist theory of truth can be launched on the basis of the same appeal to satisfactoriness which serves as the ground of all individual truth claims falling under it. The analogy with the case of scepticism is, however, inexact in one important particular. There it was held that the sceptic does not formulate his *habit* of withholding assent in the shape of a proposition and therefore that he can continue to maintain his stance without being trapped by the inconsistency manifested by a dogmatic claim. But the pragmatic conception of truth *is* formulated and even if it be equated with an attitude or 'habit', the habit must be that of *believing* the conception to be superior to other alternatives. Despite James' use of the term 'attitude' as a synonym for belief, it is difficult to see how the pragmatic *conception* of truth can qualify as an attitude. One might admit what James had earlier written about the pragmatic approach to meaning or to life being essentially a stance, an attitude, a method, not a doctrine, but a theory of *truth* is something else again. How can such a *theory* exist merely as an attitude or a habit without finding propositional formulation?[75] The move to formulation in this case as opposed to that of scepticism, is unavoidable and therefore something must answer to what is meant by making a normative claim for that formulation. James' only response is that this theory is treated the same as any other and held as a challenging hypothesis on the basis of its 'satisfactoriness'. But as Peirce had pointed out, the 'satisfactory' is an incomplete predicate; something more must be specified in the form of the 'for what' or 'to what end'.

A comparison between James and Peirce is most instructive on this point. James, responsive to ordinary experience and to the living psychology of the individual in acquiring, assimilating, modifying, rejecting or accepting beliefs, was ready to accept satisfactions as the touchstone for the manner in which the process of settling on the truth *actually takes place* in the ongoing experience of many individuals in ordinary circumstances. In this respect much of what James had to say had a *phenomenological* basis – what actually happens has some claim on our attention and is not to be set aside entirely in favour of some theory prescribing what *ought* to happen. Peirce, as the attack on 'paper doubt' and the defence of 'critical common-sensism' and fallibilism show, also appealed to what actually happens in the way of fixing thought and belief, but he differed from James in making the normative sciences – aesthetics, ethics and logic – basic, and deriving his conception of truth not so much from ordinary experience as from the history of science and the logic of inquiry. There is indeed a considerable difference here; the question is whether one need transform it into an unbridgeable chasm. When stressing his realistic stance, James was pre-pared to insist on the reality of the object as the condition for truth, let the satisfactions fall where they may, and this demand approaches Peirce's claim that with regard to every intelligible question posed the real is such as to impose on the community of inquirers at least one and at most one answer. The difference between them is one of scope and context; James had chiefly in mind the historical career of the individual *in situ,* sorting out beliefs, making unavoidable decisions with whatever knowledge he has available, acting in the particular moment and taking the consequences, etc., whereas Peirce, while not unmindful of the same concrete scene, put more emphasis on the normative constraints required for the self-controlled thought of science and philosophy. James had that more immediate per-spective and the sense of urgency in belief which one associates with the existentialists, while Peirce's thought was totally coloured by the assumption of that more expansive time scale which is the hallmark of modern science and the rationalist tradition in philosophy.

Earlier the question was raised as to whether it is legitimate to speak of a distinctive 'pragmatic' theory of truth to be set side by side with other theories that have established themselves in the development of the western philosophical tradition. If one considers Peirce and James to the exclusion of Dewey, whose views on logic, inquiry and warranted assertion will be considered in the next chapter, the answer to the question is negative, an answer thoroughly in accord with James' claim that Pragmatism is 'a new name for an old way of thinking'. This answer, however, must be carefully interpreted. In accordance with the previous suggestion (p. 52) that conceptions of truth might be divided into the two types of *conform* and *transform*, it seems clear that the emphasis to be found in Peirce and James on correspondence or agreement as essential to truth places them in the conform category. This judgement is perhaps more secure when made in relation to Peirce, but, despite James' insistence on 'workings' and 'leadings' and his belief that ideas are not merely to mirror or duplicate the world in the shape of a carbon copy, he too required that the true idea accord with or adapt to the reality to which it points and is meant to know. Dewey, on the other hand, in his attack on 'antecedent reality' and his defence of problem-solving as the transformation of an indeterminate or problematic situation into a determinate or reconstituted state of affairs, clearly placed himself outside the conform type. There are in Dewey's thought, to be sure, some residual features of the conform view, just as there is in James a tendency to transformism marked by the belief that ideas function effectively in the shaping of a real future, but in the end Dewey's instrumentalism must be set apart from the positions of his two predecessors. Moreover, as has been pointed out by others, one does not find in Dewey's writings a strict theory of truth of the sort found in the writings of those who espouse correspondence or coherence, but rather the specification of the conditions necessary for providing a warrant for an assertion. By contrast, both Peirce and James were still working within the classical conceptions of the meaning of truth. For both, however, these conceptions were not entirely adequate; neither was satisfied with a theory of truth that involved no reference to a procedure or process whereby the truth value of a proposition could be tested. This concern is, of course, consistent with the demand of the pragmatic outlook that the meaning of a concept – that of 'truth' included – must be set forth in terms of consequences, procedures, methods and outcomes. One consequence of this approach, however, was the charge advanced by critics that the pragmatists do not say what truth 'is' or means, but focus instead on the method for attaining it. The distinction implied is valid enough, but the charge accompanying it is easily neutralised. Truth, on this view, is not to be understood apart from method and test; what must not be overlooked, however, is the essentially teleological presupposition at the root of the theory.[76] Truth has to do with outcomes and results and therefore for neither Peirce nor James is it *identical* with a method or procedure. Truth attaches to a proposition or a belief as the *result* of the discovery that an expectation – in the case of explicitly controlled scientific inquiry, an hypothesis – has been fulfilled or, as one says, has been found to be in accord with the facts. This result is not to be regarded as a fortuitous or accidental affair as in the case where one 'happens' to 'hit upon' the correct solution for an algebraic equation without being able to set forth the logical process leading to that result. Truth, as the result of a process of inquiry (Peirce) or of following out the 'leadings and workings' of ideas (James), stands logically and experimentally related to that process and is not to be understood apart from it. To take James' example of the idea of Memorial Hall, one starts with the idea of a building exhibiting some more or less clear type of architectural style together with an indication of where the building stands. To check the accuracy of the idea or belief it is necessary to find a way of coming into the presence of the object to which the idea leads or points (its object), in order to determine whether the building itself actually possesses the expected characteristics and is located where it was believed to be. The one who is thus led to the object which fulfils the expectation does not stand in a merely conjunctive relation to that object as someone would were he simply leaning against the building; on the contrary, the entire process starting with the projected expectation passing through the intermediate stages and ending with the reaching of the building as the one intended by the idea must be taken into account. If the idea or belief 'corresponds' with its object, then it is 'true' in virtue of this fact. It is the idea or belief that is 'true,' not the object, but the truth of the belief is grounded in the relation of corresponding with or being in accord with its object. Despite significant differences between the views of Peirce and James on this topic, they came together in holding an agreement or correspondence theory of truth. In view of this fact, one cannot say for either of them that there is a special 'pragmatist' conception of truth. If any novel element has been introduced, it is their insistence that 'correspondence' not be conceived as a static or timeless relation having no connection with the process of inquiry and the tracing of consequences. If a label is needed, one could do not better than to call their theory of truth a theory of 'dynamic correspondence'.

3 The new conception of experience

The pragmatists were indeed concerned about those problems of meaning, of knowledge and of truth which have chiefly occupied philosophers since the period of the Enlightenment. It would, however, be a gross misunderstanding of their entire outlook to suppose that they accepted without question the priority of problems dealing with the nature of knowing. The fact is that they were revolting against the dominant trend of modern philosophy wherein the critical analysis of our cognitive equipment was allowed to overshadow all other philosophical problems.[1] Dewey was the most outspoken of the group in this regard and he not only referred disparagingly to the 'industry' of epistemology, but he denied that its problems are perennial as well. He viewed these problems as stemming from certain erroneous assumptions concerning the nature of experience which were made by the classical empiricists. Even if Dewey's criticism was at times overdrawn – he acknowledged epistemological issues in the very act of turning them into methodological ones – he was correct in the view that much modern philosophy has been so preoccupied with preliminary questions concerning the tools of thought that attention has often been directed away from other philosophical problems such as freedom, the nature of man and the bearing of science on values, which have now become the province of non-philosophers. Emphasis has too often fallen on the consideration of the language one *would* use, or the method one *would* follow if one were to deal with these problems in a rigorous way. Unfortunately, the subjunctive mood has prevailed and too often the problems which Dewey called 'the problems of men' have either been postponed or evaded on the supposition that vague, immediate and important issues cannot be treated until we have first settled the problems of the criteria of knowledge, the nature and proper functions of language, and the status of logical systems *vis à vis* the content of experience.

The clearest and most effective way of showing that the pragmatists (a) did *not* identify philosophy with the typical questions of modern critical philosophy (the problem of perception, phenomenalism and the external world, etc.) and (b) must *not* be interpreted as responding to these questions as if they were simply carrying on the 'empiricist' tradition,[2] is to call attention to their critique of classical empiricism and their reconstruction of the theory of experience along lines that reveal the basic inadequacy of the view maintained continuously on the British scene from the days of Hume to those of Russell and Ayer. The pragmatists' critique of 'empiricism' and their reconstruction of the meaning of experience are expressed at three focal points in the writings of these philosophers. Attention, therefore, will be directed, first, to Dewey's critical contrast between his own view and the conception established chiefly by Locke and Hume,[3] second, to the fundamental notions which constitute James' 'radical empiricism'; and third, to Peirce's special formulation of Pragmatism in the maxim 'Dismiss make-believes' and his interpretation of experience in terms of effort and surprise leading to the formation of new habits which establish themselves in the form of commonsense and pervasive experience.

Dewey's criticism of the empiricism which all philosophers associate with the British tradition in philosophy is well known and need not be repeated in all its details. At least four points, however, are essential: first, his refusal to identify experience with *sense content* taken to consist of absolutely determinate and singular data; second, his refusal to identify experience with *knowledge*; third, his attack on the view that experience is the *passive registry of data* already furnished or 'given' on a *tabula rasa*; fourth, his claim that experience cannot be made to form a *contrast domain to thought* because it includes inference and has a temporal 'stretch' not to be compacted into instantaneous data of the sort envisaged either by Hume with his 'impressions' or by the positivists' protocol sentences.

The valid and permanent contribution of modern empiricism, as Hegel made so clear, was its insistence that every man should see and feel himself present with every item of knowledge he is expected to accept. This demand meant a rejection of tradition and authority as grounds for the fixation of belief and appealed instead to the *encounter* with the world which each individual enjoys. The problem that immediately arises, however, can be expressed in the question: What is experience and how is it to be understood in its generic character? The classical empiricists answered these questions both in detail and with exceptional clarity of thought. In doing so, however, they envisaged experience primarily as a content or subject matter and came to identify experience as such with the deliverances of the senses and thus to set it off as a tissue of sensations and sense perceptions in contrast, on the one hand, to reason or thought, and, on the other, to the 'external world'. Experience became, in short, a body of sensible subject matter inhabiting the mind, separate in kind from thought and standing over against a world that could only be understood as 'external'. Moreover, in their genetic programme of tracing all conceptions back to an original in 'experience', the empiricists further identified it with singular and wholly determinate items, simple and clearcut given data. Dewey rejected both these identifications not only on the ground that these ultimate constituents represent what he called 'reflected products' or the result of analysis which cannot be primitive or 'first' in order, but also because experience as it actually manifests itself for conscious subjects cannot be adequately understood as content immediately present to, and contained within, an introspecting, individual mind. Under the influence of Darwinism and the belief that man and experience must be understood through the biological matrix of developing organisms interacting with a complex and changing environment, he proposed to view experience as the many-sided, funded product of a long series of encounters between self and world. Such a product involves the disclosure of the way things work and behave, the responses we are to make in their presence, the tendencies and capacities of both natural and cultural objects, to say nothing of the many contexts – moral, aesthetic, philosophical and religious – in which the world as encountered actually makes itself felt and comes to be understood. The content of experience is said to embrace *all* that can be encountered – objects, transitions, connections, events, persons, situations – and, on Dewey's view, there is no warrant for identifying this variegated content through the single characteristic of sense as if experience constituted one homogeneous subject matter. In Dewey's sense of experience, to have experience of horses, for example, goes far beyond the recording of their sensible characteristics; it means being acquainted with their habits, what they may be expected to do, and it means knowing as well how to 'handle' them or to conduct oneself in their presence. The analysis of the experience of horses into the clearcut data of the 'given' in the form of colours, shapes, etc., does not adequately convey what happens when we encounter these animals. For Dewey, what has traditionally been called the 'given' is actually a reflected product largely dictated by conceptions of what experience *must* be like if it is to deliver knowledge in a pre-eminent sense. Referring to classical empiricism, Dewey wrote, 'traditional accounts have not been empirical, but have been deductions, from unnamed premises, of what experience *must* be'[4] with the result that ideas are *forced into* experience, not as Dewey said, *gathered from* it.

One must be careful here not to suppose that Dewey was primarily concerned to distinguish between a general theory of experience and actual experiencing in order to claim that the Lockes and Humes provided the former and that he alone was focusing on the latter. This is not the case: Dewey, no less than those he criticised, was espousing a general theory of experience. It was his belief, however, that experience manifests its own character as it actually takes place, and that, unless we focus attention on actual experiencing involving the interplay between the intelligent organism and its environment we are likely to end by identifying experience as such with some limited feature or function. Whether he was altogether justified in this contention is a matter for further discussion; one point, however, is clear and it is indispensable for understanding his criticism: no *general* characterisation of experience can be given in terms of *content* or subject matter but only in terms of a *process* which in the end turns out to be a medium and a means. If this point is missed, Dewey's critique will be entirely misunderstood. The point needs to be laboured because of long-standing linguistic habits established in the minds of philosophers; consider how frequently it is said, 'let us locate the "empirical" [i.e. the sense content] part of this theory, in contrast to the formal or logical components'. The thought behind such a statement stands absolutely opposed to what Dewey was arguing for.

In considering the four focal points previously mentioned, it will be well, since they all involve negative contrasts, to indicate Dewey's positive view at the same time so that his conception of what experience *is* will emerge and we shall have gone beyond saying what it is not.

Experience and sense

Taking the biological context seriously meant for Dewey starting with a living, intelligent or language-using organism attempting to sustain itself in an environment which is partly supportive of, and partly hostile to, that attempt. Experiencing as the meaningful interaction between the subject and his surroundings is a complex affair, and is, initially at least, quite vague and inchoate in comparison with the standard empiricist model consisting of a subject or knower who stands over against the world as a spectator trying to represent it by means of clear ideas. If one views experience from the standpoint of the organism–environment model, it is not difficult to see why Dewey could not *identify* experience with sensible components known by a spectator. To begin with, these components form but one set of items in the complex of interaction, and, furthermore, the spectator stance is but one stance among others occupied by the experiencing subject *vis à vis* the world.[5] For Dewey, experience is the name for what results, a process and a funded product, from the interaction situation; experience is *simultaneously* both doings and sufferings or undergoings.[6] Consequently the experiencing subject is at once both agent and patient, receiving what is presented to it and responding in ways appropriate for a being who seeks to sustain itself in a precarious world. The reception and retention of sensible data belong to the process of experiencing but they do not exhaust it as such, largely because these data are seen by Dewey as 'already there' in finished form, whereas the organism is constantly living forward in anticipation of what is to come in the form of a challenge to be met. The large scale on which Dewey sees experience, its place in an ongoing life seeking to cooperate with nature in its favourable aspects, and to control or neutralize its indifference to man, made it impossible for him to adopt a sense-data model of experience as sensible content immediately grasped by a mind or intuitive consciousness. The significant function which he assigned to experience as man's weapon in confronting the course of events led him to a conception very different from that ordinarily envisaged by empiricists who think of experience primarily in terms of red patches, pains, the hand which I am certain that I see before me, and the like. He has a place for such observational reports as a specific stage in the pattern of inquiry, but he denied that they represent 'experience' *per se*. In a striking comment made in response to his critics, Dewey claimed that 'no living creature could survive, save by sheer accident, if its experiences had no more reach, scope or content, than traditional, particularistic empiricism provides for'.[7]

Experience and knowledge

Dewey's refusal to equate experience and cognition introduces a matter that is quite complex and disputes about it have been plagued by verbal confusion usually centring on the term 'knowledge'. If knowledge is understood, as indeed it was by Dewey, to be the *outcome* of a process of critical inquiry, then one is prevented from describing what is directly presented and encountered as a cognitive affair. That is to say, on Dewey's view, there is no immediate knowing. There are, of course, good reasons for holding such a view, especially when one considers how many claims to immediate certainties have turned out in the end to be false. On the other hand, however, Dewey did not always take sufficient account of those familiar cases where we appeal in a present situation to the established results of previous inquiries and feel that we 'just know' that an object is of such-and-such a nature without initiating a new inquiry. But leaving that issue aside, there are two more immediately relevant motives behind Dewey's refusal to equate experience and knowledge. The first has to do with his concern to deny that experience is generated by, and located in, a 'knower' in the form of an ego or consciousness which is 'outside' the world viewing it as a spectator. The second goes to the root of his general suspicion of epistemology. The first motive must be treated in connection with his denial that experience is the passive registry of the 'given' and may be postponed. The second motive makes clear why he would not identify experience as such with knowledge.

It was Dewey's contention that many of the issues constituting the theory of knowledge stem largely from the treatment of certain relativities in perception as cases of a distinction in kind between appearance and reality. He believed that if the status of knowledge is accorded to the 'appearances', insuperable problems arise that might be avoided if such appearances were not regarded as cases of knowing in the first instance. In considering the familiar examples of the stick which looks bent in the water, the coin which appears as both a flat circle and an ellipse, the doubled appearance of objects when the eyeball is depressed, etc., Dewey objected to the view, held in common even by those with opposed epistemologies, that there is but one object which is 'real' and two 'subjects' in whom the 'appearances' reside, thus supposedly providing clear evidence of the distorting influence of the knower. As against this view, Dewey argued, first, that the discrepant appearances are to be explained consistently in terms of the laws governing perspective and the reflection, refraction, etc., of light, and, second, that the truly incoherent situation would be one in which the coin, for example, did *not* appear both circular and elliptical from different perspectives. Moreover, no special significance should be attached to the designation of the experiencing subject as the cause of the object's being modified, because, as Dewey pointed out, two cameras or other light-reflecting apparatus will manifest the same result and it would be absurd to think of such devices as the source of 'subjective' distortions.

The origin of the problem of discrepant appearances, the mainstay of endless epistemological discussion, points, in Dewey's view, to a way of resolving it. 'The objection,' he declared, 'assumes that the alleged modifications of *the* real object are cases of *knowing* and hence attributable to the influence of a *knower*.'[8] He proposed instead to describe the experiencing situation as the dynamic interaction of two agents – the eye and the coin – from which results a third thing, an effect; it is only *after* this effect has come about, he claimed, that any question of knowledge arises. That is to say, when the discrepancies are taken as a problem the task is to explain, in terms of what is known about the conditions of the interacting objects, why some one perfectly real effect takes place rather than some other. It is essential to Dewey's argument that the observation of some particular effect not be taken by itself as 'knowledge' of 'the' real object and his ground for that claim is that there can be nothing 'problematic' about one observation as such, and that no question of knowledge arises at that point because 'knowledge' means the warranted *outcome* of an inquiry initiated by the recognition of a problematic situation. Whatever problem arises in connection with an observation does so only *after* the coin, interacting with the eye from one perspective, yields a different effect from another perspective and it becomes necessary to explain the discrepancy. 'But,' asked Dewey, 'why talk about *the real* object in relation to *a knower* when what is given is one real thing in dynamic connection with another real thing?'[9]

Not every aspect of this discussion of relativity in perception is relevant for determining the theory of experience. The significant point is Dewey's belief that if the result of *every* interaction between the experiencing subject and what is encountered is taken *ipso facto* as cognitive, a cleavage between reality and appearances must arise since it is bound to be supposed that contradictory 'truths' cannot be true about one and the same 'real object'. The result is that the object is retained and the appearances are located in the mind of a knower and are no longer seen as objective occurrences in nature. His proposal, later expressed in the distinction between *having* and *knowing,* is to avoid a premature cognitive investment by taking primary experience as the product of interactions which take place and are undergone or had. Knowing becomes appropriate only when problems arise and questions are put concerning the materials of this primary experience especially 'the use that is made of experienced natural events'.[10]

Dewey's distinction has contemporary counterparts in the difference cited between pre-thematic and thematic standpoints, or between consciousness and cognition, and it is clear that such distinctions are needed if the whole of experience is not to be made to coincide with theoretical knowing. On the other hand, to suppose that the distinction can be perfectly precise and without vagueness is to invite confusion. To return to the examples of discrepancy in perception, it is difficult to sustain the claim that the discrepant 'observations' are totally noncognitive precisely because their occurrence as genuine data have to be taken seriously or no problem would arise. That is, one 'really' sees the different geometrical shapes from different perspectives and at the least it sounds queer to say that one does not 'know' that in a certain perspective the coin exhibits a flat circular shape whereas in another perspective it appears as elliptical. Dewey's denial of knowledge at this point was dictated partly by his limitation of the term to *outcomes* of inquiry and not to the immediately received, and partly to his unwillingness to encapsulate experience entirely within a ubiquitous knower–known relationship. Consequently, he took the discrepant observations as genuine occurrences which may then be taken in turn as data forming the conditions of a problem the resolution of which is meant to eventuate in knowing. But it still remains the case that no problem would arise from the comparison of these allegedly discrepant data were they not taken as *veridical* reports of fact in the first instance. The most satisfactory way of doing justice to the situation of actual experiencing is to insist, as Dewey did, on the ingredience of intelligence in *all* experience which would allow for veridical observations in perception where no inquiry is involved, but to deny that experience coincides with theoretical knowing as if the experiencing subject stood in no other relation to what is encountered except that of the scientist seeking to explain it. The confusion that arises in connection with Dewey's position stems from the disjunction between experience as 'had' which, as he claimed, does not need to be known, and explicitly cognitive experience. He appealed to the former as a way of avoiding the doctrine that experience is all knowing, but he did not sufficiently make clear that what he calls 'having' is not all having but has within it veridical content including the ingredience of previous knowing.

Experience, activity and passivity

Many features of Dewey's thought could be considered under the above heading, but two points count as basic for the conception of experience: first, his refusal to identify experience with a passive registry of the 'given', and, second, the prospective reference bestowed upon experience by emphasizing its role in bringing about changes in the environment. The first point does not call for extensive discussion because it is clear that the classical empiricists did think of experience as what is imprinted on a recipient mind largely passive in character, and, since Kant, it has generally been admitted that this *tabula rasa* conception is inadequate. The experiencing subject does not function merely as a mirror for the given, but is active as a judging agent which *takes* what is presented to be such-and-such, selects, omits, emphasizes, etc., in arriving at a settled experience. Dewey did not deny the element of passivity – for him the subject actually suffers and undergoes in real interactions with the world – but he denied that the passive registry of the presented is to be thought of as experience *par excellence*. Patient observation, allowing the items of nature to disclose themselves in experience, is essential, but, for Dewey, much more is involved.

Were the prospective function of experience to be pursued in its many implications and consequences, it would bring us to the centre of the most controversial feature of Dewey's instrumentalism. Like James, who accorded to 'copy' theories of knowledge a limited validity while rejecting them as wholly satisfactory in the end, Dewey was not willing to concede that knowledge is a reproduction of the world precisely because his theory is aimed at transforming it. It was his stress on the reconstructive function of experience that led others, and not only those unsympathetic to his view, to wonder whether he had not confused the three activities which, since the time of Aristotle, philosophers had sought to keep distinct, namely, *knowing, making* and *doing*. For the bulk of philosophers in the Western tradition, to know the world is to *conform* to it as presented or given in the form of data. Knowing was thus distinguished both from the activity of the artist or artisan, and from the sphere of practice constituting ethical and political life. Dewey's insistence, however, on the role of action in inquiry – manipulation and controlled experiment – and on transforming the problematic or indeterminate situation into a coherent satisfactory outcome seems to reduce greatly the importance of conforming to what is presented, and at the same time to blur the edges of the traditional distinction between 'theoretical' and 'practical'. It is against this background that one must understand Russell's half-serious claim that Dewey's formal account of the process of inquiry is satisfied by the activity of bricklayers constructing a wall.

However, even if, as must be admitted, Dewey's theory does not do justice to conformism in experience and knowing, it nevertheless calls attention to an element which is of the utmost importance for the theory of experience. Dewey expressed the point with special reference to the temporal factor. Classical empiricism with its emphasis on the given ties itself essentially to what is past or over and done with. 'But,' said Dewey, 'experience in its vital form is experimental, an effort to change the given; it is characterized by projection, by reaching forward into the unknown: connection with a future is its salient trait.'[11] It is here more than at any other point that the empiricists divide. Dewey, and, to a lesser but still important degree, James, regarded the passive registry of the given as essentially an apprehension of finished fact or of what has *already* taken place, whereas both were concerned for what is in the *process* of coming and is *yet to come,* in the dual sense of the surprising or unanticipated, and of the expected or hoped-for consequences of some previous state of affairs. Focus on the growing edge of present experience, and on the projected future connected with the extensive present through intermediaries that are yet to come, leads to two distinct but closely related features of the new empiricism in contrast with the old. One feature concerns content, and the other function or use. In company with Whitehead, Dewey emphasized experiencing and its temporally extended or 'thick' character in contrast with the ultimate data of classical empiricism which are clearcut and apprehended atemporally precisely because they are finished and devoid of further becoming or transition. It has frequently been pointed out that the atomic bias of the empiricism of Hume, especially, stems from the fact that there is no room for an *impression* of 'tendency' or 'continuous transition'; connections are in the mind or are furnished by logic and linguistic apparatus because they are not in 'experience'. Consequently, the happen*ing* escapes and only the happen*ed* is recorded; grammatically speaking, classical empiricism made experience an affair of past, not present, participles. This fundamental difference explains why for the British empirical tradition the closer one is to the immediate or the origin of experience the clearer and more distinct are the experienced units, whereas precisely the opposite holds for the pragmatists. On their view what is primordial coincides with what James called 'the blooming, buzzing confusion'.

As regards the function of experience another cleavage breaks out between the two points of view. The older empiricism saw experience primarily as the ultimate basis of theoretical knowledge; Dewey envisaged experience as a means and ultimately a method oriented to the future and aimed at the selective control of consequences and outcomes. Santayana grasped the central point very nicely, and, although he was referring to James with whose thought he was more familiar, his comment is, if anything, even more applicable to Dewey's instrumentalism. Commenting on the Darwinian influence in Pragmatism as a whole, Santayana wrote, 'Ideas are not mirrors, they are weapons. Their function is to prepare us to meet events, as future experience may unroll them.'[12] It would be difficult indeed to find a more apt statement of the thesis that, from the pragmatic outlook, experience is not the passive registry of the given, but rather an experimental resource acquired by a being who lives forward and thus finds anticipation the primary mode of response.

Experience, inference and thought

Every student of the Enlightenment is familiar with the distinction, taken for granted by all thinkers of the period, between experience and reason. Experience was regarded as a sort of subject matter standing over against thought; it is not difficult to understand how this conception came about. The empiricists of the Enlightenment were challenging the reigning rationalism of the entire Western philosophical and theological tradition. They sought to bring the outlook represented by such thinkers as Descartes and Leibniz – the apex of modern rationalism – to the bar of 'experience' for judgement. Banish *a priori* conceptions, these critics declared; no one is bound to accept any truth which cannot be made evident in his own experience. The fundamental validity of this demand cannot be denied, and it was upheld even by Hegel, the symbol of the arch-rationalist. The development, however, carried in its wake at least one unfortunate consequence. The 'experience' that was to be the touchstone of all rational constructions, universal concepts and principles came to be understood exclusively in terms of sensible particulars with the result that it became difficult, if not impossible, to conceive of reason as being *in* experience. Even Kant, who found classical empiricism inadequate, accepted this dichotomy and insisted that the material of the senses and the pure concepts of the understanding differ in kind.[13] Dewey rejected all this, insisting that thought and experience are not antithetical because experience is 'full of inference' and no conscious experience is without it.[14] The import of Dewey's contention becomes clear only if it is seen against the background of his theory of reflective intelligence as a means of gaining a measure of control over the future. The learning capacity of the human species, its ability to overcome obstacles that make for insecurity and thus to establish a more stable existence, are, for Dewey, matters essentially related to the role performed by reflective intelligence in the course of experience. Since the future is the one temporal mode which is open to influence and control, attention focuses on inference as a power 'to use a given fact as a sign of something not yet given'[15] and the extent of that power is to be measured in terms of the extent of control over future occurrences which such inference affords. Inference must be seen as an active response, controlled by both thought and knowledge of the habits and tendencies of things and made by the experiencing subject in the midst of ongoing processes some of which are favourable and others unfavourable to human welfare. On Dewey's view, it is legitimate to conceive of inference as a going beyond the present and the presented, but *not* as a going beyond 'experience', since he did not identify experience with the present and presented. The operative idea in the new conception of experience at this point is that it includes an inferential response pointing to what is absent; when this response is well founded we have a forecast of the future and the possibility of a further response informed by plans and purposes.[16] Were experience devoid of this inferential stretch, it could not serve as a means whereby an intelligent being could intervene in the course of interactions with the environment for the purpose of influencing the course of events. Nor is this intervention confined to inference alone; intelligence manifests itself as inventive construction as well, an activity which goes beyond the analysis of what is presented. Here Dewey had in mind the activity of thought in proposing hypotheses and projecting possibilities to be tried out by appeal to future experience. But it seemed to him that such activity would have to be regarded as 'non-empirical' if experience is taken to be exclusive of thought or intelligence. He was confirmed in this view by the development of modern rationalisms which accepted the classical conception of experience, even while recognizing its inadequacies, but were forced in the end to explain how a purely formal 'reason' consisting entirely of abstract universals could enter into relation with an 'empirical' domain of atomic data. The problem persists and appears at present in the form of attempts to connect the 'input' of experience with reason understood solely in terms of pure logical and linguistic forms.

A topic of considerable importance, but one which cannot be pursued further, is the question of the extent to which Dewey's critique of classical empiricism and his reinterpretation of the nature of experience is dependent on the thoroughgoing biological, and especially instrumental, outlook he espoused. I am not convinced that the dependence here need be as complete as he thought. He set forth a richer and, one may even say, a more empirical account of experience than the traditional one, but his theory need not be construed exclusively in terms of the categories of success and failure, control and manipulation. If change and novelty are to be taken seriously, these categories may no longer be adequate to the full range of experience. Dewey's adoption of the biological orientation in thought led him to define the problematic situation in general as some form of maladjustment between the interest and the needs of the organism and the potentialities of the environment. As a consequence, success in resolving problems had to be seen largely as an affair of controlling the environment through the resources of technology, social planning and engineering. By comparison, self-control or, more important, reorientation of the self with respect to personal values and ideas, did not receive the attention they deserved. This imbalance might not have presented an insuperable obstacle in the end were it not for the emergence of another problem making itself felt across our entire culture which severely taxes the resources of any instrumental approach, namely, the rise of multiple crises of self-confidence, self-identity, and self-determination. These crises, though obviously not unaffected by the natural and cultural environments, are not sufficiently understood through an organism–environment problematic model. They represent, on the contrary, a problematic situation in which the organism – to persist in using Dewey's language – *becomes problematic to itself,* and the range of problems consequent on that development cannot be resolved solely in terms of *controlling* devices projected by an instrumental intelligence aimed at reshaping the environment. Part of the difficulty stems from Dewey's dislike for private 'minds', timeless egos, absolute subjects, etc., and as a result he paid insufficient attention to the interiority of the person and the problem that self-consciousness brings in its wake. Emphasis on problems arising at the interface of organism and environment led to neglect of those urgent concerns that erupt when the self becomes a problem to itself. One may well speak about an attack upon the environment for the purpose of overcoming its hostility, but it is not clear that the strategy for resolving the problems encountered by the problematic self can be best expressed in the same terms, nor is it to be supposed that these problems can be overcome merely by control of the political and social circumstances in which people live. The point is that there are human problems in connection with which the concept of *control* is not appropriate, and these problems signal the limits of the instrumental intelligence. It would, nevertheless, be unfortunate indeed if these shortcomings of Dewey's position were allowed to obscure the truth in his reconstructed theory of experience, which is the reason I suggest the possibility of developing that theory along lines not exclusively instrumental in character.

The second focal point in the pragmatist critique of the traditional conception of experience is found in James' 'radical empiricism'.[17] His approach differs significantly from that of Dewey in that James saw himself as essentially engaged in epistemological discussions. In comparing his position with that of Schiller, for example, James could say, 'My universe is more essentially epistemological.'[18] This is a statement which Dewey, for example, would never have made. James' contention is that Hume did not go far enough in his analysis, or, to put it another way, that he was not empirical enough. This claim reveals James' affinity with Hume, and, in fact, he acknowledged that his own position is a 'mosaic philosophy . . . like that of Hume and his descendents'.[19] Radical empiricism, however, signals a radical departure from Hume on a crucial point. James strongly rejected Hume's main contention that 'all our distinct perceptions are distinct existences' so that 'the mind never perceives any real connection among distinct existences'.[20] James regarded this claim as non-empirical in two respects; on the one hand, it omits certain features of experience, and, on the other, it represents a biased emphasis on what it includes. The full impact and specific meaning of James' criticism becomes more clear when understood against the background of his summary description of radical empiricism as involving a postulate, a statement of fact and a generalized conclusion.

The postulate is that only the experienceable is legitimate subject matter for philosophy; the statement of fact is that relations between items of experience are as much a part of experience, i.e. are as 'real', as the items related, and, furthermore, that conjunctive togetherness is on equal footing with disjunctive distinctness; the generalized conclusion is that, since experience holds together and coheres in virtue of its own connective tissue, there is no need to invoke a supervenient reason to perform the unifying function. The problem posed by this conclusion need not directly concern us; as the final chapter of *The Principles of Psychology* makes clear, James knew that the relational concepts involved in logic and mathematics are not to be apprehended as part of what is 'given' even in terms of his pure experience and therefore some special status must be accorded the rational *a priori*. More important for our purposes, however, is the second feature of radical empiricism, the statement of fact with regard to the presence of relations and conjunctions, transitions and continuities in experience. This brings the discussion back to the critique of Hume. James finds two difficulties with Hume's contention about distinct existences and the absence of any perception of a real connection between them. First, he thinks that Hume was biased in his account of experience in favour of the distinct as over against the connected. That A is 'other than' B he took to be somehow more primordial and better founded than the togetherness of C and D. For James, it is no less a deliverance of experience that the colour is 'with' the shape or that the pages of a book are experienced as succeeding each other when they are flipped, than that the colour is other than or distinct from the shape. James saw no reason if one attends to actual experiencing why the analytically distinct or disjoined should have a more secure status in experience than the conjunctions and transitions. On this account, James held that Hume had not gone far enough; he terminated his analysis of experience with disjunctions and failed to note the presence of the conjunctions.

Secondly, and closely connected, James, not unlike Dewey, was suspicious of analyses of experience in which the clearcut and precise are taken to be 'first' or basic. Clarity and precision are the *results* of analysis, 'reflected products', and howsoever legitimate they may be as such they are not to be thought of as primordial. Experiencing is initially an affair of vagueness and confusion; states of awareness have 'fringes' which portend connections with what goes beyond the directly noticed and focused content. To make the clear and distinct, whether in the form of Hume's impressions or the protocol sentences of the positivists, the *foundation* of experience is to distort it in the interest of a theory. James and Dewey were at one in their belief that classical empiricism represents not so much an account of actual experience but a consideration of what experience *must be,* a theory of what it *must* contain, if it is to serve as the foundation for knowledge. If, moreover, one considers that the model for knowledge dominant when the classical conception of experience was formed required clear and distinct impressions and ideas as a necessary starting point, it becomes evident why the primordial units of experience were conceived as atomic in character. The claim advanced by James and Dewey is that understanding experience solely in terms of its function as a foundation for knowledge taken to be certain, results in the oversimplification of highly complex episodes lived through by the experiencing subject. If, for example, there is a clap of thunder that particular sound would be taken on the classical view as a particular datum of sense to be named and identified. James held that the situation is much more complex: the clap of thunder is experienced as breaking in upon a contrasting silence which is only vividly grasped as such when the sound interrupts it and brings the stillness to an end. Such an experience is serial and transitional – the clap-of-thunder-breaking-silence – so that an experience of the silence preceding goes along with the hearing of the thunder. For James, whatever is experienced comes with associates, connections and transitions; experience has its focal points, to be sure, but it also has its fringes and these must not be ignored. To arrive at clear-cut and atomic items is not to have found the origin of experience but to have come to the end of an analysis instead. No one can take this reversal in outlook seriously and continue to interpret Pragmatism as merely an extension of classical empiricism with a few voluntaristic features added.

The key to Peirce's conception of experience is found in his rejection of privileged starting points for thought and in his emphasis on the *insistence* of experience over against the human will, including elements of surprise which confound human expectations. With respect to a starting point for thought, Peirce expressed opposition not only to the fundamental method of Descartes, but to the chief aim of classical empiricism as well. In one of his many statements intended to sum up the essence of Pragmatism,[21] Peirce proposed the maxim 'Dismiss make-believes', by which he meant dismissing the injunctions of many previous philosophers to commence with 'one or another state of mind in which no man . . . actually is'. The primary target of this criticism is the Cartesian *programme* of doubt which is to extend over the entire range of belief, but it applies as well to those who propose that 'we should begin by observing "the first impressions of sense" '. Against both views Peirce claimed that one can 'set out' from nothing other than the state of mind he is in when he actually does set out. All thought is seen as taking place *in medias res* in the sense that the actual thinker approaches the task already laden with a body of previous thought and belief which he can neither ignore nor negate at will, and within this starting point there is much that he does not actually doubt. The empiricist starting point, moreover, does not in fact represent the sort of beginning it professes, because, as Peirce insisted, the percepts that are supposed to be first are actually 'the results of cognitive elaboration' and are therefore set in a web of relational thought. One can only be deceived into thinking that he has begun with exclusively sensational foundations.

The critique of Cartesian doubt is well known, but less attention has been paid to what Peirce had to say in criticism of the traditional conception of experience. To begin with, he found himself wanting to express ideas about the nature of experience which he did not think it possible to express in terms of the accepted connotations of the term itself. In a short piece published in *The Monist* (1906),[22] Peirce cited Locke's opening statement about experience in the *Essay* with approval, but of a somewhat ironic sort. It is clear that Peirce thought some additions to Locke's definition were necessary, and, in fact, he proposed two; because, however, of his own belief that philosophy, like the sciences, should have its own technical terminology and that when a new concept is introduced a new word is required to express it, he found himself in a quandary. He was reluctant to 'displace or disturb' Locke's definition because of its neatness and authority, and yet he thought it had to be made more precise. The curious fact is that Peirce set forth the needed corrections without proposing a new term for the amended concept; he was content to point out that his two new ideas are *not* expressed by the term 'experience' which he believed should be restricted to the 'original meaning' assigned to it by Locke.[23] Peirce's two objections to Locke's definition are, first, that it fails to note 'the innate element of our directest perceptions', and, second, that it does not allow for the element of shock or surprise evoked by a new phenomenon. By the 'innate element' Peirce meant the role played by past experience and the constitution of the perceiver ignored by the *tabula rasa* doctrine which suggests a purely passive and pristine perceiver. In addition, allowance must be made for the novel and surprising which resists habitual expectation; the careless perceiver fails to grasp the novel element precisely because he too rapidly assimilates it to the normal expectation of 'more of the same'. But, said Peirce, referring to this novel element, 'to express precisely that idea you must have a new word for it; it will not answer the purpose to call it experience'.[24] The importance of this somewhat cryptic piece resides not so much in what it asserts as in what it denies. Peirce was convinced that the nature of experience cannot be adequately expressed in the terms established by the tradition which Locke began; it remains now to indicate the features of his own positive conception.

No attempt will be made to set forth Peirce's theory in terms of his universal categories; that would be too ambitious a task, and moreover, it is not necessary since the main concern is with traits of experience that eluded the classical empiricists. These features can be described without becoming deeply involved in the theory of quality, action and reaction signs, etc. To begin with, Peirce insisted that 'experience is our only teacher',[25] but by this he meant something quite out of the ordinary. 'Far be it from me,' he wrote, 'to enunciate any doctrine of a *tabula rasa*', and the reason is his firm belief that the source of all scientific theory is found in the power of the mind to *originate* true ideas, and that the role of experience is 'to precipitate and filter off the false ideas' largely in the form of surprises occurring within the course of experimentation. Surprise reveals a double consciousness present in all perception which is of an ego and non-ego directly interacting. Consider first, the percept which comes as a surprise; there is an imaginary object of a certain kind expected, but suddenly something quite different is encountered. 'I ask you,' said Peirce, 'whether at that instant of surprise there is not a double consciousness, on the one hand of an Ego, which is simply the expected idea suddenly broken off, on the other of the Non-Ego, which is the strange intruder, in his abrupt entrance.'[26] For Peirce, the perceptual judgement expressed in propositional form is something involuntary and beyond our control, and he held that it is nonsense, especially in the case of surprise, to dispute the fact that there is a real interaction and relatedness between the objects involved. *Relations,* therefore, are ingredient in experience along with distinct items or objects, and, in the case of surprises, mutual exchange and contrast make themselves evident. If, in the normal course of events, a certain result is expected and something quite different actually takes place, one is made vividly aware that the expectations, previously focused on what the non-ego or expected object would be or do, was actually a member of an inner world and that its place has been taken by the outer occurrence thrust upon us.

In connection with his analysis of surprise, Peirce laid particular emphasis on the *insistence* of experience and the tenure it enjoys *vis à vis* the human will. 'Experience which could be summoned up at pleasure,' he claimed, 'would not be experience.'[27] At times, it is true, Peirce followed the older way of thinking and identified experience with the 'world of fact' or the external world, but the mark of the difference between that world and the world of fancy or imagination is always a 'forcible modification of our ways of thinking'[28] and thus an instance on the dyadic interaction which he called 'secondness'. The crucial departure from the classical conception, however, appears in Peirce's refusal to identify experience with perception. 'Some writers,' he claimed, 'insist that all experience consists in sense perception'[29] but, while he admitted that we generally refer an element of experience to an external object, he also insisted that 'the kind of thing to which the word "experience" is more particularly applied' is an 'event' which has a temporal stretch or duration. The distinction is important and turns on the fact of change. Peirce, following Kant, held that change is not perceived because it requires the 'synthesis of apprehension' which is, as he said, of a 'more intellectual sort'. Perceptions may be seen as 'instantaneous' but the apprehension of change is not. And indeed if this is so, it would explain why, for classical empiricism, confined as it was to instantaneous sensations and impressions, there could be no *impression* for 'tendency' or 'directionality', but only for fixed or finished elements over and done with. To use Peirce's example, if a whistling locomotive passes me at high speed, as it passes the note of the whistle is lowered,[30] and while it is legitimate to say that I perceive or sense the note, it is not legitimate to say that I sense the *change* of note. 'That,' said Peirce, 'I experience rather than perceive.' In this he follows Kant for whom 'experience' can never be a matter of sensible components alone. Change is thus encompassed by experience on this view and not forced beyond its bounds as is the case when experience is confined to instantaneous sensations and perceptions.

There is a further feature of experience stressed by Peirce which is important because it is fundamental for Dewey as well, and that is the tendency of experience to accumulate or fund itself and thus to become established in the pervasive form of commonsense.[31] Commonplaces, said Peirce, are in fact 'universal experiences' taken for granted as the common basis for life; he was fond of contrasting the body of large, ordinary experience which he regarded as 'a valuable reservoir of truth',[32] with special and extraordinary experience by which he meant science and the results of research into recondite matters. Funded experience shared by all sustains a culture and assumes the form of a wisdom that can be passed on from one generation to another; as a consequence, pervasive experience attains to an instinctual status which sets it off from that special and controlled experience of detail which forms the substance of science. Since Peirce connected the having of experience with the formation of habits – the child, experiencing the pain resulting from the effort to grasp the candle's flame, acquires the habit of keeping its members away from fire – the pervasive experience of commonsense is something more than knowledge or information; it involves, in addition, patterns of behaviour or 'knowing how' to perform a task or to respond appropriately to a challenge.

As a concluding supplement to the technical accounts of the nature of experience developed under the influence of the pragmatic outlook, it is instructive to consider some connotations that have become attached to the term 'experience' itself in its ordinary use on the American scene. The influence of Pragmatism on these connotations is quite clear. Most prominent among them are first, the personal undergoing, *living through,* or enduring of situations and events, and second, the *acquisition of skills* enabling one to respond in appropriate fashion to the way objects encountered will behave, persons will conduct themselves, or systems will 'work'. According to the first connotation, to speak of medical, legal, or business 'experience' is to refer to the individual's encounter and familiarity with the materials, operations and transactions appropriate for one of these 'practices'. Although knowledge and theory are by no means excluded, primary emphasis falls on one being acquainted with, or actually having 'done' the operation in question as over against hearsay reports or descriptions handed down by others. According to the second connotation, to speak of the experienced painter, yachtsman, or politician is to point to the *ability* or capacity to perform effectively, or to indicate that a person 'knows how' to accomplish a certain aim, to resolve a problem arising or to meet an emergency, all in connection with a specific activity or field of endeavour. On both connotations, experience means interactions and transactions, commerce between the experiencing subject and whatever is encountered or needs to be handled. Undergoing, while not pure passivity, emphasizes the receptive capacity of the subject; the exhibition of skill or 'know-how' represents the active or transformatory aspect. Of central importance is the fact that the pragmatists never understood experience except in relation to the living subject oriented to the future and engaged in sustaining its life within a natural, historical and cultural setting. The reason in the end why they insisted that experience is more than knowing is found in their belief that experience is the actual career of the subject itself. Experience is what is enjoyed, endured, anticipated, remembered, achieved, and it forms the substance of human biography. Knowing as a specific concern assumes its rightful place when experience plays the role of teacher providing man with a means for self-direction and the reshaping of his surroundings. The reluctance of the pragmatists to celebrate experience in the form of the 'given' stems from their desire not to copy the world but to transform it.

4 Inquiry, science and control

The point has often been made that to understand the impact of science on American life and society it is necessary to pay attention to the dominant role assumed by technology. Theoretical science on the American scene has rarely been divorced from engineering or the ways in which scientific knowledge is set to work. That is the fact; the chief reason behind it was forcefully expressed in Dewey's conception of science as man's principal weapon in confronting the environment. If science is conceived not in terms of an exclusively theoretical ideal but rather as the manipulation of subject matter aimed at discovering patterns of law-like behaviour enabling man to control the world, the gap between so-called 'pure' science and technological applications is bound to close. Resolving a problem means *transforming* the problematic situation from which inquiry takes its rise and transformation requires effective instruments and not a mere display of theoretical ideas no matter how apt or ingenious. 'In principle,' said Dewey, 'the history of the construction of suitable operations in the scientific field is not different from that of their evolution in industry.'[1] It is therefore quite understandable that for the popular imagination in America, 'science' is not represented by the Willard Gibbses, the Einsteins, the Darwins, but by the Edisons, the Bells and the Westinghouses. The outcome is a consistent consequence of understanding science in terms of method, operation and control. Central to that understanding is the concept of inquiry as a certain kind of activity which has effects that extend far beyond the domain of theory.

It would be difficult to exaggerate the importance of the role assigned to inquiry in the thought of Peirce and Dewey especially. For Peirce it marks the middle term between the rise of doubt with its accompanying hesitancy and belief which serves as the basis of habits remaining settled until challenged by a new source of uncertainty. For Dewey inquiry is the appropriate response of an intelligent being to a situation which has become unsatisfactory or problematic and thus calls for some sort of resolution. Both thinkers saw inquiry as a determinate stage in the ongoing experience of a future-oriented individual; hence a full understanding of what inquiry means must include not only its logical and methodological structure as such, but also the role it plays in the life of the individual and the society to which he belongs. Confusion can be avoided if it is understood at the outset that the term 'inquiry' denotes a spectrum of situations extending from those that arise in ordinary experience at one end to highly complex and purposely constructed laboratory operations at the other. Many situations which ultimately call for inquiry are simply met or encountered and are seen as the result of existential causes quite external to the subject who must recognize these situations as problematic. On the other hand, laboratory situations are deliberately planned as part of an ongoing process of inquiry, so that it makes no sense to think of an investigator meeting them fortuitously. Dewey dealt explicitly with the differences between commonsense and scientific inquiry, maintaining that differences in their respective subject matters do not preclude the existence of a common 'pattern' in the two enterprises. Since considerable emphasis is placed on this community of pattern, it is wise not to approach his view at the outset with a sense of the utter discontinuity between ordinary situations and those specially instituted in the laboratory.

Suppose I arrive at the door of my office, put a key into the lock and find that the door does not open. My response in at once trying to deal with the obstacle or disappointed expectation represents a form of inquiry. I am confronted with a problem or impediment and I think instinctively about possible explanations and resolutions: perhaps I picked out the wrong key; perhaps the lock was changed in the meantime; could the key have been bent when I used it to pry open my tobacco jar?' etc. I proceed to check the alternatives with the two-fold aim of discovering the cause of the difficulty and of using this information as a guide for correcting the situation. That all of this may be done more or less automatically, unaccompanied by any focused sense of being engaged in a special process of investigation like that of science, does not mean that the logical and methodological structure of the ordinary situation may not be the same as that involved, for example, in the procedure necessary for determining whether the sulphate radical is present in a solution whose constituents are unknown. Science is thus seen as continuous with ordinary experience, at least with respect to the general pattern of inquiry; the inquiry characteristic of the sciences represents a refinement of those rudimentary trial-and-error operations everyone engages in when confronted with an obstacle which can be removed only when the grounds of the difficulty have been discovered.

The all-important difference between the approaches of Peirce and Dewey as regards inquiry has to do with the fact that Peirce was thinking primarily of the fixation of belief in both science and philosophy and thus his thought retains a theoretical thrust, whereas Dewey was concerned chiefly with the *instrumental* function of the inquiring intelligence in transforming the problematic situation so as to achieve a satisfactory outcome. While it is true that Peirce was no less concerned than Dewey to preserve integral relations between thought and action, it is also true that Peirce put more emphasis than Dewey on inquiry as leading to scientific knowledge and

D

the settling of opinion without making the instrumental or engineering consequences paramount. One can state the difference neatly by appealing to a most useful and genial ambiguity in colloquial language: Peirce aimed at 'fixing' belief, whereas Dewey aimed at 'fixing' the situation. The difference of emphasis is by no means insignificant; it explains why Peirce could maintain a version of correspondence theory in his account of inquiry and truth, while Dewey was led to set that ideal aside in favour of a transform theory which requires that the indeterminate or problematic situation which first gives rise to inquiry be replaced by a determinate state of affairs wherein the problem is resolved, not merely by answering a theoretical question but by actual manipulation and control of the relevant objects and conditions involved. Practical applications of knowledge are, for Peirce, among the conceived consequences of knowledge gained from controlled inquiry; Dewey, on the other hand, understood the pattern of inquiry solely in terms of the explicit aim of producing a transformed situation. If one thinks of the classic distinction traceable back to Aristotle, between *knowing, doing* and *making* as corresponding respectively to science, ethics and art, one can readily understand how difficulties arise in grasping Dewey's position since he seems to have blurred this three-fold distinction and to have relocated all three within the compass of the problematic situation.

In view of the fact that Peirce's correspondence-type theory of truth and of the inquiry that leads to knowledge are more readily understandable against a traditional background than is Dewey's position, it is wise to begin with the latter. A full-scale treatment would, of course, require an extended examination of Dewey's *Logic,* what it means to conceive of logic as the *theory* of inquiry or the structure of methodology and how the logical forms, including the constants, are to be construed in functional terms. Such a treatment exceeds the scope of the present discussion, but it is possible to give an acount of the pattern of inquiry as Dewey described it and also to make clear what his programme for the *Logic* was meant to accomplish.

Restating Dewey's view concisely on any topic is never easy, partly because of his tendency to write round a subject, picking up new problems as he proceeds, and partly because of his inability to refrain from interrupting a given line of thought in order to fire a shot or two at perennial opponents. Dewey was prepared, for example, to break into his discussion of any topic in order to launch an attack on the 'mental', call attention to the errors of psychologism, or point up the failure of some philosophical position to take science seriously. These asides distract attention from the main theme and are usually followed by an attempt to recapture the point through a restatement which invariably contains something novel. His entire account of inquiry is beset with these difficulties and it consequently appears as more complicated than it actually is. In what follows the focus will be on the section 'The Pattern of Inquiry'[2] in which Dewey attempted to show, *first*, how 'new formal properties accrue to subject matter' when that subject matter has been made the object of controlled inquiry, and, *second*, how inquiry into actual inquiries discloses a *pattern* of inquiry which is to serve as the justification of the 'normative' status of logical forms and methods.

In an earlier chapter Dewey set forth the theory 'that all logical forms (with their characteristic properties) arise within the operation of inquiry and are concerned with control of inquiry so that it may yield warranted assertions'.[3] And he went on to point out that this claim means not only that an examination of processes of inquiry in actual use brings these forms to light, but that they *originate* in such processes. As a consequence, Dewey was led to deny the validity of a fixed distinction between logic and methodology which has been determined in advance of the analysis of inquiry itself. And yet he claimed that in order to be valid, inquiry must 'itself satisfy logical requirements'[4] which would seem to move the discussion about in a circle. Dewey was not unaware of the problem and, in fact, raised it himself, firm in the belief that the problem is not insoluble. 'How,' he asked, 'can inquiry originate logical forms . . . and yet be subject to the requirements of these forms?'[5] The general shape of the answer to this question is that inquiry actually develops, in the course of an ongoing process, the standards to which *future* inquiry must be subject. This answer, it is clear, presupposes the all-important fact – the basis of Dewey's entire position – of science as a 'self-corrective process' which presumably operates successfully without appeal to 'standards *ab extra*' by which Dewey generally meant standards imposed by a transcendent or transcendental reason. Misunderstandings would have been avoided if Dewey had stated more explicitly that his logic was intended as the theory of 'successful' inquiry, i.e. inquiry which has already in fact issued in what he called 'warranted assertions',[6] so that whatever *normative* character attaches to the logical forms constituting the pattern of such inquiry is derivative from the validity already accorded the inquiry itself together with its outcome. The 'autonomy' which Dewey claimed for logic as inquiry into inquiry stems from the fact that, as he pointed out, a circular process is involved since such logic 'does not depend on anything extraneous to inquiry'. It is essential, however, to add that one is not referring here to 'inquiry' in some purely formal sense but to actual methodologies exhibited in the sciences and already presumed to have led to warranted assertions. In this regard it is necessary to call attention to Dewey's dependence on the history of science, a fact which stands out more clearly within the present climate of opinion than it could have in earlier decades. Dewey, in terms characteristic of many of his views, was here attempting to move beyond previous mutually exclusive alternatives which to him seemed inadequate. On the one hand, he was opposed to the selection of logical first principles on the basis of some '*a priori* intentional act', and against this view he maintained that logical forms have their sole origin within inquiry. On the other hand, although he acknowledged the validity of Mill's attempt to ground logic in methodology, he objected to his 'empiricist' approach and the doctrine of immediate certainty it involves. Dewey believed, moreover, that Mill's 'particularism', or the idea of reasoning from case to case, is not representative of actual scientific inquiry, especially in its neglect of the controlling function of hypotheses, but expresses instead Mill's own psychologically oriented theory of the way the human mind is supposed to function.

Since Dewey's account of the pattern of inquiry is intimately connected with his concept of the problematic situation it will be well to start with the concept of a situation itself. This notion has been an object of some confusion largely because it has frequently been thought of in quasispatial terms which focus attention on the 'size' of a 'situation' and the problem of determining its boundaries or limits. The reference to size or scope does seem inevitable, especially when it becomes necessary to attempt to determine how much a situation embraces and what is included or excluded from it. But in the end this way of thinking is unpromising because Dewey's way of characterizing a situation is chiefly through its *quality*; the boundary of any situation turns out to be a matter of relevance or functional relation between its constituents depending on the quality which defines that situation. Dewey repeatedly described a situation as a 'contextual whole' and this designation was meant to exclude thinking of a situation as 'a single object or event or set of objects and events'.[7] His basic reason for so thinking goes back to his conception of experience: no one experiences or judges objects and events *simpliciter,* as it were, but only within some framework of purpose and interest which marks out a context. This is not to say that *an* object or event cannot occupy a focal position in an experience; it is rather that such an object or event is always experienced in a field or 'environing experienced world' which is synonymous with a situation. It was Dewey's contention that an object or event becomes 'focal' only in virtue of its position and function within the situation which surrounds it. At times Dewey made reference to the 'total complex environment' against which a singular object becomes conspicuous, but he cannot have meant this in an unqualified sense without arriving at that 'whole of reality' which the pragmatists generally rejected on the grounds that it precludes finite terms and finite situations. For Dewey situations are finite and they are intelligible without invoking a whole of reality which ultimately contains them. Secondly, it is not clear that *every* item in a finite situation is relevant or equally relevant or enters essentially into the interest or purpose determining that situation. Some constituents of a situation may not 'count' or 'make a difference' with respect to the problem or concerns at hand. This consideration is, in fact, so important that it can be made to serve as a defining character of the entire pragmatic outlook – theoretical intelligence, according to the pragmatists, presents us with a logically *infinite* set of determinations and relations in every context; unless we have a selective principle indicating what to stress and what to ignore, we have no choice but to include everything if reality is to be adequately represented. We need, therefore, to have a way to determine what is relevant and the relative importance of factors and conditions in a situation.

A situation is determined initially by what Dewey called an immediate pervasive quality which binds all the elements in that situation into one whole. By 'quality' here Dewey did not mean specific sense qualities or dispositions such as are indicated by the terms 'soluble', 'bitter', 'yellow', which are distinguished and referred to singular objects within situations. He meant instead such qualities as are designated by terms like 'cheerful', 'distressing', 'problematic', 'confused' which 'permeate and color *all* the objects and events that are involved in an experience'. These qualities are obviously not to be correlated with the standard senses as in the case of the traditional 'secondary' qualities.[8] Every situation is identified through a pervasive quality of the above sort; it was Dewey's contention that apprehending or 'having' the unique quality of the situation provides, first, a vantage point for selecting and weighing facts constituent in it and, second, a clue as to the conceptual ordering of these data. One might say that Dewey was seeking, through the concept of a situation and its pervasive quality, to provide an 'orientation' for reflective thought. One of his examples reinforces the point. He cited, on the one hand, a situation in which facts are indiscriminately gathered, after the fashion of Russell's ants who merely gather things without a purpose or plan, and consequently lead nowhere, and, on the other, a situation in which observations are so rigidly controlled by a predetermined conceptual scheme that many items actually relevant for resolving a problem are overlooked.[9] To avoid both of these unsatisfactory states of affairs, Dewey proposed an open-ended approach: attention should be directed primarily to the *quality* defining the type of situation that confronts us because this quality provides reflective thought with its focus and orientation. The immediate bearing of the concept of a situation on the nature of inquiry is obvious: inquiry is the ordered response to any situation having the pervasive quality of being 'indeterminate' or 'problematic'.[10] Both the pattern of inquiry and the general nature of its outcome are determined by this fact.

The first point to be noticed in considering Dewey's account of the pattern of inquiry is that it does not purport to be a set of rules governing procedure which are taken as conventions or stipulations of a purely 'formal' sort. The inquiry of which logic is the theory is *selective* and concerns only those 'methods which experience up to the present time shows to be the best methods available for achieving certain results'.[11] Logic, in short, as the pattern of inquiry, is not independent of the existence of actual inquiries and must be seen in relation to the actual historical development of science. The dependence of logic on actual inquiry, however, is not to be construed as a reduction of logic to an 'empirical' science. The peculiarity of Dewey's position is that he would not locate logic in either of the two places it has traditionally occupied on the philosophical map. In criticism of transcendental conceptions like that of Kant and Husserl, or of formal conceptions like that of Russell and the mathematical logicians, Dewey urged that logic can neither deny nor ignore its dependence on actual inquiry and hence cannot constitute itself as a purely *a priori* domain. The most that can be said on his view is that logical forms which have proved themselves effective *up to a given time* can be regarded as *a priori* with regard to the inquiry at hand. This view is similar to Lewis' 'functional' *a priori,* but is not identical with it in virtue of the fact that Lewis attached a necessity to his *a priori* which Dewey did not allow. Yet, on the other hand, in opposition to Mill especially Dewey acknowledged the 'distinctive existence' of logical forms and accorded them a 'relatively' normative status. 'Logic,' he wrote, 'is not compelled, as historic "empirical" logic felt compelled to do, to reduce logical forms to mere transcripts of the empirical materials that antecede the existence of the former.'[12] This suggests a measure of independence for logical forms, but it is clearly of a qualified sort. For although Dewey did speak of these forms as having independent 'development', he insisted that the independence is 'not final and complete' but intermediate which means that they are dependent on an historical process revealing not what is perfect, but only what is 'better' than other alternatives.[13] The forms, moreover, are said to originate 'out of' experiential material and to 'introduce new ways of operating,' an idea which suggests a functional approach quite distinct from the structural realism (idealism) to be associated with the Platonic tradition and its modern representatives such as Whitehead. Not unlike Hegel, whose peculiar rationalism aimed at bringing about a coherent togetherness of the rationalist and empiricist traditions, Dewey sought to combine in a *methodological suspension* both the involvement of logical forms with experience and inquiry and their legislative function as canons which *must* be adhered to if contradiction and ambiguity are to be avoided. That legislative function, however, is always qualified by the fact that it derives ultimately, not from the depth of reason, but from methods that have proved themselves successful in the past. In this regard, Dewey stood in the end on the same ground as Peirce in his attack upon foundationalism in logic;[14] both appealed to a large circular process according to which the validity of logic is a function of its contribution to the achievement of certain cognitive results over a period of time; these results are in turn dependent for their validity upon the fact that they were reached by following a method informed and controlled by that logic. The principal difference between Peirce and Dewey is that the former allowed greater autonomy to the formal structure of abduction, deduction and induction, while the latter tried to find the entire meaning of logical forms in their function as controlling factors in inquiry.

The difference is not insignificant and can be traced back to Peirce's description of Dewey's contributions to *Studies in Logical Theory* as a 'natural history of thought' and his expressed uneasiness about the extent to which Dewey's approach can make a place for 'normative logic'.[15] On the other hand, one should not overlook the influence of evolutionary thought on Peirce's understanding of logic; that influence is most manifest in his emphasis on the growth of concepts and on the rate at which the expansion of feeling determines changes in even our most fundamental logical categories.

There is much to be said for this mediating or synthesizing position *vis à vis* the status of logic, even if it is not likely to satisfy purists at each end of the spectrum. Those who insist on preserving necessity and formality will be forced to do so at the cost of reducing the logical component either to convention or tautology and on both alternatives the relation of that component to empirical subject matter becomes something of a mystery. On the other hand logic is not an 'empirical' science and it will not do to construe it as such in order to provide an intelligible account of its role in empirical inquiry. Logic has a sort of annoying transcendence which allows it to enjoy an autonomous and independent development quite apart from the demands of specific inquiries and their consequences. A special example of this transcendence is found in the development of the non-Euclidean geometries. From a logical point of view, they represent the consistent development of the two remaining logical alternatives to the parallel postulate in Euclidean geometry without any concern whatever for the 'applicability' of these new geometries or their role in empirical inquiry. No 'empirical' theory of logic can account for this transcendence. On the other hand, no empirical inquiry can dispense with logic, and therefore some way of accounting for its role is demanded. The classical pragmatists tried to deal with this problem through what I have called the 'methodological suspension'. Methodology appears, as it were, as a third term embracing both formal structure and empirical procedure. From the standpoint of methodology, inquiry is a unified and continuous process so that no one of its constituents is absolutely autonomous. Logical forms are seen as the structure of inquiry and their normative force derives from the role they play in 'successful' inquiry. These forms stand related to empirical subject matter in two essential ways: first, they exercise control over the process through which warranted conclusions are reached and, second, they exercise authority in the consistent formulation of these conclusions and in the determination of their logical consequences.

Returning now to Dewey's account of the problematic situation which forms the matrix of inquiry, it is necessary to set forth the stages of the process embracing both logical and temporal order. Underlying the entire account of inquiry as intelligent response to indeterminate situations which can be described as incoherent, disturbed, confused, etc., is Dewey's view (essentially the same as that expressed by Ryle but set forth decades earlier) that we do not first begin with a 'mental' state and then proceed to an overt response so that it becomes a question as to how the mental which is clearly other than this response came to bear on the situation. The intelligent response which initiates inquiry and *is* indeed inquiry itself is the apprehension or recognition of some situation *as* problematic. And it was precisely because Dewey wanted to avoid exclusive emphasis on the doubt or uncertainty considered as conscious traits of an inquirer, that he insisted on assigning the quality of being indeterminate and problematic to the situation itself. As he expressed the point, '*We* are doubtful because the situation is inherently doubtful';[16] like Peirce, Dewey was insisting on the correlation of doubt with existential states of affairs which evoke that particular response. The view being rejected is that situations, actual existence, are always determinate in themselves and become 'subjectively' doubtful only in virtue of becoming related to a mind which is in doubt. Were this the true state of affairs, problematic situations could be resolved merely by changing our minds or rearranging our thoughts. On the other hand, Dewey went on to connect the problematic situation with the organism or subject which confronts it; the problematic is actualized at the interface between organism and environment. The fact that the interaction between the two is a temporal sequence and concerns the sort of response the organism will ultimately make directs attention to the *issue* or outcome of the process as the decisive respect in which the situation is indeterminate. Despite Dewey's tendency to draw on a wide variety of controlled activities as illustrations – tilling the soil, waging war, clearing a path in the forest – it is certainly *not* the case that he regarded every sort of interaction as inquiry. It is, therefore, not sufficient to define inquiry as the transformation of an indeterminate situation into one that is determinate, and indeed were this not the case, Russell would have been right in his contention that Dewey's stated conditions for inquiry are validly fulfilled by a team of bricklayers constructing a wall. An interaction becomes inquiry only when: (a) some existential consequences of operations are anticipated; (b) environing conditions are analysed in order to determine their tendencies and potentialities; (c) activities constituting the response are selected and arranged for the purpose of realizing certain potentialities and not others. The critic may say that these conditions are still too vague and inclusive to define inquiry and this is in fact the case. What is needed in addition is the judgement on the part of the subject that the situation in question *is* problematic, that it is *the occasion for the asking of intelligible questions* which can be answered only by initiating inquiry. 'To see that a situation requires inquiry,' said Dewey, 'is the initial step in inquiry.'[17] The situation calling for inquiry is said to come about from existential causes, just as the state of hunger arises, and in this case the cause is whatever there is about the situation which leads us to regard it *as* problematic. The judgement that a situation is problematic represents the first cognitive move. The next step is to determine *what* the problem is and to have grounds for claiming that it arises out of factors in the situation at hand.

For Dewey, there is no determination of a problem which does not at the same time involve in its formulation some reference to a possible solution. Question and answer are thus not logically external to each other. The question is: How is the formulation of the problem 'so controlled that further inquiries will move toward a solution?'[18] The answer to this question is given in terms of two central items – facts and ideas or meanings – which are then understood in functional terms as Facts–Meanings working together in the actual course of inquiry to bring about the sought-for resolution. Though correlative, the two components are distinguishable after the fashion of Kant's sense and understanding, or the perceptual and conceptual distinction which formed the background of discussion for Bergson, Royce, James and others. Dewey claimed, however, that in opposition to past views the two factors cannot be conceived as utterly different in kind. As will become clear, his way of connecting them was through the concept of *operation*. Turning to the factual component, the first step is to determine what constituents of the situation are *settled* or may reasonably be regarded as settled by comparison with other constituents. No situation is indeterminate in every respect, and from the standpoint of the inquirer there is no situation every one of whose features is in doubt simultaneously. If every feature of a situation were in doubt, no beginning could be made, and in actual fact there is no situation in which an inquirer actually doubts – in the sense of having specific grounds for doing so – everything. This point is crucial and it forms a coping-stone of the pragmatic outlook on inquiry and knowledge. Moreover, it seems to have gained considerable acceptance at present as can be seen in the frequently cited figure comparing the edifice of knowledge with a ship which, to be sure, leaks, but is not in fact leaking everywhere at once. If, for example, our aim in a situation is to measure the length of an object, that length is indeterminate as a desideratum, but the measuring device is not open to question; it is taken as one of the settled features of the situation.[19] The 'facts of the case' then constitute the terms which are settled and those observational features which must be taken into account by any relevant solution.

Possible solutions to the problem at hand take the form of ideas which originate as 'suggestions' consequent on the determination of the facts. These suggestions are, for Dewey, the counterpart of Peirce's abductions. They are characterized as forecasts or anticipated consequences of performing operations under observed and specified conditions; the test of their 'functional fitness' for resolving the problematic situation is found in experiment and is thus an eventual affair. Two features of the suggestions which qualify as ideas and hence as hypotheses are especially noteworthy.

First, because ideas are meanings and are not present as such in the facts of the case they require symbolic representation – concepts and propositions – which enables us to 'look' at them, criticize them and take note of their development. Second, and of greater import, is the *functional* role assigned to these meanings: they are to direct observation and aid in the determination of what in the field of observation is relevant. It was Dewey's contention that neither of these functions can be understood on the theory that an idea is a copy of a physical thing. Although he included Kant among those who failed to grasp the functional role of the idea, it is clear that what Dewey was pointing to was well stated by Kant when he wrote concerning the experimental method:

When Galileo caused balls, the weight of which he had previously determined, to roll down an inclined plane ; when Toricelli made the air carry a weight which he had calculated beforehand . . . a light broke upon all students of nature . . . Accidental observations, made in obedience to no previously thought-out plan, can never be made to yield a necessary law.[20]

The idea of a possible solution to a problem serves as a guide in the selecting and devising of operations or procedures for testing and at the same time provides clues to the proper interpretation to be given to the observed results. To take the simplest possible example, the rise of a liquid in a tube would remain as the barest observation in the absence of a guiding idea which indicates the significance to be attached to the phenomenon. The point Dewey wanted to insist upon is the functional togetherness of the perceptual and conceptual components in inquiry; the *active* work done by ideas in directing operations on and observations of perceptual content, no less than the role of the initial observations which enable us to locate and define the problem to be resolved.

Reasoning enters at the point where suggested ideas have been cast in symbolic or propositional form and the attempt is made to discover what other meanings can be derived from those already in hand. If, for example, it were assumed that there is a valid analogy between the flow of an electric current through a wire and the flow of water through a pipe, a number of interesting consequences follow, each of which provides further occasion for inquiry. Is there a formula for expressing rate of flow in terms of the diameter of the conduit? Is there a formula for expressing the resistance offered by the conduit? The aim of such reasoning is the further clarification of ideas, resulting in the determination of the relevant operations required for testing the validity of these ideas. The repeated emphasis which one finds in Dewey, along with Peirce and James, on the functional interpretation of meaning is for the precise purpose of deriving from the ideas themselves clues as to the tests required for determining where and when these ideas actually apply.

Dewey's account of the manner in which the observed facts and the conceptual components function together in inquiry is quite typical of his general position. Attention is focused not on the logical structure or internal constitution of percepts and concepts as, for example, in some of Royce's analyses, but rather on the *role* played by each in the process of inquiry. The general idea at work is well expressed in Cassirer's book, *Substance and Function*; it marks a significant point of agreement between the two thinkers of which each was aware. Dewey's contention was that only if both components are seen as 'operational' can we show how the existential observed facts can be related to a conceptual non-existential order. The operational role assigned to ideas as hypotheses or theories has already been indicated; the question that remains is: What is to be understood by the operational character of the facts? Dewey's answer was essentially as follows. The facts of the case are not self-contained because they are meant to serve a dual function: first, through them the problem is stated, and, second, they are to indicate some relevant way of answering a question or resolving a problem. The facts, then, are selected to perform these functions and only those which do so are relevant. These two functions, however, do not exhaust the operational significance of observational facts. In language far from clear, Dewey went on to claim that the basic function of fact is to serve as *evidence,* and that no fact taken in isolation 'has evidential potency'.[21]

To be tests of an idea, facts must be organized so that they 'interact' with each other, or, more precisely, they can be organized only in so far as they interact. Since no illustration is offered it is difficult to be sure of exactly what Dewey meant. It appears that he wanted to describe inquiry as a *serial* process involving experiment and at the same time to call attention to the mutual interaction between ideas and facts in this process. Perhaps the familiar example of the gas laws will serve to make Dewey's view more clear. If we assume that Boyle and Charles started out with some initial observational facts concerning the behaviour of gas samples under certain conditions, their question or problem would be whether these facts express regular or law-like correlations between volume, pressure, rate of flow through an aperture, etc. for all known gases. The testing of the idea would require appropriate experimental procedures which in turn would result in further observational facts. The latter would determine the validity of the idea that, for example, the volume and the pressure of a gas are related in a constant and regular way. These same facts, however, might also require a modification of the idea being tested as when it was discovered that not all gases but only 'ideal' gases obey the standard gas laws precisely. The interaction between fact and meaning of which Dewey spoke starts with observational facts which 'suggest' an idea as to how they are related or are to be accounted for. This idea guides further experimental activity yielding new facts which in turn tend either to confirm the idea, or to require its modification in scope or intent, or even the eventual abandoning of the idea as ill-founded. On Dewey's view, the mode in which the observations of existential facts are related to the proposed idea which is not existential is through the expression of both in *symbolic* form. That is to say, the idea as a possibility is not present existentially as the facts are, but requires expression in propositional form. The facts, on the other hand, are not just there as *presented* but are rather what are *represented* by the symbols which refer to them. Being a fact is to have a selected status in inquiry and thus to have relevance and evidential force. As long as inquiry persists, symbolic representation and the transformation of symbols continues along with the manipulation of the subject matter as directed by the ideas being tested.

One feature of Dewey's theory of inquiry especially has given rise to considerable discussion and criticism: it concerns his claim that inquiry has a *transformational* character and that the subject matter involved undergoes temporal modification. In short, to say that inquiry is a temporal process is to say more than that it takes place in time. Before considering what this transformationalism means, it might be well to note the main ground for the uneasiness felt by its critics. According to a long philosophical tradition strongly reinforced by commonsense, knowing or discovering the truth concerning the world about us requires setting aside personal prejudices and predilections in order to *conform* to that world as a reality 'given' from beyond human consciousness and will. Such a conformism stands, for example, at the foundation of such diverse views as Husserl's phenomenology and Santayana's realism; Santayana was particularly scornful of 'transcendental' philosophies for what he called their 'systematic subjectivism' and their natural *impiety* in constructing new worlds in imagination when there is a real world which must be followed and conformed to if man is to learn its secrets. This strong sense of the need to mirror or faithfully represent a given world without subjective addition or coloration seems to be totally at odds with the transformationalism Dewey described. Nor were critics at all reassured when they read Dewey within the intellectual climate created by James who talked about truth being 'made'. Since it is obvious that the conform tradition cannot be dismissed as just so much philosophical error, the important question is whether Dewey's transform theory excludes it, or whether his conception of inquiry can consistently embrace the truth in the other tradition. In seeking to answer this question, it will be necessary to raise another: to what extent did Dewey's concern to bridge the gap between thought and action, theory and practice lead him to construe inquiry in terms so completely operational that scientific investigation and engineering become virtually indistinguishable?

What exactly did Dewey mean by transformation in inquiry? No answer to this question is possible unless we consider the distinction between commonsense and scientific inquiry. Dewey's basic thesis was that two distinctive modes of inquiry are involved and that the difference between them resides not in basic logical forms and relations but in their repective subject matters. The distinction of subject matters depends on the different problems acknowledged in the two enterprises; from this difference there follows a difference in aim and in the consequences to be sought for. It is important to notice that commonsense problems are described as 'practical' in contrast to 'intellectual' and they are said to be concerned chiefly with the efforts of living creatures in an environment to determine the appropriate 'objects of use and enjoyment' within their society. The ideas and meanings involved presuppose a cultural background and find expression in an everyday language commonly used and understood. Custom and tradition prevail and, according to Dewey, in the commonsense situation 'there is no such thing as disinterested concern with either physical or social matters'.[22] Such disinterest as did exist prior to the special disinterestedness on which science is based took the form of an insistence that group interests be given priority over private needs and concerns. Science, however, demands something more, namely 'intellectual' disinterestedness which means primarily that 'meanings are related to one another on the ground of their character *as* meanings' and are not restricted to the interests of a limited cultural group. The appearance of a scientific language signals the change in outlook; everyday language with its cultural involvement and emphasis on the qualitative features of things is inadequate for expressing what is disclosed from the novel standpoint of science. The 'scientific object' is something understood in terms of relations that are indifferent to qualities; qualities figure in inquiry only in so far as they aid in instituting relations which are in themselves abstract or general and are freed from the restrictions imposed by particular times and places.

The upshot of the foregoing is that scientific inquiry necessarily involves the *transformation* of familiar commonsense objects with their immediate cultural qualities and associations into scientific objects which are shorn of these associations and are meant to have universal import. The interesting feature of the transformation, in Dewey's view, is that an *increment of meaning* accrues to things when they are seen in the context of scientific inquiry as opposed to the usual view which says that from the scientific standpoint the *qualities* of things have been 'reduced' or relegated to the status of mere appearance. Understanding a thing in terms of its relations and relational properties is seen as an addition to its total significance and not as a substitute for the world of commonsense. Scientific inquiry, then, represents initial subject matter in a new mode; accompanying this transformation goes the new aim of attaining theoretical comprehension and explanation instead of the use–enjoyment objective dominant in commonsense inquiry.

Transformation of the subject matter is not, however, the only sort of transformation involved in inquiry. That initial change is largely conceptual

in character being focused on differences in the mode of symbolic representation. In addition, overt and existential modifications are called for which
direct attention to the significance of what is done to the subject matter of
inquiry in the course of our exacting from it the answers to our questions.
To begin with, the unsettled situation which gives rise to inquiry is such
that it cannot be settled or resolved except by 'modification of its constituents'.[23] In short, the intermediaries represented by experimental operations, go beyond alterations in symbolic representation. These operations
'change existing conditions' and do not leave everything as it was before.
Here Dewey was attempting to take account of what actually happens
in empirical inquiry; he was not content merely with the analysis of
the language of science or with some purely logical account of the nature
of scientific explanation. 'Reasoning, as such,' said Dewey, 'can provide
means for effecting the change of conditions but by itself cannot effect
it.'[24] Since the ultimate aim of inquiry is the production of a settled
and unified situation, a result that takes the form of warranted assertions alone will not of itself be adequate to the task. As was pointed
out earlier, Dewey's aim was not just to 'fix' belief, but to 'fix' the situation
so that its initially unsettled or indeterminate character is existentially
modified in the direction that resolves the problem. Leaving aside for the
moment the question about the possible confusion here between resolving
a problem by arriving at a warranted assertion, and rearranging an existential situation in order to remove a physical obstacle, one must ask whether
there is any reason why this transformism could not make way for the
demand of the conform position as a stage in the process of inquiry. I
believe that there is no such reason and that in fact Dewey's conception
of the 'facts of the case' allows for full acknowledgement of the conform
position. Without a faithful representation of these facts, no inquiry can
attain satisfactory results; in short, no amount of concern for changing
the constituents of the situation to attain the end of inquiry frees us from
the obligation to conform to those facts. Dewey would have insisted, however, against those who would ground these facts in some form of sense
certainty, on their essential connection to ideas or meanings expressed in
the concepts of some system. Thus, for example, to say that water boils
at a certain degree of temperature under x atmospheres of pressure, is to
assert a firm fact, but it stands related to theoretical elements – theories
of heat and atmospheric pressure – which are also asserted when the
proposition expressing the fact is asserted. To this extent the fact is not
'brute'. Dewey, moreover, in accord with the pragmatic theory of meaning,
would further have insisted on evoking the 'operational' significance of
facts which means that they are seen as relational rather than qualitative
and that they are set forth with some indication of the procedures necessary
for determining them. As with James, Dewey's dissatisfaction with the
'copy' conception of ideas supposed to represent fact – a conception lurking

in the background of conform theories – stems from the belief that a mental duplicate is static and inert and therefore fails to express the temporal and dynamic character of fact. The idea is that if our presumed knowledge of things is to fulfil its instrumental function, it must indicate how an object qualified in a certain way as fact will behave, and how an inquirer is to proceed experimentally to verify that fact.

The other question cited above about the possible confusion between knowing and making in Dewey's account of inquiry is more difficult to resolve. Let us suppose that Dewey was basically correct in his view of the general shape of inquiry, and in his insistence on the importance of the activity involved – the intervention of the investigator manipulating subject matter with instruments, initiating changes in the working of physical systems, etc. The point is not simply that knowledge or warranted assertions when obtained are meant to have practical application or to guide conduct, but that the attainment of that knowledge itself requires activity and the handling of things. The question that arises at this point is whether the activity which results in existential changes in a problematic situation has an identical counterpart in purely theoretical research. It is not obvious that inquiry aimed at answering a question where there is no specific plan to apply the answer through specific engineering operations involves the notion of 'repairing' or putting back in order. This notion, however, is clearly required in problematic situations where there is a breakdown of some going concern or the failure of a mechanism to operate in accordance with an expected, long-standing habit. Another and perhaps better way to put this question is to ask whether Dewey's initial characterization of the unsettled, indeterminate, problematic situation is not too broad and includes under the same rubric too many diverse sorts of problematic situations. It is, to be sure, important to hold fast to the underlying and common pattern of inquiry obtaining in all such situations but it cannot be less important to pay attention o he differences involved as well. The distinction Dewey drew between comonsense problematic situations arising within the ambit of cultural life, and those belonging to scientific inquiry is clear enough. What is not so clear, however, is whether Dewey's view allows, within the confines of situations calling for scientific inquiry, for a reasonable distinction between inquiry in which the resolution of techno- logical problems is *not* the main focus and those in which it is. The con- tinuing extension of technological society and the industrialization of scientific research in recent decades have had the effect of so complicating the relation between theoretical science and technology that it is virtually impossible to draw the line between them. The bearing of Dewey's thought here is quite paradoxical. On the one hand, his characterization of science in terms of disinterestedness, the transcendence of cultural limitations and the development of an abstract, relational language shows clearly that he grasped the ideal of the founders of modern science which was to lay bare the reasons and causes of things as a matter of pure *theoria* without concern for its utility or applicability. On the other hand, Dewey was equally aware of the fact that actual scientific inquiry takes place within a cultural environment which forces upon that inquiry an involvement in interests and concerns which from the standpoint of *theoria* would be regarded as irrelevant. The curious fact is that the deep involvement of science with a technology has led recent historians and philosophers of science to take very seriously those relations between science and culture which Dewey long ago sought to express in his operational theory of inquiry. In this regard his theory takes on a new relevance not to be found in positions which assume a divorce between a purely 'intellectual' science and a contingent world of problems to which this knowledge has to be applied. And this is not all; as our awareness of the pressures to which science is subject – ideological, economic, political – increases, there has arisen a strong feeling that science needs to be 'saved' through a recovery of its older theoretical ideal which Dewey had stressed initially in his differentiation of science from commonsense. In the end it appears that Dewey was attempting to do justice to both faces of science: first, by insisting on the integrity of theoretical inquiry, and, second, by closing the gap between a purely theoretical and inert knowledge and its technological applications by emphasizing the need to manipulate subject matter in order to attain that knowledge in the first place. Whatever logical problems may remain in connection with the distinction between knowing and making in Dewey's theory, it cannot be denied that his account is pertinent in the highest degree for the treatment of those larger and vaguer questions concerning science and society which cannot be adequately treated from a purely logical point of view.

No discussion of Dewey's conception of inquiry can fail to mention the obvious connection it has with the underlying motive to control or influence the course of events. Though the environment is supportive of man, it has its hostile dimensions and these are multiplied enormously when it is expanded to include the fabric of human culture. Inquiry, itself a manifestation of the instrumental intelligence, has as its human goal the attainment of insight into the workings, habits and tendencies of things, thereby furnishing man with a weapon for subduing what makes life precarious and for enhancing the powers that sustain us. Just as inquiry is a controlled activity where, as Kant said, we are not in nature's leading strings but seek rather to exact her secrets by design, the fruits of inquiry represent new means of control over the workings of nature and the historical process. In Dewey's ultimate metaphysical view, man appears not only as the tool-maker, the animal with intelligence, but as the being whose destiny it is to control his own being in a world that harbours within itself no guarantee of success.

Peirce's theory of inquiry, in comparison with Dewey's, clearly lays greater emphasis on its constituent logical structures and their problems and it keeps more steadily in view the belief or opinion which stands as the outcome of inquiry for the one who pursues it. Much has been written on the topic. There are, moreover, numerous questions which interested Peirce that are still under discussion such as the formulation of hypotheses, the nature of deduction, and the theory of probability. These topics are beyond our present scope. Therefore, I shall focus on a facet of Peirce's view which is likely to be neglected although it is both central to his position and characteristic of the pragmatic outlook at the same time. Inquiry was seen by Peirce in its existential import as a process carried on and also undergone by a 'flesh and blood experimenter', and it is for this reason that an account of the three stages of inquiry from a logical standpoint alone will not convey the full significance of the process. In short, despite Peirce's undoubted concern to analyse the logic of inquiry, he still regarded it as an actual process which only a puzzled inquirer can carry out.

The place in which Peirce explained the nature of inquiry in direct relation to the inquirer is in one of the best known papers, 'The Fixation of Belief'. There inquiry is identified with a 'struggle'[25] to overcome doubt and 'attain a state of belief', and it is seen as having no function other than to settle opinion.[26] Like James at this point, Peirce was here concerned with what 'actually happens' in human consciousness when believing, doubting and the attempt to overcome doubt are involved. The empirical orientation of both thinkers stands out clearly; neither was prepared simply to set aside the facts revealed in our direct experience of doubting and believing in order to proceed to a theory of how we *should* determine belief. This is not to say that Peirce and James had no such theory, but only that they refused to develop it in a wholly abstract way.[27] Not least among the several points Peirce wanted to make is the equation of 'believing' and 'believing to be true'. There is no tendency in Peirce to use the term 'belief' in the 'weasel' way characteristic of some modern philosophers where believing is hardly to be distinguished from 'entertaining' an idea without conviction, or else it is equated with a sort of diminished claim in assertion where one wants to avoid the onus of making a truth claim in the hope of being allowed merely to 'believe' and letting it go at that. 'We think,' he said, 'each one of our beliefs to be true, and, indeed, it is mere tautology to say so';[28] that a belief may not in fact be true does not alter the case. And the reason cited is that the only way in which the two could fail to accord is for there to be some *actual* doubt in the situation. In the absence of doubt, belief prevails. If there is such doubt, which is to say, actual grounds rooted in the facts of the case why the belief in question may not be true or warranted, then the appropriate response is *inquiry*. It is for this reason that Peirce laid such stress on the importance of 'real and living doubt' as against the Cartesian *programme* of doubting everything and in opposition to intellectual exercises where, as he said, one simply puts the proposition into interrogative form. Critical discussion and inquiry remain unintelligible apart from actual doubt. 'In cases where no real doubt exists in our minds,' Peirce wrote, 'inquiry will be an idle farce.'[29] The point is made again with even greater force in his account of 'critical commonsensism'. There it is said that genuine doubt always has an 'external origin' in the form of a surprise, and that it is impossible to create either a doubt or a surprise by an act of will.[30]

There is no point in saying of this analysis that what it represents is 'merely psychological' as if the actual state of affairs concerning human belief is unimportant in contrast to the standard and impersonal situation that obtains in the fixation of scientific opinion. Peirce was not unaware of the role played by what he sometimes called 'feigned' doubt in scientific inquiry, and he even spoke of devising ways of attaining such doubt. In characterizing his 'critical commonsensist' who represents an advance over Scottish commonsense philosophy, Peirce cited 'the great value he attaches to doubt'[31] as long as it is genuine and not a 'paper substitute'. 'He is not content,' Peirce wrote, in describing the pragmatist, 'to ask himself whether he does doubt, *but he invents a plan for attaining to doubt,* elaborates it in detail, and then puts it into practice.'[32] The important point in all this is that if inquiry is to perform its proper function it must be initiated by a genuine doubt based on the facts of the situation which in turn indicates to the doubter some respect in which the hypothesis in question may be erroneous. In describing doubt – the third essential ingredient in experimentation – as a *feeling* of uneasiness, or irritation, Peirce must not be taken to mean that the doubt *consists* in the feeling. The feeling is a colour or tone of doubt as a state of mind, but the doubt itself is manifested as an obstacle, something which interferes with the 'smooth working' of a belief which is also a habit. With every belief goes the habitual behaviour – my own and that of the objects and persons involved – associated with that belief; doubt however, is a challenge to the habitual because it introduces hesitancy or irresolution consequent upon the interruption caused by a disappointed expectation. In both cases something more is involved than states of mind; just as the believing, on Peirce's view, is expressed in the *habit* which it informs, the doubting is to be found in the *interference* which always comes as a definite surprise.

The same holds true of inquiry. From the standpoint of the singular inquirer, inquiry is *felt* as a 'struggle' to overcome the interference which has broken the continuity of habitual action or expectation and to reach a new belief and thereby a new continuity. But, again, inquiry does not *consist* in the state of mind accompanying its initiation, but rather in types of reasoning and experimental procedure – Peirce's 'three stages of inquiry' – aimed at reaching an opinion no longer assailed by the doubt which set the process in motion. The outcome, moreover, has to be seen in relation to the entire process from which it emerges, since a central contention of Peirce's Pragmatism is that the validity of an opinion is a function of the method through which it was reached. Inquiry is called into being through doubt and sustained by the natural thrust of the inquirer to arrive at an opinion which nullifies that doubt. The underlying assumption is that doubt forms no stable basis for the formation of habits which lead to resolute action; for that, belief is required. In so far as belief is not attained, doubt stands in the way and must be mediated. Inquiry *is* that process of mediation.

The importance Peirce attached to inquiry as a continuing process is readily seen in his 'first rule of reason'[33] which, as he said, should be inscribed on every wall of the city of philosophy – 'Do not block the way of inquiry.' This imperative at the same time serves to express the *open-ended* character of Peirce's thought and indeed of the pragmatic outlook generally. It is of the greatest importance that the four examples offered by Peirce to illustrate the violations of his rule are variations on the same theme, namely that inquiry must cease or that it never can begin. These errors are the absolute assertion of the 'self-evident', the claim that such-and-such can never be known, the assigning of the status of ultimate and 'inexplicable' to some item of knowledge, the belief that some law or truth has been given its final or perfect form. It is the belief that thought is always in *transit* which defines the open-ended quality of Pragmatism, and bestows upon it that tentativeness which has often disturbed its critics. For Peirce, no less than for James and Dewey, tentativeness belongs essentially to all inquiry, and cannot, in principle, be overcome. One has simply to live with it, and accept the risk which tentativeness entails both in belief and action. The demand of action, and the need to respond to what a situation 'calls for', to be sure, cuts short the tentativeness of thought or inquiry in transit because resolute action requires firm belief; this fact, however, only serves to point up both the importance and the precariousness of the 'practical' from the pragmatic standpoint. We are constantly forced to believe and to act – *here* and *now* – against the background of a knowledge which is not final; it will do us no good to pretend that the case is otherwise. Action does not require us to convert a tentative knowledge into an absolute certainty, but it does require us to 'make up our minds' as to what is relevant and what we must believe if we are to act at all. It was the belief of the pragmatists that the inescapable demands of the situation will help to select from our store of theoretical knowledge what is *relevant* for dealing with that situation; the background of inquiry and of thought in transit, however, endures. Practice intervenes and forces us to judge, to decide and to act against this background, but the demands of practice do not alter the character of inquiry. It is simply that belief and action are always accompanied by risk.

In his 'Lessons from the History of Science' (*c.* 1896), Peirce expressed sharp criticism of those who mix 'speculative inquiry with questions of conduct'.[34] Involving one with the other leads to what he called 'sham reasoning', or withholding assent to a method until one sees the conclusion to which it leads so that ultimately the conclusion determines the reasoning -- the direct opposite of what science demands. The mark of surrender to experimental inquiry is accepting it 'in advance of knowing what its decisions may be'.[35] Defence of the priority and autonomy of inquiry over the consideration of its implications for human conduct is characteristic of Peirce's thought throughout. A similar point is made in his lectures on 'Vitally Important Topics' (1898) where scientific inquiry is equated with 'useless inquiry'[36] and any possible usefulness of such inquiry, if taken into account, is said to be a hazard to the possibility of success. Even allowing for the special circumstances which led Peirce to exaggerate the gap between 'theory' and 'importance' throughout these lectures, the passage clearly expresses his aversion to granting the anticipated practical application of the *results* of inquiry any determining force in the process itself.

In comparing the views of Dewey and Peirce on the nature of logic and the form of inquiry, it is fortunate that we are not left entirely to our own devices since we have one review and some correspondence between them on these topics.[37] It is clear that Peirce was sympathetic to what he called Dewey's 'Pragmatistic views', but it is equally clear that he was uneasy about Dewey's genetic approach to thought and what he took to be Dewey's subordination of normative logic to a 'natural history' of thought. When confronted with a challenge to the autonomy of logic, Peirce invariably tended to overstate his case and to disjoin normative logic from all relation to 'what actually takes place in the universe'. Dewey's contributions to the *Studies in Logical Theory*, it is true, lay greater stress on a genetic method than would later prove to be the case in his *Logic*. Peirce took those contributions to represent an 'anatomy' of thought to the neglect of the theory of inference and 'normative logic'; he even referred to a 'spirit of intellectual licentiousness' in the volume which suggests a failure to see 'that anything is so very false'.[38] Nothing troubled Peirce more than a display of what seemed to him bad logic in works devoted to logic, and he repeatedly expressed doubts about the validity of a 'genetical' method. Actually, his criticism is not unrestricted because, he admitted that some sciences can be studied genetically while others cannot, and he offered appropriate examples. It is interesting that he concluded this portion of his critique with a challenge – 'I should like to know what genetic logician ever came to have such close quarters with actual science as I have done.'[39] This challenge gives further evidence of what everyone who reads Peirce extensively comes to realize, namely, that he regarded his own analyses of inquiry and its structure as firmly rooted in the facts concerning the actual development of particular scientific endeavours.[40] He was not content to speak only of 'science', but focused attention on what is peculiar to, for example, physiology and dynamics, in comparison with anatomy. While

Peirce, no less than Dewey, held that there is a pattern of inquiry continuous throughout the domain of science, he did not suppose, as Dewey did, that the differences between sciences could be adequately expressed merely through the distinction between *method* and *technique*. Dewey regarded all science as exhibiting the one pattern of inquiry set forth in his *Logic* and therefore on his view there is one 'method' which defines science. Particular sciences are distinguished by differences in technique or the sort of operations required for inquiry into a given subject matter or some feature of that subject matter. Thus, for example, sociologists may employ questionnaires, whereas astronomers do not, but Dewey would have claimed that these differences in technique are not incompatible with the thesis that the same method is exhibited in both sciences. Such a distinction as Peirce drew, however, between sciences which can be studied profitably through a genetic approach and those which cannot, is surely not to be drawn solely on the basis of the method–technique distinction to which Dewey appealed. That is to say, some further analysis of the logical structure of particular sciences becomes necessary, and it is clear that Peirce was able to supply this analysis precisely because he was thoroughly familiar with the *formal* logical patterns exhibited in the three forms of reasoning he acknowledged – abduction, deduction and induction or probability – as essential for scientific inquiry. The fundamental difference between the two thinkers becomes evident at precisely this point: Dewey viewed logic exclusively from the standpoint of methodology, whereas Peirce accorded logic as a normative science an autonomy of its own. The root of the difference is to be traced back to the fact that Dewey approached science from the standpoint of his general theory of mind as instrumental intelligence, and therefore science appeared to him as the most exacting and controlled form of response to the doubtful as such.[41] The reason Dewey repeatedly and consistently described science solely in terms of method and the continuity of analysis in every field of study, is that, whatever the subject matter and special techniques required, science *is* the problem-solving intelligence or mind in its most effective form.

By contrast, Peirce did not view science primarily in terms of a general theory of mind, but rather as an enterprise made possible by man's concern and capacity to find a way of fixing belief that is responsive to external permanencies and independent of individual predilections and prejudices. Despite his emphasis on real or living doubt and on the 'struggle' underlying inquiry, both of which point to individual and personal need, Peirce was still thinking of science as a 'theoretical' enterprise aimed at the discovery of true opinions which refer to independent reals. The difference is not insignificant; since Dewey identified mind with the response to the problematic, the incoherent and the doubtful, he was forced to go further and identify it with a transformatory function which goes beyond the fixing of opinions and must ultimately result in the production of a resolved existential situation. Thought and logic exist only as functions in the process. Peirce, on the other hand, saw the transcendence factor in thought and made room for a more classical theoretical ideal which allows inquiry to go its way without being determined in its course by the concern for the further application of its results.

Taking the most comprehensive viewpoint, the final comparison suggesting itself with respect to Dewey and Peirce on inquiry is that Dewey laid all the stress on the motive to control the situation which evokes it and ultimately to reshape the environing conditions of human life. This motive is much less prominent in Peirce's writings; for him, inquiry is primarily a form of logical self-control which focuses on the manner in which beliefs are formed or, rather should be formed and thus leads to a critical awareness of those beliefs which are based on less solid ground.

5 Pragmatism and metaphysics

In considering the large topic of Pragmatism and metaphysics in what is surely too brief a compass, it will be more fruitful to indicate some of the substantive views involved than to concentrate on preliminary questions concerning the pragmatists' conceptions of the nature and possibility of metaphysics in a scientific age. Naturally, the two issues cannot be kept entirely distinct especially in a climate of opinion where the nature of philosophy and its legitimate role have become substantive questions. On the other hand, it would not be in keeping with the tenor of Pragmatism to focus attention primarily on such a question as 'How is metaphysics possible?' because James, Peirce and Dewey moved directly into discussion of issues traditionally regarded as belonging to metaphysics even if, as in the case of James especially, they sought to recast the form in which such issues are to be discussed.

The metaphysics of the pragmatists revolved around three fundamental problems: first, as F. H. Bradley correctly perceived,[1] they were concerned with the status of the distinctly human in existence. What place, they asked, has man, his experience, his activity and the culture to which he gives birth in an evolutionary universe? The centrality of this question makes it quite legitimate to speak of Pragmatism as a 'humanism' despite the considerable ambiguity which attaches to that term. Just as Hegel sought to overcome the modern consciousness that man exists in an 'alien' universe – a consequence of the Cartesian split between man's mind and the world of objects – through his speculative idealism, the pragmatists hoped to show that man is continuous with nature and that through his activity he can 'civilize', cultivate and thus create a human face for the environment. But if this is so, all that is characteristic of man, his consciousness, his foresight, his capacity to transform the earth, cannot be, as Santayana would have it, an infinitesimal and evanescent spark of light in a cosmos which is otherwise dark. On the contrary, man and his experience constitute a distinctive level of being which must be taken seriously by every account of what there is.

Second, the pragmatists were determined to show the significance for philosophy of an evolutionary viewpoint rooted in the reality of time. They saw themselves as attempting to make clear to their contemporaries the implications of evolution in much the same way that Locke and Kant interpreted the Newtonian conception of the universe to the citizens of the eighteenth century. And one point at which the pragmatists seemed most at odds with other philosophers was in their tendency to give priority to time and change over the fixed and immutable. Much of the older American philosophical tradition was rooted in Platonism; theologians under the same influence thought of God primarily as the one 'in whom there is no shadow of turning'. Consequently, Dewey's denial of 'antecedent being', Peirce's doctrine of chance and James' untidy and unfinished universe all seemed to go against established patterns of thought. Pragmatism, it appeared, was subverting the best wisdom of the past by espousing a relativism which set old and fixed foundations at nought. And yet the pragmatists themselves sought only to be true to their obligation as philosophers to call attention to the facts of contingency and the precariousness of existence, along with the *tentativeness* attaching to the conclusions reached through critical processes of inquiry. In short, they were perplexed by philosophical theories of knowing which guaranteed to knowledge some form of certainty in a world where science had to be content with something less.

There was, however, another side to the establishment of time and change at the heart of things; it is the feature most often regarded as the hallmark, not only of Pragmatism, but of American life as such – the belief in the lure, the power and the promise of the *future*. The fact of change may seem to undermine old and fixed sources of security, but change becomes less unsettling when it appears that man can have a hand in controlling its direction. The future became the principal target of the pragmatists because, as Peirce pointed out, it is the one mode of time subject to control. From this vantage point the future never merely 'comes about'; some at least of what it brings must have been *made* to happen, and it is this making which is the insertion of human will and effort into the cosmic scheme. The future is what 'makes room' for will and active intelligence. The pragmatists did not deny the reality of the past as has often been alleged; they tended rather to minimize its significance, largely because it frustrated them – there is nothing to be 'done' about it, they felt, hence why expend energy in contemplating what is over and done with when that same energy is needed for accomplishing what yet remains to be done? This outlook helps to explain why Pragmatism, in the minds of many, seemed to allow the present no more than a tenuous foothold in reality. The present in their view is not so much a dwelling place as a vantage point from which to mount an attack on the future.

Along with concern for the status of the human in existence, and a firm belief in the reality of time and change, the pragmatists argued vigorously for the reality of tendencies, potentialities and habits, traits of existence which, it seemed to them, had been either denied or neglected by empiricists and rationalists alike. The world and human life in it cannot be adequately understood if the final facts acknowledged are fixed states of affairs which in themselves are static, given and 'all there'. Each of the pragmatists in his own way held that tendencies and directionalities actually exist as part of the total facts encountered. These tendencies find their being in the form of habits and real possibilities both in persons and in things. To omit them is to omit a most significant feature of the world as experienced; it was the contention of the pragmatists that every view of the world according to which the ultimate existents are absolutely singular – the view which Peirce, for example, identified with nominalism – will be forced to deny the fact of tendency because no room can be found for it in the domain of the sense 'given', since the data of sense have generally been regarded as wholly determinate.[2] With regard to this point, it is clear that the pragmatists were going counter to the tradition of classical empiricism, and in so doing they pointed the way forward to the process philosophers for whom tendency is also a fundamental datum.

The foregoing was purposely couched in quite general terms in order to call attention to some basic philosophical conceptions that are characteristic of Pragmatism and shared by its three principal representatives. Detailed development of these conceptions with reference to the extensive writings of Peirce, James and Dewey would result in what could reasonably be called the 'metaphysics of Pragmatism' considered as a unified outlook. Unfortunately, this project could not be carried out within present limitations and therefore another strategy is called for. Since every attempt to present Pragmatism as a single position is precarious, a more accurate understanding can be attained by focusing attention on the three thinkers separately in their treatment of metaphysical themes. To this end it is necessary, first, to explain the meaning of James' 'pragmatic' treatment of some metaphysical issues; second, to consider Peirce's conception of categories and to give some indication of the substance of his 'cosmic' doctrines such as tychism and synechism; third, to set forth Dewey's proposal to identify basic philosophy with the disclosure of the generic traits of existence.

In James' discussion of such metaphysical issues as freedom and determinimism, materialism and theism or the one and the many, a certain tension becomes evident between his 'Pragmatism' with its appeal to the 'promise' or practical results which a given metaphysical doctrine holds in store for future unfolding, and his 'empiricism'[3] which focuses attention on the meaning to be assigned to abstract terms and concepts by determining what the things to which they point are 'known as' in direct experience. The difference is not between appealing or not appealing to the meaning of an idea or doctrine, since meaning is involved in both cases, but rather between two distinct ways of determining what that meaning is. In the former case James insisted that a doctrine is not to be taken 'intellectualistically' or abstractly but in terms of 'our concrete attitudes of hope and expectation',[4] whereas in the latter case the terms in which a doctrine is expressed are to be construed by consulting direct experience without any special mention of emotional and practical appeals. The difference is nicely illustrated in the one case by James' discussion of materialism, and in the other by his analysis of the one and the many.

As a matter for 'serious philosophical debate', the underlying issue between materialism and spiritualism (sometimes called 'theism') makes its appearance only when the respective doctrines are translated into prophecies concerning the world's future. So that, according to James, the 'real meanings' of the doctrines have not to do with conceptions of the inner nature of either matter or God, but with the denial of an eternal moral order and the consequent loss of hope, on the one hand, and the affirmation of both on the other. These differing prophecies are what the two warring theories of the universe 'practically' mean, and they constituted for James the interest and concern which lead people to argue about them. It is important to notice that in stating the issue in this way James did not think of himself as making a short-term 'practical' appeal, because, as he points out on several occasions, the appeal is in fact the most remote possible since it envisages a final outcome of all things.[5] That outcome, nevertheless, is no more available to us now as a matter of cognition than is the knowledge, as James would have had it, possessed by Royce's Absolute. And James would have admitted this, since he purposely translated the issue between the two conflicting metaphysical doctrines into one of faith, promise and expectations. Nothing, it would appear, can now be accomplished by way of theoretical or dialectical argument for or against either position; we simply have no way of knowing which (if either) is the case, which is precisely why we are forced to settle for the task of determining what practical difference it *now* makes if we believe that one or the other will turn out to be true in the end. Santayana's incisive remark, even if it is not wholly fair, is also not without its element of truth at this point; he wrote, 'He [James] did not really believe; he merely believed in the right of believing that you may be right if you believed.'[6]

The fundamental idea behind James' translation of some at least of the metaphysical issues he discussed into promise and prophecy is so well illustrated in a section of Kant's treatment of his antinomies,[7] that a brief development of the parallel will repay the effort. After having presented the antithetical conclusions of reason which arise in the attempt to think and to maintain certain doctrines about the world as a whole, and having indicated why it is impossible for these antinomies to be resolved on theoretical grounds in relation to the facts of existence, Kant dramatically shifted the ground of the discussion to the 'interest' which *reason* has in the conflicts. Prior to his attempt to show the ultimate consistency of reason – an aim which is not germane to this discussion – he proposed to consider 'upon which side we should prefer to fight, should we be compelled to make choice between the opposing parties'.[8] But Kant was careful to point out that the raising of this question, how we should proceed if we consulted only our interest and not the logical criterion of truth, will decide nothing in regard to the contested rights of the two parties, but has this advantage, that it enables us to comprehend why the participants in this quarrel, though not influenced by any superior insight into the matter under dispute, have preferred to fight on one side rather than on the other.[9]

Kant then went on to claim that, from the standpoint of interest, the doctrines expressed in the theses – that the world has a beginning, that the self is indestructible and free, and that there is a primordial being – are all on the side of morals and religion. He saw this interest, moreover, as a *practical* one, 'in which every right-thinking man, if he has understanding of what truly concerns him, heartily shares'.[10] The antitheses, on the contrary, are all on the side of empiricism and science; in these we have no practical interest, said Kant, and indeed they appear in what they assert to rob morality and religion of all theoretical support. Despite the many differences in outlook between Kant and James,[11] the preceding parallel is striking, For both, metaphysical issues cannot become a matter of theoretical knowledge; with regard to the materialism–thesim antithesis, for example, we simply do not know which, if either, is true, and an impasse is reached. But in view of the fact that other 'interests' than that of the strictly theoretical are involved, the case can and must be taken to another court; for James this other court was 'practical consequences', or consideration of the promise which a doctrine holds out for man in the future. The change of venue also implies that the issue cannot be discussed in 'objective' terms and quite apart from reference to man's religious and moral interests.

Santayana referred more than once to the 'agnosticism' of James although it is not entirely clear how much of his thought this designation was meant to cover. The term is certainly applicable to James' view on religious questions and to some, but not all, metaphysical ones. It is clear that he regarded certain questions (the existence of God, the reality of cosmic design, the struggle between freedom and determinism) as beyond the scope of rational speculation in the sense in which a Descartes, a Leibniz or a Hegel would have understood it. Such questions cannot be approached in objective fashion; they can be discussed only in terms of *belief* which points in one direction or another depending on the sort of 'promise' which a given *answer* affords. In this sense James was 'agnostic' and it was precisely this lack of confidence in speculative reason which led him to find the only possible meaning in religious and some metaphysical doctrines in their practical and prospective consequences. It is important to notice however, that here one must say 'some' metaphysical doctrines because there are cases, notably the problem of the one and the many and the relative merits of monism and pluralism, where James did not rest his argument solely on prophecies and promises even if he did not exclude them entirely. The notation of this fact serves to introduce the other dimension in James alluded to above as the 'empiricism' which stands in tension with his 'Pragmatism'.[12]

James was at times prepared to approach a metaphysical issue by appeal to pervasive experience already available and to attempt to determine the meaning of key concepts through what things are actually 'known as' and not only in terms of what the doctrine promises to the believer for the future. The problem of God, for example, must be dealt with in terms of practical consequences, but not so the issue of monism and pluralism. James was quite clear in his mind that certain forms of monism are false and that in the end it is the 'pluralistic universe' which represents the true conception of what there is. The analysis offered of the thesis 'The World is One' is a good case in point. Having granted the oneness to exist, even if only in the sense that we have but 'one' world to think about, James went on to ask, 'What will the unity be known as?'[13] and in answer to his own question he cited some eight senses in which unity is manifest in experience. Starting with the world as one subject of discourse, he called attention to such facts as continuity and the hang-togetherness of things, gravitation and the conduction of heat, causal chains, the possibility of a *generic unity* of all things, the unity of purpose, aesthetic unity, and the unity introduced by the One Knower associated with various forms of modern idealism. Over against all this, however, stand the multiple facts of disjunction, separateness and discontinuity, and James concluded, 'It is neither a universe pure and simple nor a multiverse pure and simple.'[14] James, so it would appear, was content to leave both features of the world as experienced on a par; we encounter many forms of unity and many types of plurality, and we are not entitled to hold any form of monism which denies the reality of that plurality. On the other hand, it is equally illegitimate to hold an *absolute* pluralism which either ignores or discounts the various grades of unity that manifest themselves in experience. And yet in the end the two features were not left on a par by James: Pragmatism must come down on the side of pluralism as the 'more empirical path' since the hypothesis of total unification represents an overdraft on our intellectual capital.

The important factor for understanding James' approach to metaphysical questions is his tendency with regard to what might be called the 'more available' issues to proceed on an empirical, even phenomenological, basis by asking for the meaning of basic concepts in terms of what things are 'known as'. That is, in discussion of such issues as monism and pluralism, the nature of the self or the meaning of causality, he was less inclined than he was in considering the problem of God or freedom[15] to translate the hypotheses into their promise or prophecy regarding the future. His refusal to consider some issues 'objectively' in terms of the subject matter and present experience betrays his metaphysical scepticism or agnosticism. For it is quite clear that when he found the 'real' meaning of an hypothesis in what it promises for the life and significance of the individual in the future, he was in effect claiming that, as regards present fact and experience considered apart from the interest of the person, that hypothesis is without meaning. In short, James, like Peirce on those occasions when he declared metaphysics to be 'gibberish', had his positivistic streak, but he sought to nullify its destructive consequences by a strenuous fideism of active commitment.

If one shifts attention from James' way of approach to metaphysical problems and considers his substantive views, there is good reason to doubt whether he would qualify as 'tough-minded' in his own sense. Or perhaps it would be more accurate to say that he was tough-minded methodologically but tender-minded in the substantive opinions he maintained. Although it is quite naïve to suppose that methods imply no doctrines, it is not difficult to see what James had in mind when he declared that Pragmatism is not a doctrine but a method which 'unstiffens' theories already on the ground by asking about their practical consequences, etc. If one connects the two columns of characteristics which define the tough-minded and the tender-minded temperaments,[16] James was 'empiricist', 'sensationalistic' rather than 'intellectualistic' and sceptical in stating and pursuing a question, and the general drift of his philosophy has to be called pluralistic rather than monistic. But there the tough-mindedness ceases; if one considers the many beliefs which James heartily supported and even made one feel guilty for not believing, they are all on the other side. He was 'idealistic' in his belief that worthwhile personal and social goals can be achieved through devoted efforts; he was 'optimistic' in his 'meliorism' and in his 'piecemeal supernaturalism' wherein God appears, like a typical American, as striving against severe odds to make things better; he was, if not 'religious' in some specific denominational sense, still very much the believer in the importance of religion in human experience; he was a 'free-willist' in his denial that men are automata or mere by-products of their environment, and in his defence of real possibilities and genuine novelty in the course of events. In summary, it would be fair to say that, in contrast with Peirce and Dewey, James could not bring himself to entertain metaphysical conceptions without considering what sort of efficacy they would have in personal life if someone were to believe them and shape his life accordingly. By contrast, Peirce and Dewey had more interest in *theoria*.

In an unpublished paper, 'The Logic of Mathematics' (c. 1896),[17] Peirce made comments about metaphysics which are at once prophetic and characteristic of his entire outlook. He saw clearly the extent to which critical discussion about the nature of metaphysics, whether it is possible, etc., had postponed the consideration of first-order questions. 'The general law of metaphysics,' he wrote, 'is little understood. The attention of thinkers has been so riveted upon the question of its truth, that they have largely overlooked the importance of determining what it is...'[18]

What Peirce called the 'general law of metaphysics' is the application to the real world of what he had previously described as the three clauses of the general law of logic. These clauses refer respectively to *fact* as existentially determinate (monad), to *predicate* as involving two and only two determinations for each subject (dyad), and to *truth* wherein there is fact and predicate together and the thought which apprehends that they are together (triad). Metaphysics, for Peirce, meant, first, the results of accepting the logical principles as valid of being and not only as regulative, and second, the extrapolation of these principles to form a general theory of the structure of the real.

The first consequence of the acceptance is that the universe has an explanation which it shares with every logical explanation, namely, the unification of a variety of items. The monadic clause of the law is expressed as the identification of being and the One; to share a common character is to share an identical being. Existence, for Peirce, always involves oppositions – attraction, repulsion, etc. – in the sense that the flower in the crannied wall stands out as distinct from the wall and indeed as over against an entire universe which could not exclude just that flower. The dyadic clause of the law is expressed in existence as opposition. If the preceding extrapolations seem somewhat cryptic, the third is even more so. Taking as a deduction from the third clause the idea that law is the 'mirror of being', Peirce concluded that the real is 'the law of something less real'[19] which can only mean that the 'would be' represents the real as law in contrast to a singular instance of it. This interpretation becomes plausible in view of Peirce's illustration – Mill's definition of matter as permanent possibility of sensation. 'What,' Peirce asked, 'is a permanent possibility but a law?'[20] The singular sensation is 'less real' than the law.

Peirce took thinking of this sort as characteristic of metaphysics and he believed that it represents a valid form of reasoning. It was his conviction that philosophers frequently fail to understand such metaphysical principles because of a tendency to concentrate exclusively on whether these principles or indeed any principles could be true.

Peirce was acutely aware both of the extent to which metaphysics involves 'extrapolation' and of the unavoidability of this sort of reasoning if we are not to deceive ourselves concerning the ultimate assumptions behind what we believe. Since Peirce took science seriously and frequently spoke disparagingly not only of 'seminary' philosophy in contrast with 'laboratory' philosophy but of much previous metaphysics as well, some have concluded that Peirce's own metaphysics may be dismissed as a mere decoration which need not be taken seriously. In the present upsurge of interest in Peirce's thought, moreover, one can detect signs of the same bias; it is expressed in the assumption that the 'real' Peirce is Peirce the logician and philosopher of science. Peirce the speculative philosopher, presumably, does not count. The fact is that such a view is not only erroneous as a description of the man and his thought, but it is short-sighted as well.

Peirce's metaphysics was rooted in his logical principles and he never tired of repeating the claim that his philosophical realism stemmed from his analysis of science and its assumptions. His favourite targets for attack were those philosophers and men of science who believe, whether explicitly or not, that science requires and even guarantees philosophical nominalism. How clearly he grasped the main drift of modern philosophy in this regard is seen in his charge that with the exception of Schelling (!), all modern philosophers have acknowledged but *one* mode of being, namely, individual fact, or what Peirce called existence.[21] And he was particularly critical of what he called 'dangerous' metaphysics, by which he meant metaphysical doctrines *unconsciously* and uncritically taken over from the past.[22] He was in entire agreement with F. H. Bradley who contended that when philosopher *x* attacks philosopher *y* for holding 'metaphysical' views, philosopher *x* is certainly assuming and usually developing a rival metaphysics of his own. 'Find a scientific man who proposes to get along without any metaphysics,' wrote Peirce, 'and you have found one whose doctrines are thoroughly vitiated by the crude and uncriticized metaphysics with which they are packed.'[23] Peirce's firm conclusion, one which reverberates throughout everything he wrote, was that there is no escape from the criticism of 'first principles'. No attempt to rehabilitate Peirce in accordance with current philosophical fashions can ignore this fact.

As was hinted previously, a full-scale treatment of Peirce's voluminous metaphysical writings is well beyond our present scope; it is, however, possible to give a brief account of his categories and of his two basic doctrines, tychism and synechism, which will be sufficient to make clear the cosmology and ontology underlying his Pragmatism.

To follow Peirce's thinking about categories from his 'New List' of 1867 through the numerous writings of the 1890s on the same subject, is a Protean task to say the least. The story embraces not only a plurality of expositions and applications of the fundamental categories – logical, psychological, phenomenological, metaphysical – but different views as well of their origin and status. There is, however, a consistent drift in the conceptions expressed in firstness, secondness and thirdness, even when Peirce's language changes as it frequently does. Such consistency is less evident when one considers the question of the source of these categories. Peirce had several different approaches. One was to find the categories inherent in the 'elements of all experience', another was to derive them from an analysis of the phenomenon as such, and still another was a return to Kant's table of categories and its dependence on the forms of judgement. It is not suggested that there is any fundamental incompatibility between these approaches; they simply represent different points of departure each of which leads in the end to the same fundamental conceptions – *quality, fact*, and *law*. More problematic is the matter of the status or validity of the categories which leads to the ultimate question of the relation between logic and metaphysics. The most persistent view which emerges from Peirce's numerous discussions is that logical principles are basic and that from a metaphysical standpoint they are to be seen as truths of being and not merely as regulatively valid.[24]

This claim expresses Peirce's advance beyond Kant, revealing at once his own realistic outlook and what he had learned from Hegel about the need to understand categories in their role of determining what *is*. It is clear, however, that Peirce was troubled over the proper justification of his categories. In one place[25] he could argue that each category has to 'justify itself by an inductive examination' which can attain to no more than an approximate validity, whereas in his development of the categories[26] 'from within', he could ask why 'there should be these categories and no others' and then find the reason in the most fundamental characteristic of the mathematical hypothesis of number. These tendencies can be synthesized if one attends to the two main influences at work in his thought. On the one hand, there is the thoroughly Kantian conception of categories set forth in the 'New List' of 1867. There a conception is said to serve the function of reducing a manifold of sense to unity and its validity depends on the impossibility of attaining this unity without introducing that conception. On this basis Peirce proceeded to develop the notions of being, substance and the intermediate conceptions of quality, relation and representation, starting with the universal conception of the present in general or 'It'. In some notes on this paper written at various times later on,[27] Peirce claimed that Kant was right in holding that the fundamental categories of thought are dependent on logic, but he criticized Kant's 'hasty' treatment of both the logical division of propositions and the categories themselves, and indicated his own concern to find 'logical support' for them. To this end Peirce began to consider the relation of the categories to each other and, like Hegel but with a quite different conception of logic in hand, sought for their justification in a *system* of interrelated concepts which are necessary because indispensable. Like Hegel again, Peirce was interested in determining the manner in which fundamental conceptions develop out of each other so that, as he said, 'deep study of each conception in all its features brings a clear perception that precisely a given next conception is called for'.[28] Though both Peirce and Hegel were critical of Kant for setting forth the categories full-blown, as it were, on the basis of a table of judgement simply taken over from traditional logic, and both sought for a form of systematic interrelationship between categories issuing in a necessity that would justify the claim 'these categories and no others', the two differed widely in their manner of working the matter out. Whereas Hegel developed what Peirce called a 'dilemmatic method' for the evolution of thought which cannot in the end be separated from the internal dialectic of self-consciousness, Peirce appealed instead to formal logic and mathematics, hoping to find the ground of the necessary characteristics of mathematical hypotheses in 'some truth so broad as to hold not only for the universe we know but for every world that [a] poet could create'.[29] If Hegel went beyond Kant by the rehabilitation of dialectic as the positive and creative advance of thought, Peirce went beyond Kant first by going back to Leibniz and then by coming forward again with his own evolutionary conception of thought cast in terms of mathematical logic. Peirce was not averse to acknowledging a 'general similarity' between his method and that of Hegel, but he regarded the latter as too circumscribed and not well suited for a high degree of exactitude in thinking.[30]

The foregoing discussion indicates the problems Peirce envisaged with respect to the justification of categories. One point, however, stands out quite clearly: Peirce was ready to accept the Kantian conception of categories as functions of unification in thought, but he was determined to interpret these logical conceptions and principles as 'truths of being', thus giving a realistic turn to his doctrine and moving away from a 'transcendentalism' of regulative principles.[31] Whether Peirce succeeded to his own satisfaction, or our own, in establishing his case must remain an open question. One would, however, do well at this point to follow a suggestion which he made in his 'Second Essay on Categories' (*c.* 1894); there he suspended inquiry into the question: 'How far it is justifiable to apply the conceptions of logic to metaphysics?' on the ground that, important as that question may be, it is not paramount to the determination of what the categorial conceptions actually are.[32] In short, it is necessary to locate and analyse the categories before the more basic question of their justification can be pursued.

As was mentioned previously, the task of analysing and developing a list of categories occupied Peirce over several decades and the results he achieved are expressed in a sufficient number of formulations to lead to some bewilderment. This variety cannot possibly be reflected adequately in any brief account; it is important, however, to see that a number of factors serve to explain the different versions and that they do not stem solely from Peirce's having altered his views. Much depends on the context in which the categories are being developed, whether it is logical, phenomenological, metaphysical, etc., and while one can detect basic, persistent meanings throughout the analysis and application of firstness, secondness and thirdness, caution must be exercised in order to avoid the assumption that conceptions which must be taken as correlative are on that account identical in meaning. One illustration will serve to clarify the point. Quality, fact and law are the names assigned to what Peirce sometimes called the 'metaphysical categories' and these are said to express the 'matter' of phenomena, while the logical categories are identified as the monad, the dyad and the triad (polyad) and these express the 'form' of experience. The two sets of conceptions are correlative, i.e. quality is understood as monad without otherness, fact is understood as dyad with action and reaction, and law is understood as triad involving something like object, other and third or the respect in which they differ. The important point is that the two sets of categories, though obviously correlative, 'do not precisely correspond' and must not be taken as identical in meaning. A dyad, for example, composed of monads which represent, in Peirce's language 'their sole matter' is said to belong to the category of quality which is the material mode of being possessed by the *monad*. Confusion can be avoided if one is careful not to identify the various conceptions of firstness, secondness and thirdness which are indeed correlative conceptions but which differ in meaning depending on the particular mode they are meant to express.

There is sufficient consistency in Peirce's several accounts of the categories to permit one to select as basic the conceptions of *quality, fact* and *law*. By quality Peirce meant a primordial suchness, illustrated by a sense of redness, a prolonged musical note, a feeling of grief or joy, which is a partial determination but neither abstract nor involved in relation to another. Quality is not restricted to the familiar features which one associates with the special senses, colours, sounds, etc., but includes as well such characteristics as 'tedious', 'heartrending', 'noble'[33] which are not 'located' as it were, or assigned to the functioning of an organ. It is not the sensing or the feeling as psychological events to which Peirce called attention but the quality as such making itself manifest in any phenomenon. Quality is said to be *sui generis* and indescribable and its suchness holds it apart from being nothing at all. Quality 'is a mere abstract potentiality'[34] which, in accordance with Peirce's realism, has its own tenure as a mode of being. In maintaining, for example, that red things in the dark are still capable of transmitting light of a certain wavelength, or that a bar of iron has some degree of hardness where nothing is pressing on it, Peirce was launching an oft-repeated attack upon both conceptualism and nominalism. On his view, a sense-quality is no more than a 'possibility of sensation' but he insisted that it is precisely the being of a possibility to remain such when it is not actualized. For Peirce, possibility was not a merely 'logical' category; there are real possibilities and his belief in them as essentially *ways* of behaving was the ground of his rejection of the view that the only mode of being is the present existence of individual fact.[35]

Quality as a category manifests itself when we view the universe of phenomena solely in its *monadic* aspect, that is, attending only to suchness without reference to existence, to parts or components, or to relations of any sort. It is the quality-element in experience which Peirce was trying to apprehend and therefore it is important that we do not confuse this element with what we say about the category of quality itself when it is articulated through the concepts of generality, partial determinateness and potentiality. In this regard Peirce was no less concerned than James to lay hold of experience in its own integral character, but he was far less inclined than James to see the process of articulation as a source of distortion or a threat to that integrity. For Peirce, phenomena in their concreteness are complex and heterogeneous, but this fact does not prevent us from attending solely to their monadic aspect in order to disengage the category of quality.

Contrary to traditional views of qualities as 'inhering' in subjects, Peirce's view represents quality as a 'may be' which, when actualized, is ingredient in every experience as a pervasive unity. Quality is not itself an occurrence for that would involve an object, a dyad, etc., all of which takes us beyond the monadic level of suchness. Qualities may not indeed be realized and, if they are, something more than quality will necessarily be involved. One must, however, abstract from this 'something more' in order to focus on the quality as such. Dewey was right in his perception that Peirce in his theory of firstness as quality was not offering a new candidate for the 'given' within the context of epistemological discussion, but pointing instead to the unity and integrity of all experience, including that of noting and expressing the character of firstness itself.

No account of firstness, however brief, can ignore the panpsychistic form which it assumes in virtue of Peirce's doctrine of feeling. This interpretation of firstness is the counterpart to his logical interpretation of the monad as the *term* in distinction from the proposition which correlates with the dyad. The first point to notice is that in the philosophical climate within which Peirce was writing, the word 'feeling' had legitimate status as a technical term indicating immediate or undifferentiated consciousness. This fact is made evident in the writings of James and John Stuart Mill, Bergson, Bradley and William James. One must not, therefore, understand the term in accordance with its more ordinary usuage ('I have the *feeling* that such-and-such is the case') because this implies a cognitive claim already identified in advance as weak or lacking objective support. For Peirce, feeling is 'that kind of consciousness which involves no analysis, comparison or any process whatsoever . . . which has its own positive quality which consists in nothing else'.[36] Feeling, then, is the immediate *feature* of consciousness and, as such, it is whole and entire; however, in the immediate present which is instantaneous there is no consciousness in the feeling since, as Peirce said, 'feeling is nothing but a quality, and a quality is not conscious; it is a mere possibility'.[37] Quality, when actualized, is just 'there'; it is the immediate as such. Peirce was very far, however, from saying that the immediate exhausts consciousness and the phenomena to which it is directed, for experience embraces not only quality but struggle, resistance and effort; in short, experience means transactions with the other. The thought of relation to the other leads directly to the next category, *secondness,* the basic meaning of which is duality and action, but its specific meaning varies with the context involved. From the standpoint of consciousness, secondness appears as struggle; in the context of metaphysics and cosmology, secondness is identified as existence and fact; within the sphere of logic, secondness means the dyad.[38]

Since we cannot trace secondness through all its contexts, a selection of essential conceptions will have to suffice. One can grasp the meaning of the second category most adequately by concentrating on the conceptions of action and reaction, the distinction between ego and non-ego, and the identifying features of fact. In the first case, secondness is mutual action as when one seeks to unlock a door and feels the resistance of the lock which will not open, or when one pushes a chair out of one's way and feels the resistant force of inertia in hands and arms. Such action and reaction have manifold and subtle forms in Peirce's view so that we need not think exclusively of overt activity situations involving gross physical effort. Consider an example in the sphere of thinking. In order to be examined, an hypothesis must maintain itself as a steady and persistent meaning which stands over against the inquirer. The same is true of the sum of a column of figures which I set out to check against those figures and discover that it is correct. When I verify the sum I encounter the resistance of the other and its integrity as *the* correct answer. Perception exhibits the same secondness as action, but with the normal emphasis reversed. When one is actually moving a chair the consciousness of manipulation stands out as distinct from whatever resistance is felt due to some unevenness in the floor or to surface friction. In perception, the effect of things on us far outweighs any sense we may have of modifying them.

The situation in which one experiences the contrast between ego and non-ego is a further manifestation of secondness. Encounter with the unexpected as, for example, the shock experienced when the third step of a familiar staircase suddenly gives way and our habitual action is thwarted, contains within itself what Peirce calls a double-consciousness. In the awareness of the shock there is also the awareness of the other, the non-ego, as in fact different from my expectation of what it would be. I thus meet what is established beyond the limit of my own action, expectation and volition, and I do so in the duality of action and reaction. Peirce took the reciprocal character of the relationship seriously so that in his view it is not the case that the ego side is taken as something securely known while the non-ego side is merely a dim awareness. My awareness of myself as ego, as other than the non-ego encountered, also comes into view, and in fact the conception of the double consciousness is what stands behind Peirce's denial of intuitive self-consciousness and his claim that self-consciousness is essentially a discursive affair. Otherness, then, is decidely symmetrical except at the point where independence becomes manifest as the *existence* of the other. Independence as existence is illustrated in the case[39] of the man engaged in debating with himself whether an external world exists and is knocked down by another whom he jostles in the street. It is the other, i.e. the one who interrupts the sceptical reflection, who is said to be independent and it does not seem that in this case independence has the same obvious symmetry which attached to 'other' taken in a minimal sense.[40] On the other hand, when Peirce said that something has a mode of being not in itself but in its being over against a second and called this the *existence* which belongs to fact, he was taking the relation as symmetrical, i.e. the existence is on *both* sides of the duality.

One must be careful to balance the account of secondness through the development of consciousness with the corresponding analysis of secondness as fact, or that aspect of the phenomenon which is fact since fact always involves a particular time and place. From the most general standpoint, Peirce aimed to distinguish fact from both quality and law, that is, from possibility as well as from that generality which includes the contingent necessity of law or thirdness. Consequently, it is necessary to exclude from the category of fact all generality, whether of the negative sort characteristic of the merely potential (quality) or of the positive type peculiar to conditional necessity (law). As a result of these exclusions, there is left for secondness as fact the contingent or what 'happens' to be actual, and what is unconditionally necessary because devoid of reason, and usually described by Peirce as *brute* force.[41] 'The fact,' said Peirce, 'takes place', and this means that it acquires a 'here and now' in the relation of opposition and otherness to whatever stands over against it. Existence means 'having a place' in a total collection marking out a universe.[42] Among the dozen features said to define fact, the most important (along with the basic conception of otherness, involving action and reaction) is that a fact is always *individual;* the two, however, cannot be equated since Peirce referred to law as 'general fact' in contrast to individual fact. Being individual means primarily the self-assertive character of a fact, and, from a logical standpoint, it means being determinate with respect to every possibility or quality, i.e. the fact either has or does not have the quality in question. The invocation of the principle of excluded middle serves to distinguish fact from the general which is always partially indeterminate.

The third category, or thirdness, was variously identified by Peirce as law, general meaning, thought, sign or representation and the triad; once again, the context determines which conception is made the major focus of a given analysis. Naturally, this category assumes a place of paramount importance in Peirce's thought, since only through thirdness is the discrimination and articulation of any categories possible at all. However, he repeatedly cautioned against an idealism that would so completely encompass reality in thought that the independent tenure of first and second would be lost or obscured. It was his standing charge against Hegel that he did not make adequate provision for secondness in his passion to express the systematic togetherness of things and the totality of reason. The triad, to be sure, encompasses first and second, but their being is by no means exhausted in *being thought*. Thus Peirce's thought aimed at preserving a realism with respect to quality and existence within the confines of a system which he nevertheless did not hesitate to describe as a kind of objective idealism.

Thirdness always involves triadicity of some sort, whether it be a case of comparison, the interpolation of a third *between* two items, or a conclusion which can be validly drawn from no less than two premises. In all such cases, thought, meaning and generality are present, as can be seen from two examples cited by Peirce aimed at showing, first, that a triadic relation is *not* the same as two successive dyads, and, second, that thirdness has a pecular relation to the future. We are asked to consider the relation of *giving*; A gives B to C. This relation, said Peirce, 'does not consist in A's throwing B away and its accidentally hitting C',[43] for that case would represent no more than two dyads, whereas giving is a transfer of something one owns to someone else and therefore requires thought and meaning, neither of which is present in the relation of action and reaction. Exactly the same point is illustrated in James' proposal to take the idea of an object, translate it into a recipe or plan for reaching that object in a series of steps and then estimate the idea's validity in terms of its success in bringing the one who followed its lead into the presence of the object. Mere co-presence with the object – such as is illustrated by someone leaning against it, picking it up, or throwing it – is a dyad and does not allow for either knowledge or validity. For knowledge to exist it is necessary that the object, into whose presence one is brought by following the lead of the idea, be the same object that was *meant* so that the successful outcome is the final step in a purposive process. The one thus checking the idea is not merely *conjoined* with, set over against the object reached, for both relations are dyads, but is in the presence of the object that was thought or intended and hence a triad is involved.

The qualification of future reactions through thirdness as meaning was nicely brought out by Peirce in his approval of Royce's claim that the 'meaning' of a word and our 'meaning' to do something are not unconnected. There is, to be sure, a difference between the two, but they are not worlds apart as might be assumed if one were to locate the meaning connected with a word in the 'mind' and the meaning associated with the act intended in the spatio-temporal world. Consistent with much that he wrote on other occasions, Peirce connected both cases with future reactions; 'meaning' to *do* something is said to be a case where the consequent reactions of things with each other will be in conformity with whatever it is that informs the mind of the one who intends the act, whereas the 'meaning' of a word is found in the way it might or would tend to mould the conduct of a person believing a proposition in which the word itself was a proper constituent. In the case of overt action, emphasis falls on the future as *tense* and the form assumed by the brute reactions that *will* ensue; in the case of words or signs, emphasis falls on the future as the 'might be' tendency of a meaning which is believed to direct action.

There can be no question that in a 1903 version of the list of categories Peirce identified thirdness with *meaning,* and insisted upon its reality in experience.[44] To fortify his position he sought to argue that meaning is not reducible to either quality or reaction, first, because meaning requires triadic relations, and, second, because no triadic relation is expressible in terms of dyads alone. The first point is well illustrated by the example above about the relation of 'giving' as involving a meaning which is absent in the brute contact of two objects. If, in a crowded train, I 'just happen' to jostle someone with my shoulder, that is a dyad; if, however, from exasperation or anger, I 'shove' someone out of my way, that is a triad and cannot be represented logically without reference to at least *three* distinct items. The giving and the shoving manifest thirdness; the jostling which 'just happens' is a case of secondness.

The second argument, having to do with the irreducibility of triads, is trickier and was frequently expressed by Peirce through his existential graphs wherein he maintained that whereas *n*-adic relations can always be compounded from triadic relations, no triadic relation can be compounded from monads and dyads alone. His intuitive illustration of the point is most instructive. If, he said, I see a man on Monday and a man on Tuesday, and then say of the latter, 'He is the very man I saw on Monday,' it is legitimate to regard the identity as directly experienced. He is here taking identity as symmetrical and allowing it to be a matter of direct recognition. If, however, I see a man on Wednesday and say, 'That is the same man I saw on Tuesday,' I cannot go on to say as well, 'That is the same man I saw on Monday' without interpolating another premise, namely, 'The man I saw on Tuesday is the same man I saw on Monday.' The conclusion is drawn from two premises and the relation is therefore triadic. Between any two appearances the relation of identity is permissible as dyadic, but between any one and two others it is not. I can identify the Wednesday appearance with the Monday appearance *only* in virtue of having identified the Wednesday appearance with the Tuesday appearance. As should be evident, we have here but a special case of the triadic relation which Peirce took to be the basis of the classical syllogism. In this context it is cited as an example of the reality of thirdness or meaning in contrast to quality and reaction. This 'reality', moreover, is not inert, but shows itself as a power, first of self-control, and ultimately of control over the other.

At least two other characterizations of thirdness need to be mentioned because they figure prominently in Peirce's theory of signs and in his interpretation of nature. One is the triad involved in what Peirce called representation – sign, object and interpretant – and the other is the conception of thirdness as law. A brief analysis of the act of comparison, though indeed a special case, will serve to show the general thesis for which Peirce was arguing. To compare any two items is to bring them into relation to the third item which serves as mediator and enables us to express some similarity or dissimilarity holding between the original pair. Peirce's example in his earliest statement of the categories[45] is the comparison of the letters p and b. If we imagine one turned over on the line of type as an axis and superimposed upon the other, the mediating image is that when one is thus manipulated it represents a *likeness* of the other. The presupposition, of course, is that the two letters are compared in the most general sense with respect to shape. We might have compared them with respect to the colour in which each is printed, how long it takes to draw each, etc., but in each case the logical structure is the same; the two are each viewed in relation to some *third* and through the mediating element some representation of the two in relation to each other results. Peirce was careful to call attention to the broad sense of 'representation' involved – words represent, portraits represent, a weathervane represents, etc., but the formal meaning of the function remains the same. In calling the mediating representation an *interpretant,* Peirce had in mind the translation situation in which an 'interpreter' stands between two speakers and says, in effect, 'what the word "goose" means to you is what the word *Gans* means to him.'[46] What the interpreter as translator thus expresses is that a certain sign in one language stands in the same relation to some object as another sign in another language stands to the same object. It is upon this basic principle that the whole of Peirce's semiotic is based. The massive detail of his scheme is the result of his analysis of the many modes of representation and their logical structure, the kinds of signs, both as regards material and function required, and the purposes for which they are employed. It would be eminently fair to say that long before the 'linguistic turn' in philosophy was taken, Peirce had worked out a framework within which the nature and function of languages, both natural and artificial, can be understood. On the other hand, it would be quite incorrect to think of him as in any sense a 'linguistic' philosopher, not only because of his philosophical realism and his insistence on beginning with experience and its funded result in commonsense, but in virtue of a declaration such as the following which is by no means atypical:

As before, it is not the usage of language which we seek to learn, but what must be the description of fact in order that our division of the elements of phenomena into the categories of quality, fact, and law may not only be true, but also have the utmost possible value, being governed by those same characteristics which really dominate the phenomenal world.[47]

Whereas many contemporary philosophers have invoked the name of science either to discredit explicit ontological positions or to establish some form of lingiustic nominalism as *the* position consistent with science, Peirce viewed science as unintelligible unless rooted in realistic assumptions. And even if it is dubious, as I believe it is, to use science – the epitome of reality as *known* theoretically – as a way of supporting some particular conception of the general shape of things, it is still of the utmost significance that Peirce did not see in modern science any foundation whatever for nominalism, nor did his interest in signs lead him to adopt a linguistic approach to philosophy.

Much of what Peirce wrote about thirdness has to do with the concept of law, bringing in its wake the further conceptions of generality and habit. The close association in Peirce's mind between law and his most generic characterization of tiredness as representation becomes evident in the claim that law is a grasp of thirdness in the phenomenon 'from the outside only' and must be supplemented by the conception of thought.[48] Thought is generality, and hence is neither quality nor fact. Thought is produced and developed, whereas quality is independent of time and realization; thought is general both in the sense of being communicable and of referring to all *possible* things, whereas fact is individual and no collection of facts constitutes a law because a law specifies, beyond the limit of past fact, how facts 'that *may be,* but *all* of which never can have happened, shall be characterized'.[49] Though Peirce frequently claimed that law requires 'a peculiar kind of subject' – thought or mind – it would be a total misunderstanding of his position to suppose that for him laws are only in the 'mind', while the facts that embody law stand over against thought in their individualized status. Such a view would be nominalism all over again, and he rejected that position repeatedly. Law represents habit, tendency and potentiality *in the items* exhibiting law-like behaviour, and therefore law has to be seen as the dynamic presence of thirdness or generality in existence. Law is grasped in thought as representation and therefore comes into view at the level of thirdness, but it must be remembered that, in accordance with Peirce's Pragmatism, thought is never unrelated to *habit,* a conception which applies not only to human behaviour but to the things of nature as well. Law, then, like thought, has to do with the possible and potential in behaviour, but neither law nor thought is ever identical with any individual instance of behaviour or any finite collection of actions, reactions and facts.[50]

The foregoing consideration of thirdness as representation and law provides a good foundation for understanding Peirce's theory of mind and nature in so far as they are expressed in and through this particular category. Unfortunately, space does not allow for further development of thirdness in its more strictly logical form as the triad. In view, however, of the central importance of this conception for Peirce's logic, and especially the logic of relatives, it is essential to say something, no matter how brief, about triads and triadicity. Once again, many types are involved and, in Peirce's scheme, not all triads are 'genuine'.[51] Three and only three conceptions are required for defining the genuine triad – *object, other* and *third* – and just as 'other' is the distinguishing idea of the dyad, 'third' is the idea characteristic of the triad. In view of the close connection asserted between the genuine triad and representation, it is not difficult to see that the paradigm cases for Peirce will be those involving intent or relations of an 'ideal' sort. We are asked to consider the meaning of a contract. *A makes a contract with C,* and it involves a one, another, and a third, namely, the contract D which both sign and thus relate themselves so that conditional rules govern their conduct in all respects specified. Although reference is made to experience and to dyads of fact, the contract itself is not a matter of positive fact, but is conditional and intentional and it cannot be identified as such with any finite number of cases or completed acts governed by it. The root of the triad is the principle of relationality; with respect to any two, it is always possible to interpolate a third or some relation obtaining between them. The extent of Peirce's conviction about this principle can be seen from his claim that if someone says of two items, A and B, that they have *no relation* to each other, he has succeeded in stating the relation which does obtain between them, assuming, of course, that such a total disjunction of 'other than' and nothing more actually obtains. Since, however, the terms of a triad may themselves be polyadic, the triad remains as the irreducible relationship from which to build the logic of relatives.

A final point to be stressed in relation to Peirce's categories is the matter of their interdependence. This topic is complex in the extreme, but it is of basic importance since one may be inclined to think of the three categories as having the independence they seem to have acquired as a result of the ease with which Peirce distinguished his basic conceptions from each other, i.e. that quality is not fact, that fact is not general and that law is neither quality nor fact. It was necessary for Peirce to make these distinctions in order to disengage and articulate the characteristics of the *phaneron,* but having done so, it was also part of his task to explicate the *togetherness* of the categories and thus to see them as applicable to each other.[52] In Peirce's first attempt to compile a list of categories,[53] he employed a threefold distinction between *abstraction* (precision), discrimination and dissociation as a means of setting up a hierarchy of modes of 'mental separation' among ideas. Although he did not always apply the same terms in using this distinction it is possible to give a clear, even if only rudimentary, conception of how they express connections between categories. According to Peirce, we can imagine sound without melody, but not melody without sound, and this type of separation he calls 'dissociation'. Secondly, there are conceptions which cannot be separated in imagination, but in connection with which we can suppose one without the other. His example is that we can suppose uncoloured space, but we cannot dissociate space from colour. This type of separation he called 'precision' or prescinding. The third mode of separation is that of 'distinction' where one element cannot be supposed without the other – it is not possible to imagine or suppose a taller without a shorter – but where it is still possible to distinguish the two. Applying these conceptions to the categories, he claimed, first, that they cannot be dissociated from each other 'nor from other ideas'. The latter addition would seem to indicate the continuity of all thought in a universe of discourse. The key conception is that of 'precision'; firstness can be prescinded from secondness and from third-ness, but secondness cannot be prescinded from firstness nor can thirdness be prescinded from secondness. Quality may be supposed without existence – action and reaction – and thought or signs, but existence cannot be supposed without quality, and signs cannot be supposed without action and reaction.

This rather abstract characterization of the relations between the categories does not adequately convey what Peirce had in mind. A better understanding is forthcoming if one attends to his actual application of the categories to each other. There is, he said, a firstness of firstness, a firstness of secondness, and a firstness of thirdness. By this he meant that when we attempt to get the clearest conceptions of the categories we are striving to grasp them in themselves as pure. The firstness of firstness is quality, literally pure and simple. The quality, for example of *King Lear* as a tragic play is universal and *sui generis,* pure firstness. The firstness of secondness is the apprehension of the blind compulsion in action and reaction as existent event taken all by itself. The firstness of thirdness is the apprehension of meaning *per se* as is exhibited in a thought which necessarily follows from another thought and can be realized in no other way. While, however, a firstness of all three categories is possible, there is no secondness of pure firstness, because that would involve the existence which is excluded from the conception of quality as such. Moreover, there is no thirdness of either pure firstness or pure secondness, because that would involve the conception of mediation excluded from both. There is, however, a secondness of thirdness which is met whenever there is a con-sidered or purposeful response to an action or event which presents a challenge of some sort.

Peirce worked out categorial interrelationships of the sort here indi-cated with incredible patience and in the greatest detail, frequently correct-ing previous formulations by pointing out some degree of inaccuracy in them. For example, he repeatedly identified firstness with *possibility,* but he came to see that possibility implies a relation to existence, 'while uni-versal firstness is the mode of being of itself'.[54] The upshot is that 'possibility' and pure firstness are not precisely equivalent in meaning. This consideration led him to claim that a new word – firstness – is neces-sary. Or again, consider his circumspection with regard to the category of secondness. In numerous places secondness is identified through the experience of *willing* and through perception, the former being regarded as a sort of paradigm. But upon reflection, Peirce saw that willing cannot be pure secondness because willing involves purpose and the *representation* of the act as a *means,* both of which signal the presence of thirdness. Like Whitehead, Peirce was extremely sensitive to the problem of finding appropriate *philosophical* terminology, and he was fully aware of the tension that exists between accuracy and communicability. His development of the categories particularly gives evidence that for him accuracy came first and he was prepared to bear the onus of volumes of writing studded with neologisms and bizarre terminology rather than to perpetuate inaccuracy in analysis.

In addition to Peirce's elaborate categorial scheme for expressing the generic structure of reality, his metaphysics also included certain general cosmological doctrines largely bound up with the evolutionary foundation of his Pragmaticism. Among these are his theory of chance in reality or *tychism,* and the conception of continuity or *synechism.* Each is complex and a few basic ideas must suffice for conveying the conceptions that determine his pragmaticistic universe.

As is clear from many writings, Peirce held fast to his belief in the reality of natural laws as operative and exhibited by the regular behaviour or habits of the things that exist. He did not, however, believe that law-like behaviour is ever *exact,* nor would he allow that the inexactitude of empirical determinations is to be explained entirely in terms of an error factor. In short, Peirce believed in the objective reality of *chance* in the universe and, for him, this meant a rejection of any total or unmitigated necessitarianism. In arguing against a mechanical philosophy, Peirce was arguing against the familiar thesis that the state of things at any given time, together with the invocation of 'immutable laws', completely determine the state of things at every other time.[55] Peirce was quite unpersuaded by the claim that this thesis can be maintained as a 'postulate' or 'presupposition' which is demanded by science,[56] partly because he regarded scientifiic inference as probabilistic and dependent on sampling, and partly because he refused to allow that a proposition designated as a postulate can be accorded equal validity with evidentially supported *premises* in scientific reasoning. The matter is actually more complicated than at first appears because Peirce did not believe that probabilistic or experiential inference involves any postulates beyond the *provisional* claim that further experience of the material under investigation will accord with the pattern established by the fair sample from which we argue. He insisted instead that a postulate is 'the formulation of a material fact' which is not among the premises, but whose truth is necessary for the validity of an inference. The postulate is such that the fact it involves must either present itself in experience or not; if it does, it becomes a premise and is no postulate, and if it does not, then there is ground for holding that the case can be otherwise than the postulate asserts.

If the necessitarian thesis cannot be supported as a postulate, perhaps it can be shown to be true or rendered highly probable by observation. In considering this line of argument, Peirce translated the thesis into the claim 'that certain continuous quantities have certain exact values'[57] and argued that these can never be ascertained by observation alone since the factor of error cannot be eliminated and necessarily involves mathematical calculation. But Peirce did not rest the case there; he did not allow that the facts are all fully determinate and that the deviation or error is to be put down to the conditions of observation. On the contrary, he insisted upon *both* regularity in nature and error in observation, but he believed that the regularity is never exact and that the ultimate cause of the error is the inexactitude or the existence of chance in nature. Chance and regularity, however, are not to be conceived as dipolar opposites; regularity Peirce did not deny and he even referred to chance as a spontaneity 'which is to some degree regular',[58] but what he did deny is that the universe, especially in its organic complexity, can be understood solely in terms of a regularity which means exact repetition in the sense in which the cycle of a machine may be said to recur exactly.

The underlying consideration here is found in Peirce's evolutionary outlook and his unwillingess to believe that the diversity and complexity of developing organic systems can be explained by invoking law which represents the exact repetition of the same. Central to Darwinian theory was the concept of individual variation *within* the species; Peirce did not see how this fact could be accounted for without a form of spontaneity and a degree of irregularity. Seen from another perspective, law or regularity, though it serves as an explanatory principle, must itself be explained. Peirce's idea is that regularity is the result of the formation of habits, but that the latter become possible only if there is plasticity and spontaneity in the universe. The mention of habit serves at the same time to call attention to another motive for Peirce's tychism – his concern to deny that nature is closed to mind and to find a way of expressing some continuity between the two. 'I make use of chance,' he wrote, 'chiefly to make room for a principle of generalization, or tendency to form habits which I hold has produced all regularities.'[59] The so-called immutable laws of nature, then, are not ultimate, but are the expression and indeed the outcome of tendencies, associations and habits which spread and grow. Denying the necessitarian thesis, Peirce claimed, 'gives room for the influence of another kind of causation, such as seems to be operative in the mind in the formation of associations, and enables us to understand how the uniformity of nature could have been brought about'.[60]

It is clear that Peirce regarded his tychism or evolutionary cosmology of growth as a foundation or, if not that, a necessary first step in the development of his doctrine of continuity or *synechism* which expresses the basic nature of mind. Peirce's robust belief in the applicability of precise logical and mathematical concepts to speculative questions is nowhere more forcibly illustrated than in his development of this doctrine through the concept of the infinitesimal. The underlying thesis for which Peirce was arguing is 'that ideas tend to spread continuously and to affect certain others which stand to them in a peculiar relation of affectibility'.[61] Recognising the centrality of the act of comparison as requisite for saying that ideas are similar, different, etc., Peirce attacked the question: How can a past idea be present? He dismissed the view that a past idea cannot be in any sense present because that would make our knowledge of the past 'mere delusion'. His solution was that the past idea cannot be wholly past, but can only be 'going' or be 'less present than any assignable past date', so that any present is connected with the past 'by a series of real infinitesimal steps'.[62] Relying on his claim that there is no consciousness at an instant but only in an interval of time,[63] Peirce concluded that we are immediately conscious through an infinitesimal interval of time. In this interval we perceive in the mode of immediate feelings the temporal sequence of beginning, middle and end. And if the present is viewed in this 'thick' way as duration, we can say, Peirce held, that 'the present is half past and half to come'.[64] A present instant is such that it never fails to be contained by an infinitesimal duration.

Peirce's ultimate aim in setting forth the conception of synechism was to explain how ideas affect each other, leading to generalization, communication and the formation of a continuum of reasoning or inference. Peirce's main target was, once again, nominalism, here understood as the belief that ideas are utterly individual and distinct in their absolute determinateness and do not affect each other but are governed by absolute uniformities of an external sort. If there is no reason in such necessitated uniformity then, said Peirce, the uniformity is coincidental and must be put down to chance. If, moreover, the uniformity is said to extend over an entire infinite future, we are confronted with nothing but an *idea*. According to the position Peirce was maintaining, all ideas have their intrinsic quality as feeling and as such they possess an energy to affect other ideas with a force which varies in accordance with temporal position and a tendency to bring other ideas with them. The upshot is that the continuity of ideas is what makes reflective thought possible; its characteristic modes of deduction, induction and hypothesis formation are explained by Peirce in terms of associations and habits which express themselves in reactions appropriate for the purpose of the particular reasoning process involved. The 'laws' governing mind are not nearly so rigid as those governing matter since, according to Peirce's panpsychism, matter is essentially 'frozen' mind which has become so throughly habituated that its range of surprises is quite small. Mind is subject instead to 'gentle forces' and its living character shows itself in an amount of 'arbitrary spontaneity' never to be eliminated. In this regard mental action is always subject to uncertainty.

If James saw metaphysical issues as urgent and ultimately connected with conduct and the quality of human life, and Peirce regarded them as extrapolations or 'guesses' rooted in science and logical analysis about the intrinsic character of nature and mind, Dewey had a conception of metaphysics different from both. It is at once more secular than James' (and without his moral and religious overtones) and far less bold or 'speculative' than that of Peirce. Bernstein was, nevertheless, quite correct in noting the similarity between Dewey's conception of metaphysics and Peirce's idea that philosophy is based on phenomena so pervasive in experience that one 'usually pays no particular attention to them'.[65]

Dewey aimed to give an account not only of the nature of nature and experience but of the nature and function of metaphysics as well. The latter topic comes first as a matter of logical priority. To avoid confusion one must bear in mind that Dewey drew a distinction between 'metaphysics' and 'philosophy' and, while there are places in his writings, especially references to the history of philosophy, where the two terms are used interchangeably, the distinction in question must not be overlooked. Metaphysics meant for him reflective analysis aimed at disclosing what he called the 'generic traits of existence' or the pervasive features which manifest themselves in *every* specific subject matter which defines or marks off a distinct field of inquiry. Stars and galaxies represent the specific subject matter of astronomy, plants of botany, insects of entomology, etc. Each of these subject matters exhibits diversity and individuality; these are generic traits cutting across all subject matters and hence form the subject matter appropriate to metaphysics. Philosophy, on the other hand, is understood as a reflective enterprise of *criticism* pointing in two directions. There is first the task of interpreting or functioning as a liaison between the technical languages of special areas of inquiry, and secondly, a focusing on the goods or values ingredient in science, art and social intercourse. Dewey liked to think of this view as in accord with the traditional conception of philosophy as wisdom which is not knowledge but which at the same time cannot dispense with knowledge. Like science, philosophy has its instrumental value and it would be quite fair to say that for Dewey philosophy stands to culture, society and history as natural science stands to nature. Science aims at a knowledge of things in their interrelationships which leads to control and the transformation of precarious existence into something more stable. Philosophy aims at the good of society through the critical appraisal and ordering of the values inherent in the various dimensions of life and experience – social, political, economic, moral, aesthetic and religious. Consideration of the relation between philosophy so conceived and metaphysics will be postponed until Dewey's conception of the nature and method of the latter has been developed.

The first point is that ultimate origins or causes are not the proper concern of metaphysics. Following essentially the line inaugurated by Kant and pushed to extremes by the positivists, Dewey held that 'a question about ultimate origin or ultimate causation is either a meaningless question, or else the words are used in a relative sense to designate the point in the past at which a particular inquiry breaks off'.[66] Questions about the world *en masse* cannot be given a determinate meaning; in so far as they make reference to some specific trait or phenomenon in the world they can be interpreted distributively as questions belonging to specific inquiry and resolved in terms of the actual and overt interaction of natural factors which explain the trait or phenomenon. There is no formula for the world 'as a whole'. 'Ultimate' with respect to explanation has only a relative sense; one explanation may be more 'ultimate' than another in the sense of pushing an inquiry beyond any assignable limit, but wherever we stop we are always dealing with finite and specific states of affairs. If, however, all significant questions are specific and become the province of a special science, what is left for metaphysics? James had raised this same problem when he cited the development of modern science out of the bag of questions previously assigned to 'natural philosophy' so that, as one question after another was translated into specific terms to be treated scientifically, the philosopher was left with a bag which ultimately turns out to be empty. Dewey's response was to ask whether there are ultimate, in the sense of *irreducible*, traits which manifest themselves across the whole spectrum of scientific subject matters, and, if there are, such traits would form the appropriate subject matter of metaphysics. While not attempting to develop a metaphysics in the paper under consideration, Dewey did single out such traits as specifically *diverse existences, interaction, change,* and *evaluations* involving time and determinate direction as generic traits of the universe we know. These traits can be studied profitably in themselves as long as we are careful to avoid two errors. First, no explanation of a phenomenon or occurrence is legitimate if it results in the disappearance of the phenomenon. Dewey repeatedly insisted on this anti-reductionism as an essential feature of a metaphysics which respects primary experience and upholds the reality of initial occurrences which set the process of explanation in motion. Analysis and attempts to explain always result in the disclosure of more than we started with, but never with less. Second (and this point is the distinctive feature of Dewey's naturalism or scientific neutralism) the generic traits are not to be accorded any special or honorific status such as is illustrated in Aristotle's identification of 'first philosophy' with theology or a superior kind of knowledge. Metaphysics is not involved with creation or eschatology; in Dewey's formula, there are beginnings and endings *in* nature, but nature, as such, has no beginning or end.[67]

Before returning to the question of how metaphysics is related to philosophy as criticism, some attempt must be made to show what Dewey meant by empirical method in philosophy and how the conception of nature which is at the centre of his thought embraces both material events and mind in the form of meaning. From one end to the other, Dewey's philosophy exhibits the same recurrent pattern; the beginning is always *primary experience* which means whatever is done, suffered, undergone, or encountered in any way by the human organism in the natural world. From this storehouse of experience and things experienced emerge numerous types of reflective thought in response to questions, problems, interests, concerns, frustrations, incongruities which present themselves to a living being existing and seeking to persist in an environment which affords no advance guarantee of success. Since reflective thought – the concepts and theories of the sciences and philosophy – arises out of problematic situations in primary experience, it must be brought back again to that experience for the purpose of seeing to what extent it successfully performs the functions – interpretation, understanding and control – for which it was first introduced. This cycle represents at the most basic level what Dewey meant by calling his version of Pragmatism 'instrumentalism'. The key term is 'function' rather than 'action' taken in the narrow and immediate sense of 'doing', since the most important types of functioning concern the role played by ideas, arguments, theories and philosophical vision. For Dewey, the validity of an idea is to be determined by estimating the success with which it performs a function, which is to say, realizes some purpose or end in view, and it is only in some cases that the purpose is control of overt action.

One of the basic theses of the metaphysics set forth in *Experience and Nature* is that the very existence of natural science testifies to the essential connections between natural existence and experience as a reliable medium of disclosure. Experience is not an evanescent subjectivity, nor a veil or screen standing between the subject and the 'external' world, but rather the principal medium and means whereby the world is encountered, enjoyed, appraised, transformed into a human habitation. Experience, therefore, must be the starting point for all reflective thought, philosophical as well as scientific. But, like Peirce, Dewey did not understand this empiricism to mean starting with simple data of the senses as an ultimate 'given' since he regarded this notion itself as a 'reflected product' which does not represent primary experience, but rather a way of conceiving what our contact with the world must be if 'experience' is to serve as an incorrigible foundation for knowledge. Primary experience consists of all the encounters, the doings and sufferings of experiencing subjects in the surrounding world. It is this experience which sets the problems and provides the data for the construction of secondary objects of reflection; these come into play when we move from the direct experience of water as a liquid in which salt dissolves to refined concepts for understanding that phenomenon such as temperature, molecular structure, viscosity, etc., which take us beyond sense contact with the things of macroscopic experience. The question is: What is the relation between primary experience and the secondary products of reflection? Dewey's answer was meant to express the fundamental conception of empirical or *denotative* method characteristic of both science and philosophy on two different levels of abstraction. The function of the objects of reflection is to *explain* what happens in primary experience; the distinctive feature of the process involved is the need for a return to primary experience as a means of discovering with what success the refined objects have performed their function.

Primary experience is what is encountered in what one might call the normal course of events; it involves a minimum of reflection in contrast with what is experienced as the result of regulated inquiry – spectral bands, deflected light, vibrating membranes – guided by theory. Primary experience would embrace, among other things, 'seeing' whereas inquiry demands 'looking' or, more precisely, 'looking for'. It was Dewey's contention that the pattern established by science requires a return to primary experience as a necessary condition for testing the products of reflection. He cited Einstein's prediction, formulated on the basis of refined products or theoretical conceptions, that light will be deflected by the sun's mass, and the subsequent return to the primary experience of an eclipse as a means of testing the theory. The recourse to primary experience is guided by the fact that we know what we are looking for and can interpret what we find accordingly. Philosophy, however, Dewey claimed, has invariably failed to complete the circle and has left its reflected products hanging, as it were, in logical space with the result that the elucidatory role of these products in relation to primary experience has been lost. In explaining this role, Dewey wrote:

Well, they [reflected products] define or lay out a path by which return to experienced things is of such a sort that the meaning, the significant content of what is experienced, gains an enriched and expanded force because of the path or method by which it was reached. Directly, in immediate contact it may be just what is was before – hard, colored, odorous, etc. But when the secondary objects, the refined objects, are employed as a method or road for coming at them, these qualities cease to be isolated details ; they get the meaning contained in a whole system of related objects ; they are rendered continuous with the rest of nature and take on the import of the things they are now seen to be continuous with.[68]

Whether this statement makes sufficiently clear the explanatory function of scientific concepts and theories may well be doubted; its implication for philosophical concepts, however, is clearer. Failure to use secondary products as a way of pointing back to something in primary experience was said by Dewey to have three important negative consequences for philosophy. There is, first, no effort to test the refined products, although it is clear that this cannot mean in the case of philosophical principles the sort of verification possible in the case of the eclipse. What it does mean is that we are to ask of a philosophy whether it ends in conclusions which, 'when referred back to ordinary life-experiences and their predicaments, render them more significant, more luminous to us, and make our dealings with them more fruitful?'[69] Secondly, without return to primary experience the things and events with which we began are not enlarged and enriched with the sort of meaning which the philosophical perspective affords. Finally, unless connected once again with ordinary experience, philosophical notions become 'abstract' in the pejorative sense of dwelling in a realm of their own, and never descending to influence the actual scene.[70] It is important to notice that despite the force of Dewey's 'instrumentalism' and the belief that he made all thought merely a means to action, little emphasis has been placed in this account of the role of reflected products on their capacity for making possible the manipulation and control of things and events. Instead, the stress falls on understanding and the enlargement of meaning bestowed on primary experience when it is approached in a reflective way.

Dewey's concern for retaining the integrity of primary experience was intimately connected with his belief that non-empirical philosophies are bound to establish an utter divorce between the experiencing self and the natural world because they insist on relegating the most intensely significant and personal features of experience to a merely subjective status in the mind. Despite Dewey's extensive reliance on science – he could even speak of appealing to the findings of science as taking the place of supposedly outworn moral traditions – Dewey nevertheless repeatedly inveighed against the ubiquity of the cognitive relation and especially against any position which identifies the thing as known with the 'real' object in an eminent sense. The point he had in mind is both valid and particularly pertinent at a time when mathematics and physics seem to be the only intellectual endeavours exempt from the suspicion of ideology and subjective bias. 'When real objects are identified, point for point, with knowledge objects,' Dewey wrote, 'all affectional and valuation objects are inevitably excluded from the 'real' world, and are compelled to find refuge in the privacy of an experiencing subject or mind.'[71] As against this selective bias Dewey was arguing in favour of equal rights for all the aspects and dimensions of things as disclosed in experience. This point is brought out in his discussion of the problem illustrated by the famous 'two tables' of Eddington; what is the relation between the macroscopic and directly encountered table which is solid and on which I write and that same table conceived in accordance with physical theory as a dance of electrons with great spaces between them?[72] Dewey's answer was that if we regard the table as it is apprehended in terms of physical theory – the table as *known par excellence* – as alone the 'real' table, then the table as it appears in every other context in experience, whether of use or enjoyment, will be demoted to subjective status and thus removed from nature, reappearing only in the secret recesses of individual mind. Dewey opposed this particular selective bias as a substantive philosophical position, but it led him as well to question any and all selective emphasis in philosophy.

Here a new problem presents itself. Philosophy, one supposes, should provide insight, illumination and some way of distinguishing what is worthwhile and substantial in experience from the momentary, insignificant and deceptive. To ignore these distinctions in order to avoid the charge of selective bias can result only in a philosophy which does no more than repeat what is familiar to everyone in our most obvious experience, i.e. that there are tables and chairs, hopes and fears, persons and nations, etc. If classical philosophies were guilty of selective bias in emphasizing being, God, substance, the good, the self as that reality in terms of which everything is to be understood, did they not at least have the virtue of offering a vision, an outlook from which all things could be ordered and their relative significance and import be determined? It is not without importance that decades ago realists like Montague and others urge precisely this sort of criticism against Dewey's metaphysics, charging that his desire to avoid reductionism drove him to an indiscriminate inclusion of everything that is and happens without any regard for the distinction between what is fundamental and what is derivative. The question then is: What response could Dewey make to these criticisms? He had in fact two retorts, one concerned with specific cases of selective emphasis and one directed to the problem of selective emphasis as such.

Selective emphasis, he admitted, is not only unavoidable, but 'is the heartbeat of mental life'. 'To object to the operation,' he said, 'is to discard all thinking.' Like James and Royce, Dewey attempted to deal with the justification of selection by invoking *purpose* as manifest both in the domain of ordinary experience and science.[73] In each case Dewey took it for granted that concentrating, for example, on the area of a building lot to the neglect of its height above sea-level, or noting the temperature of a solution while disregarding its colour, represent purposive selection based on what is judged relevant and is totally without prejudice with respect to the reality of what has been omitted from consideration. The case in philosophy, however, is said to be different. There, Dewey charged, philosophers have either concealed their selective biases or made an illegitimate, reductive use of them. His task was to show how empirical method in philosophy makes possible the admission of selective emphasis at the same time that these undesirable consequences are avoided. The illustration to follow clarifies this point, but first a general comment on the several examples Dewey cited is in order. The most interesting feature of the entire discussion is found in the subtle way in which Dewey caused his own philosophical naturalism to stand out against the background of cases of selective emphasis which he regarded as illegitimate. This fact is all the more noteworthy in that Dewey's claim for the validity of his own view was not represented by a direct attack on the substance of the positions supposedly based on invalid selective emphasis. Instead he depended entirely on the claim that whereas other philosophers conceal their selective biases, he made his own a matter of public record. The importance of this point for clarifying the role of method in philosophy will become apparent from the following illustration.

'Another striking example of the fallacy of selective emphasis,' Dewey wrote, 'is found in the hypnotic influence exercised by the conception of the eternal.'[74] The permanent, he claimed, provides us with an opportunity to rest and to enjoy a sense of security, and appeal to the invariant makes it possible for us to understand and to deal more effectively with the precarious and unstable reality which confronts us. In this sense Dewey admitted that the permanent 'answers genuine emotional, practical and intellectual requirements'.[75] The contexts, however, in which we respond to insecurity and uncertainty in experience by invoking the permanent are all *particular*, while philosophy – 'thinking at large' – generalizes out of bounds, as it were, and embarks on an absurd search 'for an intellectual philosopher's stone' which, unrestricted by any particular purpose, leads to the conception of an intrinsically eternal reality that is ever the same and out of time. Dewey, it should be noted, did not consider whether there *is* an eternal reality as many philosophers in the past have maintained, but confined himself instead to the question of philosophic method. The problem of the eternal does not arise because the illustration is already assumed to be an instance of a fallacy. It is in fact what Dewey called '*the* philosophical fallacy' – the converting of eventual functions into antecedent reality. It is, however, not clear that Dewey avoided confusing two quite distinct ideas. On the one hand his contrast is between a response which is appropriate for a specific context and the 'wholesale generalization' which is assigned to philosophy. On the other hand there is the contrast between eventual functioning and antecedent existence. His argument remains unresolved at this point, although it is clear that both contrasts raise the question of the validity of selective emphasis which, as Dewey admitted, is necessary for reflection in all its forms.

Dewey's answer was that empirical method requires the open and candid specification of the actual selective emphasis being made. Such emphasis cannot be avoided, but it can be made public. The choice involved can then be regarded as one more factor to be taken into account, to be examined and assessed. It is clear that Dewey was thinking of the purposeful selection of concepts and principles which form the basis for a philosophical system. Philosophical thinking is thus an experimental affair in the sense that the thinker clearly and specifically indicates the 'intellectual simplifications' that have been made and how they were arrived at. 'It places before others,' he wrote, 'a map of the road that has been travelled; they may accordingly, if they will, re-travel the road to inspect the landscape for themselves.'[76] By following out the consequences of the selections made we are to see not only how those selections function in the way of interpreting the world, but also to determine the extent to which we and others reach the same conclusions drawn by the thinkers who first marked out the path we have followed. 'Every system of philosophy,' Dewey said, 'presents the consequences of some such experiment.'[77]

While it may well be doubted whether empirical method in Dewey's sense can be as successfully applied to philosophy as he believed, there can be little doubt that he perceived something of paramount importance for the problems posed by philosophical disagreement and conflicting points of view. The insight is also to be found in Hegel and failure to take it seriously has been one of the shortcomings of all 'critical' as opposed to speculative philosophy. The insight is that it is not possible to estimate the validity of concepts or principles selected for emphasis simply by logical analysis which leaves out of account how these concepts and principles function or work in the interpretation of actual subject matter. If, for example, one were interested in determining the relative merits of Russell's logical atomism and Whitehead's philosophy of organism, it would be necessary not merely to analyse the meaning of the basic concepts involved but to relate the ideas and principles of each view to primary experience in order to judge the extent of their explanatory power. Can an atomism make room for organic systems or must it reduce them to something else? Can an organic theory allow for the disjunctive in experience and the items that are externally related? Such questions can be answered only by viewing the respective philosophies *at work* in their treatment of the same primary experience. Without the return of abstractions to experience, they become 'mere' abstractions which do no work and cannot be critically compared except in the most formal way. A distinctive feature of Dewey's conception of empirical method in philosophy is the demand that every selective abstraction be required to confront the continuum of experience out of which it arose. No abstractive feature is suspect simply because it is abstract; if that were the case no thought would be possible at all except as a means of distorting rather than illuminating the contents of experience. The aim is to understand how abstractions actually interpret the world, and what difference they make in the illumination of primary experience.

Like James, Dewey was inclined to emphasize the distinction between *methods* and *doctrines,* and he thought of the contribution of empirical method in philosophy as not involving doctrines. But surely if you tell someone how to proceed in thought you cannot avoid making assumptions about the nature of the subject matter and the purposes to be fulfilled. That this is the case is made clear when Dewey went on to point out two further fallacies which it is alleged can be avoided only by following empirical method. These fallacies clearly involve substantive philosophical doctrines. In addition to showing the proper way to deal with selective emphasis, empirical method, Dewey claimed, also condemns the separation of subject and object, and avoids the proclivity of philosophers to give absolute priority to the objects as *known* at the expense of their other features which derive from human association, art, industry, and the many contexts in which things are experienced as enjoyable, troublesome, perplexing, threatening, etc. The separating of subject and object, for Dewey, meant the disconnection of *what* is experienced from *how* it is experienced in the life of the experiencing subject. Experience is not just *content,* but includes as well *context* and the many dimensions of meaning – political, moral, religious, aesthetic – in which that content figures. The integrity of experience means the togetherness of what is encountered and the subject who encounters it. If the two are separated the result is two non-communicating compartments, a world of bare objects 'out there', and a realm of subjects standing over against nature encapsulated within their own 'experience'. The stage is thus set for at least two of the principal acts in the drama of modern philosophy. First, knowledge itself becomes a major problem: how can subjects transcend their own 'experience' and attain knowledge of the 'external world'? And, as Dewey rightly pointed out, stated in such a way the problem is insoluble because *all* the valid data present to the subject are 'internal' and no escape from the circle of subjectivity is possible. Secondly, the powerful influence of modern individualism resulted in exclusive concentration on internal experience itself as a citadel of certainty so that the world of nature was forced into the background. Experience, it came to be believed, is experience not of nature but of experience itself, a conclusion that was inevitable since if we cannot reach the external world we must be content with what we have before us as an immediate certainty. Against all this Dewey argued that 'we primarily observe things, not observations', and affirmed the view that ordinary experience is firmly rooted in a decisively realistic bias. It is possible to make observing itself and its conditions an object of attention and inquiry, but to do so is a matter of special investigation and even then the acts of observing studied would be the focus of attention as ordinary subject matter distinct from the observations of the investigator. This part of Dewey's defence of empirical method in philosophy coincides largely with his attack on both classical empiricism and the Cartesian starting point.

The third mistake from which empirical method is said to free us concerns the primacy and ubiquity of the knowing relationship in interpreting the world. The issue here is less simple than at first appears. The first point is that Dewey understood knowing in a quite restricted sense; it occurs only as the outcome of controlled inquiry and therefore coincides largely with science. In denying that it is legitimate to identify an object as such with the object as described and explained in terms of the refined, microscopic concepts of the sciences, Dewey was seeking to avoid the consequence that whatever in the way of quality or significance is omitted from the scientific account is thereby declared 'unreal'. In short, if only the known object is 'real', all of its features as disclosed in other contexts must be set down as 'appearance'. One aspect, then, of the attack on the primacy of knowing coincides with Dewey's attack on reductionism. Much more, however, is involved. His critique implies that the many other contexts in which the real is encountered and interpreted where no explicit or controlled inquiry is involved – moral,[78] religious, aesthetic – fall beyond the sphere of knowledge, belonging instead to the domain of what is 'had' or directly experienced and has no need to be made an object of knowing in the strict sense. Although Dewey added the proviso that what is thus had does not *need* to be known, it may well be doubted whether his severely circumscribed conception of knowing and the exclusions it entails does not in the end contribute to a further widening of the gap between what can be discussed critically and what is merely 'emotive' and thus beyond the reach of rational discourse. That he would have vigorously opposed such a consequence is clear enough, but his thought is not without its own touches of the sort of *scientism* which makes that consequence inevitable.

Before returning to the postponed question of the relation between philosophy as criticism and metaphysics, an attempt must be made to indicate Dewey's substantive metaphysical position articulated through his conception of the generic traits of existence. The central point of his position can be summed up in a formula: where others saw substances, entities and fixed characters, Dewey saw functions, processes and stages of development distinguished by their place in and contribution to some determinate outcome. In this sense, Dewey was a 'process' philosopher upholding the primacy of events over 'elements' or 'things'.

This comprehensive feature is well illustrated by his appeal to the generic trait of *organisation* as a means of providing a theory of the physical, the psycho-physical and the mental. Here it is necessary to keep in mind the underlying idea of *interaction;* thing, object, organism, subject are never considered in isolation, but only in thoroughgoing relation to an environment. The reciprocal interaction is so much emphasized that one is inclined to think of all the determinations of existence recognized by Dewey as taking place at the point of contact or interface between discriminated items and not 'in' the items themselves. The problem under attack is focused by the Cartesian dualism of living and non-living reality, although in Dewey's view the problem is much older since it is supposed to go back to the Christian dualism between flesh and spirit.[79] What is needed is a new way of conceiving the distinction between the living and the non-living and Dewey's proposal was to begin with a description of empirical traits. 'The most obvious difference,' he wrote, 'between living and non-living things is that the activities of the former are characterized by needs, by efforts which are active demands to satisfy needs, and by satisfactions.'[80] Needs are essentially tensions in energy distributions resulting in unstable equilibrium; efforts appear as movements affecting the environing objects in the direction of restoring the equilibrium; satisfactions mean the actual recovery of the pattern of equilibrium which set the process of interaction in motion.

According to Dewey, the difference between, for example, the plant and the inanimate iron molecule is not one of substance, i.e. the plant does not have 'something in addition to physico-chemical energy'; the difference is to be found in the *way* in which the energies are 'interconnected and operate' and in the different consequences which follow. The distinctive difference is that animate bodies show the tendency to recover, restore and maintain an equilibrium over a time or a history, whereas the inanimate do not. In Dewey's example, the iron shows no tendency to retain itself as such and readily oxidizes, nor does it have the capacity to modify its interaction with other elements so as to perpetuate itself in a pure state. Living bodies, or organisms, on the contrary, show both tendencies.

If we go a step further and ask about the distinctive features of organisms as such, Dewey's answer is that the organism or the 'psycho-physical' displays the need–demand–satisfaction cycle, but that we must not think of the prefix 'psycho' as the addition of something 'psychical' or as the negation of the physico-chemical level but rather as the manifestation of additional properties, namely, the capacity to elicit support from the environment. The procedure of denoting characteristic traits, functions and consequences, Dewey believed, delivers us from certain philosophical problems which have been framed in such a way as to make them insoluble. Referring to his own analysis, he wrote, 'Thus conceived there is no problem of the relation of physical *and* psychic',[81] and the reason is clear: the two, taken supposedly as entities with mutually exclusive properties, cannot be related in an intelligible way, but if they are conceived in terms of 'levels of increasing complexity and intimacy of interaction among natural events'[82] then no contrasting 'substances' appear which have to be 'reconciled'. On Dewey's view, much discussion of the 'mind–body' problem is misguided because if one begins with totally disparate entities the only possible outcome is a form of reductionism in which one or the other is declared to be 'real' and the respective other becomes 'appearance' (this happens in some forms of the so-called 'identity theory') or else the initial dualism is reinstated and we have the original problem all over again and no solution. Empirical method requires that we start with the fact that a bio-physical organism and the capacity to use language and read signs are together in the human subject; the former is identified by the need–effort–satisfaction pattern and the latter by the *prospective* use of signs for the control of eventual functionings. No theory is viable which does not start with the fact of this togetherness, and no theory is viable which ends by denying that fact on the ground that we cannot explain the 'possibility' of this togetherness. Dewey was, in effect, arguing for an 'emergent' theory of mind understood in terms of denoting additional properties and functions manifested throughout the many types and levels of cosmic events. Inanimate objects, in comparison with psycho-physical organisms, do not respond to qualities of situations as such, and, at a more complex level, only a being possessing mind can respond to the *doubtful* as such. A response of that complexity embraces not only the apprehension of the incoherent and problematic but the attempt to locate and resolve the difficulty as well. 'Body–mind,' said Dewey, 'designates an affair with its own properties,'[83] and in order to describe and understand it we must attend to what actually happens in the situations of discourse, communication and participation. 'Body' represents the continued and conserved operation of factors in the interaction with the environment; 'mind' represents anticipation and the intentional use or reshaping of the environment in accordance with ends in view. Like Whitehead who used unfamiliar terminology to avoid unwanted connotations, Dewey was especially concerned about the difficulty of expressing what the human subject actually shows itself to be in experience because familiar terminology has enshrined within it the connotations and nuances of two distinct worlds, an 'inner' and an 'outer'.

The foregoing has been intended primarily to illustrate what Dewey meant by the empirical method of denoting functions and consequences as against a philosophy of substances. The persistent application of this method results in a naturalistic pluralism in which there is no overriding unifying term, except that of nature itself which was, for Dewey, a distributive affair embracing whatever can be met or encountered. Whatever unities exist are conceived by Dewey primarily in terms of method. The parallel here between the interpretation of experience and of nature is instructive. Just as experience is to be understood not in terms of some quality such as 'sense' or 'mental', but as a *way* of encountering the world (nature) and discovering its secrets, nature must be understood not as the 'physical' or 'material' but rather as all that can become the object of empirical method. In both cases, there is no reference to the reality as a 'whole' in any way except in terms of *method*. One might say that this attitude represents the ultimate in humanism: whatever unity is possessed by nature, the cosmos, the world is dependent on its becoming an object of investigation and transformation by human beings.

Dewey had a way of defusing traditional philosophical disputes by discovering either that they had been wrongly formulated or that each side was in the wrong for supposing that everything could be explained from its perspective alone. The strength of this approach lies in the way it forces a return to experience, but its weakness is found in our sense that long-standing metaphysical issues are not so easily resolved. Consider, for example, Dewey's account of the relation between philosophy and metaphysics. To begin with, there is an ancient and extremely difficult problem standing behind Dewey's distinction between philosophy as 'criticism' and metaphysics as the delineation of the generic traits of existence. The problem points to the double-barrelled character of philosophy manifested from the beginning of reflective thought and represented by the contrast between the orientation of Plato and Aristotle. On the one side, philosophy made its appearance in the sober garb of dispassionate inquiry which in due course emerged as science with attention focused exclusively on the ways of things, their kinds, levels, structures and causes. On the other side, philosophy also meant concern for the 'things that matter most', for wisdom, for guidance and for insight into those distinctively human problems which have haunted moralists, artists, religious prophets and political leaders since the foundation of human society. The history of philosophy can well be written as the story of the tension between these two sets of fundamental concerns; the very existence on the present scene of a gulf between analytic philosophies inspired ultimately by a scientific ideal, and existential and phenomenological philosophies motivated by interest in social, moral, religious and aesthetic values, testifies both to the perennial character of the problem and to the divided consciousness which results when no mediating position has been developed. Dewey's conception of metaphysics answers to the scientific aspect of philosophy and his conception of philosophy as criticism answers to the concern for wisdom, for a *sapientia* which does not issue automatically from the steady increase of information. The question then is: How did Dewey envisage the relation between the two?

The answer, though it appears at first to be concerned only with the two faces of reflective thinking, actually represents Dewey's conception of the proper relation between knowledge and valuation and embraces his claim that valuation must become subject to the method of intelligence. The basic point is that the traits disclosed through metaphysical analysis and manifested in existence of every kind – qualitative individuality, regular relations, contingency, need, movement and arrest – are traits of the same universe of nature in which man lives and of which he is a part. According to Dewey, the universality of the traits 'is source both of values and of their precariousness; both of immediate possession which is casual and of reflection which is a precondition of secure attainment and appropriation.'[84] Apart from the difficulty of seeing in exactly what sense the universality of these traits is a 'source' of value, the point Dewey was making is fairly clear. The task of criticism, of judgement and of valuation must be pursued within nature; if it is to be carried out in a rational way it must be informed by knowledge of what is. Metaphysics provides 'a ground map of the provinces of criticism'[85] and in so far as the traits disclosed are not separate but are 'intimately intermixed', matters of importance are essentially matters of the degrees and ratios of the mixture. To say, for example, that every existent has individual quality and is contingent is true enough, but it does not take us very far; to say that *this* existent has these traits is to initiate a series of questions about their relationships to each other and to still other traits. Although Dewey clearly meant to point to the togetherness of the traits plus the degree and type of their interrelation, the illustrations he offered actually point instead to the difference between the trait as universal and its manifestation in a specific situation. Thus, he said, merely to note the fact of contingency has nothing to do with wisdom, but to note contingency in relation to 'a concrete situation of life' is the beginning of wisdom. The principal point, however, remains; the problems of human concern which are at the same time the objects of criticism can be treated intelligently only if we have reliable knowledge of the general shape of the world in which they arise. The success or failure of philosophy as criticism is, then, a function of the adequacy or inadequacy of the metaphysics on which it is based.

As was indicated above, the discussion of the relation between metaphysics and philosophy led Dewey by an indirect route to the fundamental issue of the relationship between value and existence. The topic of this chapter may be brought to a conclusion by setting forth briefly the position he developed. The basic fact of the organism–environment polarity is said to contain the basic human predicament, namely, that the sustaining of life is not guaranteed in advance, but is dependent on adjustments, transformations and adaptations within a nature which both helps and hinders human effort. This predicament defines the actual situation of man and it becomes aware of itself, Dewey said, with the appearance of mind. At that level it becomes possible to pass beyond the 'coerced' adjustment of part to part which holds for the physical and biological levels, and to search for the meanings of things, to make plans and policies based on the known characters of objects and events and to anticipate future outcomes with the aim of transforming what is basically a precarious existence into something more stable. Dewey's naturalism here remains intact; he claimed that mind and knowledge do not break man's tie with nature but only modify it, whereas his standard complaint against modern idealisms was that they appeal to the fact of knowledge as a means of elevating man above nature or of establishing him as a kind of god within the natural order. On the premises of idealism, Dewey argued, man can no longer be seen as continuous with nature.[86]

More important, however, than the preservation of the outlook of naturalism is the matter of relating valuation to existence. Dewey's basic formula is quite clear and represents the principle which he applied throughout his thought. In existence the immediate corresponds to the quality of things and situations which are *had* or enjoyed; to pass beyond the immediate to knowledge requires mediation or the institution of inquiry (critical method) aimed at reaching warranted conclusions. These conclusions represent the qualification of the primary experience from which inquiry set out but they are not on that account immediate since they represent the outcome of a process. In the sphere of value, marked by interest, need, desire and the presence of alternatives in both judgement and action, the immediate corresponds to reports of what has been regarded as satisfying, pleasant, agreeable, and to what has been approved through authority, custom and tradition, including the judgements of previous philosophers and moral theorists. But just as, on Dewey's view, there is no immediate knowing, there is also no immediate valuation. In both cases, the immediate serves as a source of material shot through with problems which can be resolved only by instituting a critical process. To use the distinction central to his theory of valuation, when we say that something has been deemed *satisfying,* we do no more than report a fact, but this fact does not settle the problem of evaluation, it only serves as an occasion for raising the critical question: Can the *satisfying* also be judged as *satisfactory?* In short can actual preferences, likes, dislikes, approvals, etc., carry credentials that make it possible to discuss them critically? Dewey saw the fundamental error in subjective or emotive-type theories of value or ethics long before their heyday; if there is no disputing about 'tastes' that is only because a 'taste' is seen as nothing but a sheer personal reaction cast in the form of a pronouncement ('I dislike this wine'); if that is all that is expressed nothing more can be said. If, however, some ground, some reason, some condition is specified, critical discourse is possible as can readily be seen when the person adds, 'I dislike this wine because it has a bitter after-taste.' Dewey perceived that if the *conditions* of desires fulfilled or frustrated are specified, criticism can follow, whereas first-person reports of likings and dislikings considered in themselves are bits of autobiography which can never be discussed as evaluations. Consequently, he proposed the concept of the 'satisfactory' as the critical term. To say that something is satisfactory means that on the basis of (a) knowledge of what we want to achieve in a given situation – an 'end in view' – and (b) knowledge of the capacities and tendencies of whatever is to serve as means and instrumentalities, we can say that the item in question meets the conditions and satisfies the demand placed upon it. The satisfactory is what has been judged capable of fulfilling some purpose or of meeting some demand. In Dewey's language we say of the satisfactory that 'it will do' in the double sense of referring to a future outcome – 'it *will* do' – and to its fittingness to contribute to that outcome – 'it will *do*'.

In the end, Dewey's concern to connect metaphysics with philosophy understood as criticism was rooted in his contention that if subjectivism in evaluation and practical 'idealism' based merely on imagination are to be avoided, knowledge of the capacities and tendencies of things must serve as a foundation for judgement in all those situations – moral, religious, political, social, educational, etc. – involving ends and values. Criticism may not itself be knowledge in the strict sense, but it cannot be effectively carried out without knowledge of things and their tendencies. It is, moreover, not just scientific knowledge that is needed, but metaphysics or all the results of analyses aimed at disclosing the general shape of things. 'To note, register and define the constituent structure of nature,' Dewey wrote, 'is not then an affair neutral to the office of criticism, whose chief import is to afford understanding of the necessity and nature of the office of intelligence.'[87] Intelligence marks, for Dewey, the intersection of knowledge and wisdom; judgement based on intelligence stands higher than either knowledge or wisdom taken separately because judgement means the continual synthesizing and adjusting of value conceptions to our knowledge of existence and vice versa. Dewey repeatedly claimed that instead of perpetuating the traditional dualism between knowledge and action, philosophers should concentrate on the all-important difference between action which is 'fluid, slavish, meaningless' and action which is 'free, significant, directed and responsible'.[88] The difference between the two depends on the presence of reason or intelligence as an instrumental force. The assigning to reason of this instrumental role together with Dewey's repeated attack on a timeless reason not involved in contingency, have led critics to the conclusion that he denigrated reason and severely compromised its autonomy. This criticism is not without merit, but it is based on an assumption which needs to be examined. The fact is that on the American scene there has always been a strong tendency to express the value of something by showing that its presence makes an important difference, that we cannot get along without it; in short, that it performs an indispensable function. Dewey was fond of saying that people think they honour reason when, as it were, they put it in a glass case to be admired and contemplated, whereas the true regard for reason is shown by those who put it to work and who dare to follow its lead whenever action – including deliberation and judgement – is called for. Kant, it will be recalled, summed up the meaning of Enlightenment by adapting a motto from Horace – *sapere aude* – and giving it a characteristic twist. To Kant it meant 'Dare to use your own reason', and if we add to that the social dimension so prominent in Dewey's thought he and Kant were not far apart.

6 Pragmatism and religion

Too many thinkers on the American scene have either confused religion with morality or supposed that religion is, as Matthew Arnold put it, nothing more than morality tinged with emotion which means that religion has no distinctive character of its own. Royce long ago pointed out that the encounter between religion and science presents a less challenging problem than that posed by the rivalry between the religious and the moral. The latter pair are 'near relations' rather than total strangers and are thus capable of intimate conflicts. As Royce saw, scientific knowledge as such cannot be successfully turned into a substitute for religion, but morality as the earnest quest for self-realization readily appears as self-sufficient in its rational secularity by contrast with the uncertainties of religious belief in a sceptical age.

The general problem is of basic importance and it has a special significance not only for the pragmatists, but for American life at large. Failure to understand that religion and morality are closely related and quite distinct has led, on the one hand, to a graceless moralism often decried by critics from abroad as self-righteousness, and, on the other, to that fanaticism which stems from endowing contingent principles guiding human conduct with the divine authority associated with religion. The problem, therefore, of properly understanding the religious and the moral and of relating them to each other in a fruitful way is not a merely theoretical affair since failure to resolve this problem has clear and unfortunate consequences.

Two factors in the American situation have worked in the direction of dissolving the religious into the moral so that the distinctive nature and role of the former becomes obscured. Scepticism about the viability of religious concepts, and especially an anti-intellectualism which sets religion over against 'theology' taken in a pejorative sense, have resulted in the belief that religion must be conceived as a wholly 'practical' affair of moral principles and precepts. Moreover, disillusioning experiences with religious persecution in a pluralistic society has created an undercurrent of uneasiness about the potentialities for conflict between rival theologies and doctrinal systems. Thus Peirce, for example, could refer to theological creeds as 'the articles of war' from which the centrality of love had been expunged.[1] This uneasiness has often led to the ready acceptance of what appears to be a simple and obvious solution: dispose of the religious ideas and beliefs about which men dispute and concentrate instead on the task of becoming 'good men', a matter presumably upon which all are agreed regardless of religious creeds. Believers in this solution advise us to stop talking about sin and grace, and return to the Gospel of Jesus expressed in the Sermon on the Mount. The supposition is, of course, that this sermon consists entirely of moral prescriptions which are clear in themselves and need only to be put into practice without any involvement in theological discussion. That this supposition is false becomes obvious by consulting the text itself. 'Blessed are they that mourn: for they shall be comforted', for example, is not a moral prescription and, apart from interpretation in terms of other conceptions, such as the idea of God and of the Kingdom which Jesus preached, it makes no sense.[2] For as everyone who has studied any form of religion knows, it is not identical with morality. Religion concerns what one *is*, a pervasive quality of life and a total orientation of the person, whereas morality concerns what one is to *do*, and although it is obvious that the latter must be consistently related to the former, the two are not the same.[3] If one asks where the pragmatists stood as regards this issue, a clear but surprising answer can be given. In view of their common emphasis on action and on the construing of ideas in terms of behaviour and practical consequences, one would expect them to accept forthwith some version of religion which identifies it with rules and principles guiding conduct. Such, however, is not the case. Although James, Peirce and Dewey gave full weight to religious belief as an active force in human life and were far from underestimating its 'practical' importance, they saw its distinctive character *vis à vis* other aspects of experience. James, for example, in stressing such ideas as the reality of the unseen, the role of the subliminal self in conversion, and the difference made by the divine in the depths of the person, clearly felt that religion involves more than moral precept. Peirce, moreover, identified religion as a cosmic affair essentially bound up with evolutionary love and while he did not specifically include it in his triad of normative sciences – aesthetics, ethics and logic – it is internally connected with all three. Despite numerous disparaging words about theology, Peirce was by far the boldest of the pragmatists in the speculative direction, attempting to give meaning to some of the traditional attributes of God and setting forth a highly original argument for God which is surely one of the most interesting pieces of philosophical theology written in this century. Dewey, though anxious to separate the 'religious' in experience from 'religion' as a substantive reality and to minimize dependence on creeds, nevertheless did not understand the adjective in primarily moral terms, but associated it with the problem of unifying the self and with a living faith in an active relation between the actual and the ideal. The pragmatists were, to be sure, engaged in reworking traditional religious ideas and beliefs in the light of new information springing from a developing technological and increasingly secular culture. Consequently, they rejected much that had become established as part of the American religious heritage. They were determined, nevertheless, to treat the subject along basically empirical lines, allowing religion to disclose itself as a distinctive feature of human life; they did not seek to legislate in advance what its nature must be.

Since it is impossible to encompass within the confines of a chapter all that our three representative thinkers had to say about God, religion, religious experience, faith, etc., it will be necessary to select. The obvious and most relevant focus for discussion is the picture of religion which emerges when it is seen from a distinctively pragmatic standpoint. The Conclusion of James' *Varieties*, for example, expresses the consequences of conceiving God 'pragmatically', and Peirce was quite definite in connecting his anthropomorphic theism with Pragmatism. Dewey's *A Common Faith*, moreover, represents an analysis of religion which follows from his theory of experience and the application of empirical method, both of which find roots in his instrumentalist version of Pragmatism.

At the outset it is necessary to call attention to some problems and confusions that have arisen subsequent to James' introduction of 'religious experience' as a technical term in the *Varieties*.[4] The point is important because it might be thought that the pragmatic theory of religion rests in some peculiar sense on 'religious experience' understood as something psychologically specific. This is not so because Peirce did not use the term, and Dewey viewed it with suspicion. Since James discussed the nature of mysticism at some length and filled his pages with illustrations of experiences which have come to be identified as 'mystical' in a broad sense, it should not be surprising that the term 'religious experience' came to be synonymous with 'mysticism'. This development is unfortunate since religion is not coextensive with mysticism as a distinctive type of spirituality, and if 'religious experience' is to be retained as a fundamental concept it should not be identified with what is but one religious form among others. For, after all, James spoke of 'varieties' of religious experience, and he devoted attention to many religious situations not essentially mystical in character. There are, moreover, other difficulties with the term, since it has come to mean a subject–object complex in which a subject 'experiences' God as an object among others, much as a person 'experiences' a table or a chair. The problem attached to this conception, apart from its assumption that God can be conceived as an 'object', is that, as Whitehead correctly pointed out, there is no consensus of opinion about this sort of experience. This approach, moreover, perpetuates the subject–object view of experience to which the pragmatists were opposed. Nor is this all; Dewey attacked the conception of religious experience taken as analogous to the experience of sensible objects because of its use (or abuse) as a means of 'proving' the existence of God, and argued instead for the quality of the 'religious' in experience. This is not the place to settle the question of the viability of the concept of religious experience for the philosophy of religion; suffice it to say that the

F

concept must not be taken as a hallmark of the pragmatic interpretation of religion. The pragmatist held that religion and experience are intimately connected, but from that fact alone it does not follow that the connection is expressible solely in terms of 'religious experience'.

Many books which have established themselves as works of major importance nevertheless suffer the misfortune of partial appreciation and a failure on the part of readers to see them as integral wholes. James' *Varieties* furnishes an excellent example: the vivid first-person illustrations contained in the descriptive or 'phenomenological' part of the work have overshadowed the conclusions at which James arrived and have caused us to lose sight of the fact that these conclusions are not mere afterthoughts but represent his attempt to offer both a unifying formula for all the phenomena set forth and an hypothesis of a psycho-philosophical kind aimed at dealing with the problem of truth in religion. The characteristic beliefs and psychological consequences cited must be understood as inductive results derived from the facts adduced; James was not proposing his own 'definition' of religion to be developed dialectically, but rather claiming that religion is to be understood primarily through the situations whereby it discloses itself. The indispensable and generic characteristics of religion at which James arrived are that the visible world is seen as part of a wider spiritual universe from which it draws its significance; 'union' or some type of harmonious relationship with that unseen order is the true end of man; and prayer or inner communion is a process whereby the spiritual world makes itself felt in the world of ordinary experience. The latter belief is the one most closely associated with the 'pragmatic' interpretation of religion. The psychological features characteristic of those who have reached the 'faith state' take the form of a new zest or vitality which adds itself to life like a gift, together with a sense of assurance and peace expressing itself in loving affections to others.

In considering these results, James was entirely aware (as some philosophers of religion have not been) that the study of religion cannot be a substitute for the living reality since knowledge about a thing is not to be confused with the thing itself. But more importantly, and much to his credit, James realized that the psychological, anthropological and historical study of religion does not (except inadvertently and by implication) raise the question of the truth or validity of the religious outlook in the light of 'other sciences and general philosophy'. But it was precisely the latter question which James proposed to raise. Before coming to his fundamental hypothesis, he felt obliged to justify his own standpoint in relation to the scientific outlook of his time and especially to meet the frequently voiced objection that religion is outmoded and is no more than a carry-over from a pre-scientific era when superstition was unchecked by reliable knowledge of the world. James' defence is most significant because it reveals his tendency to think in terms of a basic tension between the religious stance and the standpoint of science, whereas Peirce by contrast based his Neglected Argument for God on an analysis of the conditions required for the success of scientific reasoning. The antithesis, however, is neither deep not ultimate since James was himself a person of considerable scientific training, and if one keeps in mind the context of the discussion it is clear that his major concern was not to attack science, but rather to argue that the interest of the individual in his destiny is a constant factor in human life and history, not to be ruled out simply because science has helped to disclose past connections between religion and superstition. On the other hand, James was strongly opposed to the claim that the personal viewpoint of the individual can be ignored or regarded as illusory merely because it is ignored from the standpoint of scientific objectivity.

The importance James attached to man's inner states which he described as 'our very experience itself', helps to explain why he so repeatedly elevated the purely individual and private above the social factor in religion, and why he made feeling basic and relegated conceptualization or 'theory' to a secondary status. Every phenomenon of conscious life appears in two contexts or dimensions, an impersonal and a personal; it can be studied, analysed, described and explained as 'any' phenomenon of that type without regard for the individual whose experience and personal history include it as a unique part of a unique biography. When we deal, said James, *'with private and personal phenomena as such, we deal with realities in the completest sense of the term'*.[5] By contrast, the cosmic and the general are but 'symbols' and devoid of what he called the 'unsharable feeling' or the 'pinch of his individual destiny' which a person has when he grasps an experience as an essential part of his own life. Regardless of the many dark chapters there have been in man's religious history, the religious concern persists in the form of concern for individual destiny and in that form it cannot be superseded because it belongs to the structure of human existence. Since James took feeling to be the distinguishing mark of individuality, it is no accident that his first conclusion is the identification of religion with *feeling*; by comparison, theories and doctrines are regarded as secondary. Feeling, moreover, is seen as immediate and thus as contrasted with thought and inference. Like Jonathan Edwards, James identified religion with having a 'sense' of some sort; he calls it a 'sthenic' affection or an excitement of a cheerful and expansive nature, which freshens vital powers, overcomes melancholy and gives to the subject a zest and a meaning transfiguring all ordinary objects and experiences. The 'faith state' is both psychological and biological; it performs an essential function since it is a foundation on which men live. Religion in this sense endures and will continue to do so precisely because it meets a universal need.

Now, were the popular conception of Pragmatism correct, there would have been no need for James to carry his analysis any further; religion is seen as meeting a specifiable human need successfully and no further questions of truth or validity are necessary. The discussion, however, does not follow this pattern in the least. Although James believed that the intellectual content of the faith-state may very well be 'minimal', he was fully convinced that it cannot be zero. Therefore, he moved on to the 'intellectual content' of religious experience in order to consider the question of its truth. This content is expressed as a general two-fold structure manifested in all historical religions. It consists, first, of a felt uneasiness or a 'sense that there is *something wrong about us* as we naturally stand', and, second, of a resolution or a 'sense that *we are saved from the wrongness* by making proper connection with the higher powers'.[6] In a passage remarkable for its unalloyed Hegelianism, James claimed that in so far as an individual 'suffers from' and 'criticizes' his wrongness, he is to that exent 'consciously beyond it' and in two directions at once. First, a 'better part' of the self comes into view at the moment of self-consciousness and with this self the individual identifies himself; secondly, he thinks of this better self as being continuous with 'more of the same quality' in the universe beyond.[7] This general scheme is adequate for interpreting all the phenomena associated with the divided self and its struggle, the surrender of the 'lower' self and the change of personal centre together with the sense that whereas the helping power is beyond individual consciousness one is nevertheless intimately related to it.

At this point the discussion takes a rather surprising turn: James admitted that all the experiences he had considered are 'only psychological phenomena' even though they have 'enormous biological worth' in sustaining life, and hence that it is necessary to raise the question of the 'truth' of the claim about the higher self and the 'more' of its quality in the surrounding universe. In a curious footnote,[8] James said that by 'truth' here he meant something additional to 'bare value for life', and yet he went on to claim that it is a 'natural propensity of man' to believe that whatever possesses this life-value is thereby certified as true. It is surely remarkable that whereas James on more than one occasion gave the impression that 'value for life' is indeed his only criterion, he was here looking for the 'something additional' which smacks of the very 'intellectualism' he repeatedly rejected in attacking rationalist opponents. The point concerns only the internal consistency of his approach, but it is important nevertheless because it shows, first, that James was not in fact content with an appeal to 'value for life', and, second, that he understood the inescapability of the question of truth or validity if there is to be a *philosophy* of religion in addition to the descriptive enterprise of phenomenology.

The philosophical task centres on the question of the reality of what James described as the 'more' which is continuous with the higher self and the sort of relationship to that reality which manifests itself in religious experiences. He hoped to provide a 'reconciling hypothesis' which would at one and the same time represent the result of an impartial study of religions and provide a point of contact with the scientific standpoint, something which James thought the theology of his time had failed to establish. The use of the term 'hypothesis' signals James' renunciation of any claim to be providing 'coercive' argument,[9] and hence it would be quite legitimate to say that he was closer to the Augustinian tradition of 'faith seeking understanding' than to those offering proofs for God. In framing a conception of the exterior power or unseen order to which the 'more' in experience refers, James was consistently following his programme of finding an interpretation which is neither parochial nor dogmatic. We cannot, he said, place ourselves at the standpoint of a particular theology – Christian, Jewish, Buddhist – because that would exclude other religions. The description of the union or communion of the self with the saving power, moreover, must be couched in terms sufficiently universal to be recognizable by psychologists studying religion from a scientific standpoint. Here James revealed his own background and bias; psychology is given a privileged position in the interpretation of experience. This selective emphasis stems both from the intimate involvement of the self in religion and the central role accorded to feeling for understanding religion in all its forms. With remarkable insight, James seized upon the concept of the 'subconscious self' as the mainstay of his resolution. The hypothesis is that whatever the 'more' may be on the 'farther' side of the relationship, on the 'hither' side it is the subconscious continuation of our conscious life. The two-fold virtue of this conception, as James saw it, is that it allows for a point of contact with scientific thought and does justice to the claim of theologians that an exterior power is involved since in the subconscious there is a sense of control from beyond the person which blunts any supposition that what happens is due solely to individual effort or will.

James could then present his account of 'the farther limits of this extension of our personality' as essentially an over-belief of his own, a fact which he candidly acknowledged. The central thesis now is: *'the conscious person is continuous with a wider self through which saving experiences come.'*[10] Religion as represented in the experience of the individual means being related to what James sometimes called a 'mystical' world which is not the visible one described and explained by science, but an unseen order or source of transforming power. It is about this unseen world that James made the characteristic claim which is at the heart of his 'pragmatic' interpretation in opposition to a number of idealistic conceptions which he rejected. The contention is that the unseen world is not 'merely ideal' in the sense of being no more than a meaning or an interpretative standpoint from which to view facts, but rather a source which *produces effects* in the everyday world. Referring to this mystical world, James wrote: 'when we commune with it, work is actually done upon our finite personality, for we are turned into new men, and consequences in the way of conduct follow in the natural world upon our regenerative change.'[11] And, he continued, what produces effects upon a reality must itself be a reality and not merely a conception to be entertained or contemplated. This over-belief contains the innermost kernel of James' 'piecemeal supernaturalism' and he insisted upon it in opposition to then current idealistic theories up-holding an Absolute or God who apprehends everything *totum simul* and seems to make no difference at particular points in the course of experience. He directed the same criticism against what he called 'universalistic' super-naturalism or the casting of a total divine blanket over a world which is otherwise left precisely the way it was before. In short it appeared to James that on all totalistic views God makes no difference. Since it is of the essence of James' Pragmatism to maintain that reality, truth, validity cannot be conceived except in terms of making a difference somewhere and some-when, it follows that his piecemeal supernaturalism and the particular new effects taking place in the world through regenerative change represent the core of his Pragmatism in religion. This part of his thought is more impor-tant than the much-publicized will to believe. It is not that believing under the well-defined conditions set forth in his famous essay is unimportant, but rather that there the emphasis stressed the way of approach rather than the substance. Piecemeal supernaturalism as James' final interpretation of the phenomena set forth in the *Varieties* is all substance, because it means nothing less than the construing of God in pragmatic terms as the power resolving the uneasiness which defines the human predicament for particular individuals at particular points in existence. For James, to be God is to be able to bring about these differences.

By contrast with the approach of James, Peirce's treatment of religion is more cosmic in its orientation, more speculative in nature and without the psychological element which was inevitable in someone of James' back-ground and interest. Where James saw a certain tension between religious faith and the scientific outlook, Peirce, holding fast to his version of Prag-matism, was bent on showing that a proper understanding of the operation of reason in science has close connections with the conception of God. Perhaps the most striking contrast between the two thinkers is to be found in their divergence over the social principle in religion. For James, religion is found in the consciousness of the individual, whereas Peirce, like Royce and Dewey, emphasized its social dimension in religious communities and the opportunity they afforded for the critical comparison and sharing of experience. Peirce, to be sure, attacked the conventionalism and exclusivism of churches and religious bodies, but his knowledge of Western church history together with his doctrine of evolutionary love led him to appreciate the role of continuing communities in transmitting past experience and in consolidating those perceptions of instinct and commonsense which he regarded as essential to religion. 'Religion,' he maintained, 'though it begins in a seminal individual inspiration, only comes to great flower in a great church coextensive with a civilization.'[12]

For Peirce, religion finds its roots in instinct and sentiment and it is necessarily derivative from experience. If a person has no experience or 'sense of' what religion is about, he will not overcome the deficiency merely by resorting to some explicit process of reasoning. In one place Peirce defined religion as 'a sort of sentiment, or obscure perception, a deep recognition of a something in the circumambient All'[13] together with an acknowledgement on the part of the individual that he stands related to this 'A and Ω' as a finite being. Because of the total involvement of the self in this relationship, religion belongs to what Peirce called 'vitally important topics'. A word of caution is necessary in dealing with the lectures assembled under that title,[14] because they express a divorce between instinct and reason, and between practical and theoretical concerns which scarcely does justice to Peirce's Pragmaticism and his doctrine of continuity. There is no doubt that Peirce saw religion as drawing its life primarily from instinct and sentiment, but it is also clear that the force of the distinction between instinct and reasoning expressed in the lectures of 1898 is exaggerated and not for purely philosophical reasons.[15] The point to be adhered to is that instinct, sentiment and direct perception are the seminal factors in religion; they point to an initial engagement of the self which does not allow for any theoretical distance. Despite the fact that Peirce spoke of religious *beliefs* as conceptions upon which one is prepared to act with risk, in comparison with the *opinions* of science which involve neither action nor risk, he was wary of identifying religion itself with belief because belief implies mediation and some theoretical distance. '. . . it is absurd,' he wrote, 'to say that religion is a mere belief. You might as well call society a belief, or politics a belief, or civilization a belief. Religion is a life, and can be identified with a belief only provided that belief be a living belief – a thing to be lived rather than said or thought.'[16] It would, however, be a great mistake to suppose that because in Peirce's view religion is founded on immediacies it also ends there. Were that the case most of what Peirce had to say on the subject could be ignored. Religion sets out from experience and instinctual perception as illustrated, for example, by his account of the way in which the hypothesis of God starts in musement and how in the end religious faith comes back to determine our conduct and the basic orientation of life. But between these two termini there is the activity of rational reflection which is aimed at interpreting and developing the implications of the experience with which the cycle began. Included in this body of reflection are Peirce's conception of evolutionary love, his *Credo* or personal expressions of belief about God, and, finally, his paper on the Neglected Argument. The latter is not only original in its main objective, but it reveals as well how clearly Peirce grasped the peculiar problem which religion – the offspring of immediacy and faith – presents to anyone seeking to justify it or make it intelligible through rational dialectic.

No one can succeed in harmonizing all that Peirce had to say about

God and religion, but, as with most of his philosophy, sustained reading reveals a persistent core of ideas which make it quite possible to draw defensible distinctions between this core and idiosyncratic statements. For example, when exasperated by the difficulty of making much headway against the initially high degree of vagueness in theological ideas, Peirce could speak of metaphysics and theology as 'gabble'; that this, however, was not his characteristic position can be seen from the careful attempt he made to analyse the conception of God's purpose, and the perceptive way in which he dealt with the distinction between 'reality' and 'existence' in his argument for God. Problems about Peirce's philosophy of religion there may be, but confusion there is not. His 'agapasm',[17] both as a practical gospel and as a technical account of evolutionary development is quite clear, his statement of beliefs about God is candid and free of hedging, and the Neglected Argument leaves one in no doubt as to what he hoped to show about the need for a coordinator of the universes and how experience and reasoning cooperate to bring about the result.

The theory of evolutionary love has two sides: on the one hand, it represents Peirce's reading of the Johannine theme that 'God is love' in opposition to the 'gospel of greed' while, on the other, it expresses a conception of evolutionary development which is distinct both from pure chance and from mechanical necessity. Peirce objected vigorously to every form of the doctrine which says that progress depends on everyone striving to realize his own interest and advantage regardless of what happens to his neighbour in the process. This idea is well known as 'Social Darwinism' and it has generally been supposed that it represents an application of the Darwinian conception of a biological struggle for existence to economic, political and social life. The fact is that, as Peirce correctly noted, the relationship should be reversed. The fundamental idea that private self-seeking results in universal benefit to society had already found clear expression in the early eighteenth century in Mandeville's *Fable of the Bees*. '*The Origin of Species*,' wrote Peirce, 'merely extends politico-economic views of progress to the entire realm of animal and vegetable life.'[18]

As against the philosophy of unqualified individual self-assertion – what Peirce called the 'gospel of greed' – he set the law of love or Gospel of Christ which says that we are to sacrifice our own perfection to that of our neighbour, and to merge our individuality in sympathy with the persons around us. Peirce was particularly exercised over the charge that those who reject the greed philosophy are merely 'sentimentalists' because he believed not only that the 'natural judgements of the sensible heart' should be respected, but that his agapasm had better rational foundations than the *laissez-faire* doctrines with their appeal to the workings of a natural harmony of self-seeking individuals. It should now be obvious that in this regard all the illusions were harboured by Peirce's opponents.

There is a particular feature of Peirce's concept of love which deserves mention because it plays an important role in his treatment of the modes of evolution and the relation between agapasm and the other two evolutionary forms, tychasm and anancasm. Love, Peirce maintained, has no proper contrary but embraces even what appears to negate it – hatred, for example – as an imperfect stage of itself. He was perceptive in every area about which he thought and wrote: no better illustration is needed than his noticing this point, one which many theologians have missed. 'The love that God is,' he wrote, 'is not a love of which hatred is the contrary; otherwise Satan would be a coordinate power.'[19] Whether the Bible contains any speculative solution to the classical problem of evil may well be doubted, but this much is certain: no ultimate dualism of coordinate powers – God and Satan – is countenanced. Satan remains a creature circumscribed by the divine love, a point which is expressed symbolically in the Book of Job where Satan is allowed every power over Job but that of life and death. Peirce drew on this tradition, defining the negative as a degenerate case which needs to be transformed by the circumambient power of a light which in itself contains no darkness. As a real power in the scheme of things, love creates independent beings and then moves to harmonize the workings of these creatures in relation to each other. As Peirce pointed out, this conception calls for the sympathetic acknowledgement of the other as a person and forbids the unbridled self-seeking prescribed by the greed philosophy. Peirce did not regard the utilitarian formula as the proper antidote to 'rugged individualism' because, as he said, love is directed to persons and not to abstractions of the sort represented by the 'greatest happiness for the greatest number'.

The essentially religious and ethical doctrine of love based on the Johannine formula was seen by Peirce in comprehensive terms having cosmological implications. 'Everybody can see,' he wrote, 'that the statement of St John is the formula of an evolutionary philosophy which teaches that growth comes only from love.'[20] And in his characteristically perceptive way he noted that this is not a simple doctrine of 'self-sacrifice', but rather a positive concern for the other – 'the ardent impulse to fulfil another's highest impulse'. Agapasm meant for Peirce a mode of evolution operative throughout the cosmos, and it is clear both from his statements and illustrations that it is in the growth of life and mind that the force of love is chiefly manifest. Thus it is not surprising that he claimed that evolutionary love is precisely the sort of development demanded by the doctrine of synechism, the core of which is his philosophy of mind.

One must bear in mind that in Peirce's time Darwinism was not yet firmly accepted and was by no means looked upon as a foregone conclusion requiring no further philosophical interpretation. The door was therefore open for speculation about the *nisus* of the evolutionary process and the relative merits of the different agencies or forces thought to be at work. Peirce recognized three modes of evolution each of which is operative to some extent in shaping the course of things but he regarded only one as adequate for explaining the cosmic process in its entirety.[21] The modes are evolution by fortuitous variation, sporting or chance; evolution by mechanical necessity, internal and external; and evolution by creative love. His discussion of these modes is applied to the historical development of human thought; one must, however, bear in mind that it presupposes much lengthier discussion in which he had treated the doctrine of necessity, evolutionary theories in relation to the physical world, and the place of mind in the cosmic scheme. The idealistic undercurrent of his synechism breaks out in full force in the philosophy of evolutionary love where the aim is to explain those habits most intimately connected with the growth of *ideas*. It is, therefore, entirely appropriate that he should turn to the development of religion and philosophy for the purpose of assessing the relative merits of the evolutionary modes. It is impossible not to see in all this Peirce's fascination with Hegel's attempt to lay hold of the 'logic' of temporal development – 'the whole idea of the theory is superb' – but whereas in the end Peirce rejected Hegel's system as a 'pasteboard model' he much approved of the enterprise it represented and was determined to arrive at a better resolution of the main problem with the aid of synechism and the logic of relatives. The irony, more evident as Peirce becomes better known, is that his religious and speculative ideas do indeed represent Hegelianism in a 'strange costume'. That costume, as is now clear, is a garment cut from tychism and agapasm, neither of which, in Peirce's view, is reached in Hegel's philosophy.

With regard to the growth of thought, tychasm means 'slight departures from habitual ideas in different directions indifferently'[22] which is to say that the development is constrained neither by external circumstances nor by logical pattern and hence that it issues in unforeseen results. Anancasm, by direct contrast, consists in new ideas 'adopted without foreseeing whither they tend',[23] but totally constrained by factors either external to the mind as part of the environment or internal to the mind as logical consequences. In neither case of anancasm is the primary focus on the ideas themselves as in agapasm where the adoption of mental tendencies takes place neither heedlessly (chance) nor blindly (necessity) 'but by an immediate attraction for the idea itself . . . by the power of sympathy, that is, by virtue of the continuity of mind'.[24] The illustrations of three ways in which this continuity manifests itself are not only instructive in themselves but give evidence as well of the utter indispensability of Peirce's idea of community as the foundation of logic and indeed of all that can be and be thought.

In these examples Peirce was thinking chiefly of the spread or suffusion of ideas in historical circumstances involving both individuals and communities. In the first place, he said, a habit of mind or thought may 'affect a whole people or community in its collective personality'[25] and as a result be communicated to individuals sufficiently in sympathy with that community to grasp the thought even if no one of them could have attained it through his or her individual understanding alone. The history of religion is filled with instances of the phenomenon Peirce had in mind. The cluster of ideas and beliefs which, for example, served as the basis of the ancient Hebraic religious community is older by far than the long line of individuals, beginning with Moses and lasting until the great prophetic figures of the eighth and seventh centuries B.C., who were affected by those ideas and sought to interpret their meaning. Amos did not 'invent' the concept of the divine justice, nor Hosea the concept of the divine forgiveness; each discerned the attitudes, habits, motives behind these notions within the context of an ongoing religious tradition and, through the medium of their particular experience, brought them to clear consciousness.

A second case cited has to do with an idea affecting an individual directly where the individual is able to apprehend it, 'or to appreciate its attractiveness' only in virtue of standing in a sympathetic relation to others. Peirce's example is the experience identified as the conversion of Saul in the New Testament; unfortunately, Peirce did not analyse his illustration but it is not difficult to understand what he had in mind. He was clearly thinking of the problem posed when one must interpret a vivid experience or a thought which comes suddenly to mind but is unable to appeal to some context of meaning or to a surrounding community of belief. Saul's celebrated experience on the Damascus road – the flash of light which momentarily blinded him and the sound of the accusing voice – might have been taken as no more than a fainting spell of no consequence had he not grasped and interpreted it in terms of an ancient tradition, alive and present in his consciousness, which reached back as far at least as Moses. That tradition was filled with records of personal experiences whereby men were called to be prophets or were 'converted' and thus reoriented in their direction and style of life to a new life and a new being. Peirce's point is that a purely 'private' experience unaccompanied by the interpretation of a community of ideas could make no sense. These ideas are not entirely internal nor are they the exclusive property of any individual; they come to a person as the result of sympathy and participation in a community of shared experience and belief.[26]

This aspect of Peirce's agapasm played a major role in his theory of the historical development of thought and it formed the basis of his belief in the reality of what others have called the 'spirit of an age'. Despite a confession of his inability to offer a 'cogent demonstration' of the thesis, Peirce was convinced 'that mere individual intelligence will not account for all the phenomena'[27] exhibited by the spread of an historical religious tradition or by the common thought patterns of an historical era. Part of the evidence he had in mind was culled, not from religious history, but from his extensive knowledge of the history of science. He took very seriously the many recorded instances of great ideas occurring simultaneously and independently to different individuals possessed of 'no extraordinary general powers[28] and he repeatedly insisted that the greatest of human intellectual achievements have invariably surpassed the powers of individuals supposedly working entirely within their own resources. To appreciate this contention is also to appreciate the force of Peirce's insistence on the reality of community as a distinct level of being. Community was not for Peirce an 'ideal' to be realized so much as a fact of a complex sort and he found it easier to doubt the reality of absolute individuality than the continuity of mind which a community represents.

Despite this insistence on the force of continuity in the growth of ideas, there is a third variety of agapasm which has to do with the actual occurrence of a significant or momentous idea to an individual. An idea, Peirce said, can affect an individual quite apart from his 'human affections' and solely in virtue of the 'attraction it exercises upon his mind'.[29] He called this phenomenon the *'divination* of genius' and attributed it to the continuity between the human mind and God as the coordinator of the three universes described in Peirce's cosmology. It is this idea of a correlation between the natural light of reason and the structure of things which is at the root of the Neglected Argument, a fact giving further evidence of the continuity of Peirce's own thought. There is no inconsistency in his maintaining both that ideas occur to individuals and that their growth depends on a community or social continuity of thought. Every individual finds himself living as a part of some community or tradition of thinking, and, moreover, no novel idea especially is ever fully comprehended by an individual in an immediate flash of insight. Interpretation is required and, as Peirce repeatedly pointed out, interpretation is a temporal process involving a series of ideas each of which represents the significant interpretation of its predecessor.

Attention was called earlier to Peirce's claim that love does not stand related to hatred as its contrary or coordinate opposite but rather embraces the negative as a degenerate case and seeks to transform it into a likeness of itself. He availed himself of this principle in his attempt to show that tychastic evolution with its fortuitous variation – the seeming contrary of the purposiveness of agapasm – is a 'degenerate case' of agapasm and therefore cannot be regarded as its opposite. 'Tychastic evolution,' he wrote, 'like the agapastic, depends upon a reproductive creation, the forms preserved being those that use the spontaneity conferred upon them in such wise as to be drawn into harmony with their original, quite often the Christian scheme.'[30] The difference between the two evolutionary modes, however, consists in the fact that the progress of evolution as envisaged by tychasm depends on the distribution among the survivors of the talents possessed by those who have been rejected, whereas, according to agapasm, the growth or progress is due to 'a positive sympathy among the created springing from continuity of mind'.[31]

It is difficult, if not impossible, to reconcile all that Peirce wrote about the modes of evolution. It is clear that he personally regarded agapasm as the most adequate theory and the account of change most consistent with the rest of his thought. It is equally clear, however, that he did not think of his doctrine as having been 'proved', although he was convinced that there is good evidence in its favour. Tychasm and anancasm, moreover, even though they are conceived as 'degenerate' cases, enjoy some tenure in the cosmic scheme; indeed were this not the case it would be difficult to explain his own illustrations of the operation of these modes. His account, for example, of the development of the Christian attitude towards the world starting with the Gospel of Mark which betrays no animus against a wicked world, passing through the bitterness expressed against all but a small portion of the human race in the Apocalypse, and ending with the utter rejection of philosophy and secular culture to be found in the writings of the Latin Church Father Lactantius (*c.* A.D. 320), is set forth as an extended instance of a *tychastic* development within the history of religious thought.[32] The reason for describing this development as tychastic has to do with a contrast between the outcome of a line of thought and the ideas at the root of its development. Wherever human thought is found to move by 'imperceptible degrees' in a way contrary to the purposes which animate that thought and against the highest impulses of the thinkers involved, a tychastic action is at work. Though chance is manifested in a development of this sort the process itself is intelligible because we can trace the movement whereby the diametrically opposed belief is reached, a fact which distinguishes tychasm from anancasm where a given habit of thought is overthrown cataclysmically and a more powerful habit takes its place.

Though an opponent of necessity as a cosmic doctrine, Peirce nevertheless acknowledged the working of anancastic evolution (both internal and external) even if he entertained doubts about some of the examples one might cite to illustrate the point. Brute force or 'plain war' – a relation bordering on pure secondness – stands at one end of the spectrum and forms a limiting case of external influence on people's minds. The fact is that no case involving ideas and opinions could be a matter of pure secondness from Peirce's standpoint because signs are necessarily involved and hence thirdness. A belief imposed by sheer authority – if such there be – and unaccompanied by a grasp of at least a minimal rationality upon which it might be based, could be regarded as a case of external anancasm. At the other end of the spectrum there is internal necessity constraining thought, a form of anancasm which Peirce thought was represented by Hegel's logic and the process whereby he developed an internally consistent system of categories which 'must' follow each other in a determinate order. Between these two poles stands the growth of thought under the constraint of facts or evidence. Peirce regarded this case as ambiguous in that the externality of the facts would seem to indicate *external* anancasm, and yet he was too much aware of the actual development of science to suppose that even there the sheer force of evidence simply produces knowledge as a necessary outcome.[33] The development of ideas consequent upon the study of external fact was said by Peirce to be on the 'border' between the two forms of anancasm. This view should not be surprising since it reflects the delicate balance of Peirce's whole philosophy on the boundary between realism and idealism.

Despite his acknowledgement that the modes of chance and necessity do actually manifest themselves in the evolutionary process, it seems clear that Peirce regarded their scope and explanatory power as limited by comparison with evolutionary love. Tychasm and anancasm are adequate for making intelligible local weather conditions, as it were, for relatively short periods, but only agapasm truly expresses the cosmic weather and the drift of the evolutionary process itself over the entire distance. It is in this sense that the other modes are contained within the pattern of the whole, not as coordinate forms but as degenerate cases. The striking fact about Peirce's agapasm and one which sheds light on his Pragmatism as a whole is that while agapasm first makes its appearance in the form of a religious belief and orientation, it is not left in that more immediate form but is made instead to serve as the basis of an evolutionary doctrine embracing not only the cosmos but human history as well. This is a far cry indeed from the avowal of the thesis that 'all thought is for the sake of action'.

Turning now to Peirce's *Credo*,[34] the first point to be noticed is that it has been almost entirely neglected in studies of his thought. The neglect is undoubtedly due to a sense of incongruity and even of disbelief in the face of the fact that a 'scientific' philosopher so deeply involved in logic and mathematics should have directed his attention to matters theological. And yet the fact remains; it remains, moreover, because of Peirce's regard for experience and openness of mind. He did not refuse to deal with any topic merely on the ground that some theory precludes it in advance. There is more in the *Credo* than can be discussed here, but concentrating on the first article, 'The Reality of God', will suffice for focusing at least three ideas basic to his entire philosophy. One is the idea of vagueness, and the other two concern the place of instinct and instinctual belief in religion, and the force of the distinction between *existence* and *reality*. These topics are significant not only in their own right, but also because they further clarify the bearing of Peirce's Pragmatism on the philosophy of religion.

The distinction between reality and existence figures largely in Peirce's thought and was by no means introduced solely for dealing with the question of God. In accordance with his categorial scheme, existence is manifested in secondness or action and reaction of something 'with other like things in the environment',[35] so that whatever 'exists' in this sense is an item among others in a system of reciprocal relations of the sort indicated in Kant's third analogy. Peirce was quick to perceive that no theologian of the Western religious tradition had ever thought of God as 'existing' after the fashion of an object among other objects in such a reciprocal system. Following the usage of Duns Scotus, Peirce insisted on the terms 'real' and 'reality', understanding them to mean, in contrast to figments, 'that which holds its characters on such a tenure that it makes not the slightest difference what any man or men may have *thought* them to be . . . the real things characters will remain absolutely untouched'.[36] Existing is a way of being in Peirce's view to think interms of the occupancy of a place among in Peirce's view to to think in terms of the occupancy of a place among others in a limited system.[37] Unfortunately, too many discussions about God have been vitiated at the outset because no attempt is made to consider the sort of being appropriate in this case; instead, the usual procedure is simply to assume the familiar concept of existence applicable to tables and chairs. The difficulty, moreover, is not confined to discussions about God because the assumptions of the familiar concept invite such questions as: Does the self exist? Do numbers exist? Do nations exist? etc., and there is no denying that many philosophers would rather accept the paradox of answering these and similar questions in the negative than re-examine their assumptions about existence.

Peirce was circumspect not only about the matters of reality but also about the concept of God itself. He refused to substitute the favourite expression of eighteenth-century thinkers, 'Supreme Being', for the term 'God' and for two reasons: first, because the two are not equivalent in that the former implies only being and supremacy, thus omitting other connotations, and, second, 'God' is a vernacular word. All such words, in Peirce's view, have two outstanding characteristics: they are *vague,* and they are *better understood* than other words. These two features are crucial for Peirce's doctrine of God because they involve both his Pragmatism and his 'critical commonsensism'. For Peirce, it must be remembered, *all* terms are to some extent vague; no term is absolutely precise or determinate in all respects, and no term whatever is absolutely vague. 'Critical commonsensism' lives on a continuous spectrum of the more or less vague and the more or less precise. The degree of vagueness or precision depends on the subject matter and the purpose at hand. Peirce regarded the word 'God' as the vaguest term in use, but he also believed that it is precisely in virtue of this vagueness that the term functions effectively in the expression of an instinctual perception and belief.

Peirce had much to say about vagueness, but he returned ever and again to the same two points;[38] in so far as a concept, sign, representation is vague, to that extent the principle of contradiction does not apply to it. With respect to the term 'animal', taken in a vague sense, it is false neither that an animal is male, nor that it is female. Any proposition is either true or false when its identity has been determined, i.e. when the meaning of the constituent concepts has been made explicit to a high degree, but the condition does not hold in so far as these constituents remain vague. The second consideration with regard to vagueness is that a vague sign is one which reserves for some other sign or experience the task of completing the determination with the exception of generality; in this case the task falls to the interpreting mind. This much may be called the logic of vagueness; it remains to be supplemented by what might be called the Pragmatism of vagueness. This part of the doctrine concerns the relation between the degree of precision possible and necessary in a given case to be determined by the purpose involved or the end in view. It might be supposed (a philosopher's natural assumption) that in every case the one requirement is to substitute precision for vagueness but on Peirce's view this is not so. With respect to discourse about God, he held, the vague, vernacular term 'God' serves its purpose well and certain attempts to make it more precise not only change its meaning but lead to contradictions as well.

Such a view may indeed seem surprising, especially for a thinker who is known to many chiefly through his attempt to show how ideas are to be 'made clear'; if, however, one takes into account the religious context under discussion, the surprise vanishes because Peirce's view brings out genuine features about belief in God invariably overlooked by those who have no great concern for the subject matter except in so far as it provides material for 'logical analysis'. The point on which Peirce insisted is that there are instinctive beliefs which are 'far more trustworthy than the best established results of science'[39] but which are necessarily couched in vague terms and cannot be rendered more precise without bringing about confusion and contradiction. The appreciation of this point is dependent on a willingness to take seriously the actual situation within which beliefs come into being and perform their function once they have become established. No one is likely to dispute the claim that the term 'God' is a paradigm of vagueness, but the case is not unparalleled as is shown by Peirce's example of the deep-seated belief in the presence of order in the cosmos. On the one hand there are, as Peirce said, no laboratory experiments which provide a more secure foundation for this belief than that provided by instinct and common-sense and, on the other, if anyone proposes to specify *precisely* what 'that order consists in', he will be unable to find adequate logical support. The belief, nevertheless, persists as part of the stock of commonsense beliefs which are so pervasive that only an undaunted Cartesian could claim to doubt them.

The application of this point to belief in God is both novel and arresting it may even be said to form something of a test case for Peirce's variety of Pragmatism. Like James, Peirce wanted to take fully into account the actual situation in which a belief arises and takes hold of an individual; an abstract 'logic of belief' without a believer does not suffice. Following this line led Peirce to claim that 'pretty nearly everybody' believes in the reality of God, understood in a certain sense, if they are clear and candid concerning what they do not in fact have firm grounds for doubting and hence actually believe. As will become clear in the succeeding analysis, Peirce's case for belief in God's reality rests on instinctual foundations; it is a belief which wells up almost against one's will when one contemplates the constitution of the universe and the coordination of its parts. The question which seems inevitable at this point (and perhaps it, too, has instinctive roots) is: Can the matter really be that simple? Centuries of discussion and controversy about the nature and reality of God seem to suggest either that the belief is ill-founded, or that it can be maintained only with the most astute and overwhelming arguments. According to Peirce's Pragmatism, however, belief in God is an instinctive one which no one can doubt in the strong sense of doubt which goes beyond doubt on paper, principle or programme.[40] Nevertheless, no dialectically oriented philosopher is likely to be comfortable with this view as it stands because of an ineluctable sense that if the belief is to be maintained something 'better' and 'more rational' than an appeal to instinct must be found. This sense may represent a form of the philosopher's fallacy, but it is difficult to stifle. No better illustration of the problem can be found than that given by Peirce in his assessment of what Hume accomplished with his philosophy. According to Peirce, Hume showed that one winds up with 'silly paper doubts' if one proposes to set commonsense aside and be 'perfectly rational'. Reasoning is illegitimate or 'unreasonable' not when it is bad reasoning or is based on faulty premises because both can be corrected. Further reasoning is illegitimate when we reach a proposition which is perfectly satisfactory and beyond suspicion. Peirce's point is that since Hume, on his own admission, had arrived at premises perfectly satisfactory to himself there was nothing more for reason to do. 'But,' said Peirce, 'he seems to be dissatisfied with himself for being satisfied'[41] and it is precisely this dissatisfaction which represents the desire to 'improve' on commonsense or to provide for it a dialectical support with which it is not naturally endowed. Peirce was not free of this desire himself and indeed it is difficult to see how any philosopher really can set it aside, for if one rests his thought with commonsense it is always 'in the end' that one does this, i.e. as the result of a dialectic in which other foundations are shown to be less reliable. Peirce was very much aware of the tension between instinct, commonsense and direct perception on the one hand, and the force of reasoning on the other. It is in fact one of the subtleties of the Neglected Argument that it was meant to do justice to both sides by providing *rational grounds for holding that the deliverances of direct perception are trustworthy.* Before considering that discussion, however, it is necessary to consider Peirce's account of the manner in which the idea or hypothesis of God comes about in the first place, for, as he repeatedly claimed, in every case it is abduction which sets the process of critical thought in motion.

What Peirce had to say about the rise of the idea of God in his *Credo* is very close to the account set forth at the beginning of the Neglected Argument. One is to begin by contemplating the physical universe from a vantage point which Peirce called 'musement'. Musement is perhaps more a mood or attitude than a point of view, and it is animated by the purpose of casting aside all special or serious purposes in order to be open to the pheno-

menon of the universe as it presents itself on a clear night with an uninter-
rupted expanse of stars. This encounter provokes both wonder and thought;
wonder at the simplicity of the solar system in comparison with the vast
number of dark bodies in existence and thought of the amazing intelligence
exhibited by the lower animals and even by insects to say nothing of the
human mind together with the even higher level of intelligence which may
perhaps exist on other planets. In the course of such musement, said
Peirce, 'the idea of there being a God over it all'[42] will be suggested and
may even seem to impress itself upon the mind as the natural outcome of
'drinking in' such thoughts. One must not at this point suppose that musement and its fruit is meant to be a cosmological proof for God; musement
represents only the abductive stage in which the hypothesis of God presents
itself. The assessment of that hypothesis is the aim of the paper on the
Neglected Argument.

Peirce's idea of God is not only frankly anthropomorphic but he
insisted as well on the inescapability of the fact because we are forced to
think within the limits of human experience. Hence he did not hesitate to say
that there is no more adequate way to conceive of God than 'as vaguely like
a man'.[43] And, in attempting to convey what a pragmaticist means by 'God',
Peirce appealed to an 'analogue of a mind' capable of influencing one's
entire life and conduct. Contemplation and study of the universe, like
extended acquaintance with a man of great character, results in our coming
under the sway of his mind. The ability to predict the course of nature
which is the fruit of scientific knowledge is, for Peirce, 'proof conclusive'
that we can catch a fragment of God's thought even if we cannot literally
think any of his thoughts. The question, moreover, whether there really *is*
such a being is the same for Peirce as the double-edged question whether
physical science is no more than a figment of the human mind, and whether
those whose conduct has been determined by contemplation of the universe
in all its dimensions are in touch with a truth beyond what can be seen and
handled. Peirce characteristically discounted the force of argument in favour
of the force of love precisely because the appeal is to instinct which is
either above or below the argumentative level. Peirce was so convinced of
the essential rightness of his approach that it seemed to him impossible for
anyone to consider the universe seriously in the mood of musement and not
come to the same conclusions concerning God which he had reached himself. Such an approach is in the end not a dialectical one but rather an
invitation in an empirical and pragmatic mode to see for oneself how the
matter stands. There can be no question that Peirce did not lay great store
by coercive proof in the sphere of religion; nevertheless, despite the ultimacy
he accorded instinct and direct perception, he did not leave either without
a peculiar kind of dialectical support.

Not many modern thinkers have felt as acutely as did Peirce the
special problem posed for the religious consciousness of harmonizing

experience and thought. Without participation or personal engagement the religious dimension of life does not come into view; to this extent the Pascals, the Kierkegaards and the John Wesleys are correct. On the other hand the varieties of religious experience are such that uninterpreted and unsifted phenomena – the sheer 'encounter' insisted upon by some contemporary theologians – cannot be left unsupported; they require not only an interpreting word but some ground for believing in their authenticity as disclosures of a reality transcending individual consciousness. The peculiar problem presented by religion is that whatever dialectical support is forthcoming must not take the form of a *substitute* which renders experience and participation unnecessary. The scientist, secure in his reasoning, may, as in the famous case of Einstein's unconcern for the eclipse which helped to establish his theory, regard the experience as secondary, but in religion that would be disastrous because experience is the heart of the matter. In short, as Peirce well knew, whatever reasons there may be must be *reasons* for believing in the trustworthiness of experience, not *reasons* which make that experience superfluous. This point is nicely illustrated in Peirce's ingenious article, 'A Neglected Argument for the Reality of God' which first appeared in the *Hibbert Journal* of 1908.[44] Unfortunately, a full-scale treatment of that paper is beyond our scope; much however can be learned from attending to its bearing on the important relation between experience and reasoning to be found in any discussion about God.[45]

To begin with, Peirce distinguished an 'argument' from an 'argumentation' and, while this distinction does not play as significant a role as one might have been led to expect, it is important in its own right.[46] An argument is defined as *any* process of thought 'reasonably tending to produce a definite belief', and an argumentation is an argument proceeding on 'definitely formulated premises'.[47] An argument, therefore, can proceed with vague terms and it can include the meditative development of an idea which is properly neither deductive nor inductive but is aimed at the formation of an hypothesis. The discussion falls into three parts: it starts with musement or a meditation on the three universes of experience, their wonders and their connections, issuing in the hypothesis of God's reality; it passes on to *the* 'N.A.' which is in fact a commentary on the initial process of reasoning (called by Peirce the Humble Argument) and some implications, and ends with a study of scientific methodology which involves a comparison between the thought process of the muser in the first stage and man's general capacity for framing hypotheses which are testable and thus lead to scientific knowledge. The central point which must not be missed in this whole complex discussion is that the second and third processes of reasoning, but especially the second, are meant to furnish rational support for the trustworthiness of the first process – the Humble Argument – *but they do not and cannot take its place.*

Musement is a kind of 'pure play' of the mind which, on the one hand, is guided by the object of contemplation, and, on the other, progresses in accordance with the 'attentive observation' of the muser and the direction which his internal conversation assumes. The object of musement in the context of religion is the origin and growth of the three universes together with the relations and coordinations which exist between them. These universes, largely parallel to Peirce's three categories, are 'mere Ideas' or possibilities, the brute actuality of things and facts, and signs or the active power to establish connections between objects and minds. The muser is in a state of 'wondering' about the relevant togetherness and coherence of these three universes in a cosmic scheme, and his wondering is to be unfettered by any philosophical 'oracles' such as 'whatever is, is a sensible singular', or 'it is not the business of science to search for origins', etc. Peirce's injunction 'Do not block the road of inquiry' is in full force where musement is concerned. In addition to contemplating the variety to be found in each universe, the muser will attend to the homogeneities and connections both within and between the universes, and thus will encounter the unmistakable fact of growth as a type of occurrence found in all three universes. 'This,' said Peirce, 'is a specimen of certain lines of reflection which will inevitably suggest the hypothesis of God's reality.'[48] It is not that these phenomena could not be explained by chance plus a small 'dose of a higher element', but that such an explanation would itself need to be explained, a regress which is halted by the concept of God as *Ens necessarium*, or the ultimate, purposive ground of each universe.

The foregoing line of meditation and reflection Peirce called the Humble Argument because it is capable of entering into the experience of *anyone* who will follow the track of musement and is by no means confined to the learned. He could not, of course, maintain that everyone *must* come to this insight because that would run counter to the empirical appeal to what one in fact does apprehend under particular circumstances. But there is no question that Peirce regarded the continuity of commonsense and instinct to be sufficiently powerful to lead the 'normal man' who meditates sincerely not only to entertain the hypothesis but to be so stirred by it that he will endeavour to shape his entire life in accordance with the idea that the coordination and growth of the universe is purposive. This consequence is precisely what, according to Peirce's Pragmatism, is meant by the person's *believing* the proposition in question.

There are few, including James, who have been as acutely aware of the subtle interlacing of the logical and psychological or experiential aspects of this central religious belief. The Humble Argument traces out a meditative and reflective pattern which must be undergone and not merely read about; for the muser it is meant to induce a sense that the cosmic scheme cannot 'just have happened' but is the expression of a coordinated purpose. And as Peirce pointed out, the initial conviction is likely to be so powerful that further critical reflection will almost certainly be stifled. Peirce might have left the matter there, siding in all things 'with the mob',[49] and in a quite specific sense he did just that. The first article of faith is an instinctive affair, and in view of this fact Peirce regarded the Humble Argument as the essence of living belief. But in an equally specific sense, he did not leave the matter there and the next step in his reflection shows his true originality. Peirce saw that in religion sincere appeals to experience and seeing for oneself cannot be forced; they cannot be determined by what one *must* see, and for this reason he was prepared to leave the Humble Argument intact as a meditation in which all may engage. It is, however, possible to make the process of thought involved in the Humble Argument an object of further analysis and reflection in order to see whether it exhibits traits characteristic of processes of thought in other contexts. The Neglected Argument – the second argument in the 'nest' – is Peirce's original contribution to this discussion. His argument points out that the Humble Argument is the natural fruit of free meditation and is thus an illustration of man's instinctive general tendency in retroduction – the spontaneous conjectures of instinctive reason which are the only source of advance in knowledge in that they alone furnish what deduction and induction work together to test – to apprehend and embody ideas in theoretical cognition. The Neglected Argument, then, is a commentary on the Humble Argument and asserts that the latter represents the results of the same attunement between reality and the human mind which makes all science possible. 'There is a reason, an interpretation, a logic,' Peirce wrote, 'in the course of scientific advance, and this indisputably proves to him who has perceptions of rational or significant relations, that man's mind must have been attuned to the truth of things in order to discover what he has discovered.'[50] One must not suppose that Peirce had fallen back into the traditional cosmological argument for God based on the cause-and-effect relationship; it is essential to note what he said about the relation between the initial meditative process leading to the hypothesis of God and the argument concerning the attunement of the human mind and reality. About the Neglected Argument he said, 'Of course, it could not, any more than any other theological argumentation, have the value or the religious vitality of the Humble Argument; for it would be only an apology – a vindicatory description – of the mental operations which the Humble Argument actually and actively now set in a wider interpretative context which is further expanded by the lives out.'[51] The Humble Argument retains its experiential force, but it is third process of reasoning leading to the discovery that this argument is 'nothing but an instance of the first stage' of scientific discovery, 'the stage of observing the facts, or variously rearranging them, and of pondering them until, by their reactions with the results of previous scientific experience, there is "evolved" an explanatory hypothesis'.[52]

Throughout the entire discussion there is no hint whatever that the musement which gives birth to religious insight is to be superseded by any argument. What the arguments do is to provide critical grounds for holding that the meditative process and its outcome in the Humble Argument are trustworthy in virtue of the fact that they represent the same working of the mind which is necessary for the attainment of scientific knowledge. The religious significance of this approach will be lost, however, if the initial stage of musement is passed over and the second and third arguments are taken by themselves as constituting but another form of a theistic argument from design or purposive adaptation. The pragmatic context of the entire discussion was underlined by Peirce in his comparison of the hypothesis of God with hypotheses advanced in non-religious contexts. In the first place when an idea such as the idea of God springs from the intimate experience of musement the force of conviction is likely to be so great that further justification will seem superfluous, a marked contrast to strictly scientific inquiry. Secondly, the hypothesis of God is so vague that only in exceptional cases can experiential consequences of the sort required of scientific explanations be derived from it. As Peirce pointed out, however, the force of the difficulty is counterbalanced when one considers that this hypothesis has 'commanding influence over the whole conduct of life of its believers'[53] something which is not true of avowedly theoretical hypotheses. All life may be subject to the cosmic habits of the environment, but no one determines the quality and orientation of life in accordance with the kinetic theory of gases. Religious belief in Peirce's view is not scientific knowledge but neither is it mere fancy, wish-fulfilment or the expression of 'emotion'. Religion is rooted in instinct and commonsense and its central belief comes to consciousness through the same process of retroduction which is the ultimate source of all scientific knowledge. In the end Peirce's view goes beyond and between the two alternatives which are generally regarded as exhaustive. Religion rests neither on sheer immediacy of experience, nor on the proofs for God's existence stemming from classical theism. There is a third alternative which brings together the two extremes and Peirce's thought represents this alternative with clarity and force. Religion is founded on experience, meditation and direct perception but that experience needs to be properly interpreted and dialectically developed. Instinctive belief, for Peirce, is wiser than it knows and that wisdom is brought to light and articulated in the Neglected Argument. Neither experience as instinctive belief nor dialectical thought is sufficient by itself. Without the Humble Argument the Neglected Argument falls to the level of 'apologetic', but without the Neglected Argument the Humble Argument will not sustain itself in the face of criticism.

Dewey's interpretation of religion or more properly his theory of the religious in experience represents something quite different from what is to be found in either James or Peirce. In contrast with the former, Dewey placed little or no emphasis on the first-person experience which James took to be the essence of religion in all its forms. Making such experience central appeared to Dewey as a prime example of the psychological bias which he not only regarded as the hallmark of modern philosophy but which he constantly struggled to avoid in his own thought. On the other hand Dewey had no such speculative concern, as did Peirce, to consider the cosmological implications of a basic religious idea. By the time Dewey came to devote special attention to religion and the religious in *A Common Faith* (1934)[54] he had already fully developed a naturalistic and pluralistic metaphysics strongly opposed to many traditional religious ideas such as that of a transcendent reality, a ground of being, or a beginning and ending for nature. Dewey's task in interpreting religion pointed in another direction; it was to find for religion a predominantly experiential meaning within the life of man and the confines of his world, both physical and cultural. His view is by no means a reductionist one, despite its appearing in that guise to many of his opponents. The reason it is not lies with his notion of 'the religious' and his attempt to lay hold of a distinctive dimension of experience not to be reduced to any other. This notion merits the centre of attention largely because it is positive and constructive in character and intent; it must not become obscured or over-shadowed by the polemical atmosphere Dewey frequently created whenever his thought turned in the direction of religion. He was critical, and often with good reason, of traditional religious beliefs and practices; as a consequence those favourably disposed towards religion were inclined to engage him on polemical grounds and thus to lay greater stress on what he opposed than on his own positive contribution to the understanding of religion and its role. This unfortunate consequence can be avoided if all concerned would bear in mind the two focal points which proved to be the most sensitive issues between Dewey and his critics.

First, Dewey, like many other thinkers on the American scene, tended to speak in wholesale fashion about 'organized religion' and usually in highly critical terms. Anyone acquainted with the history of religion, and especially the story of strife, war, contention, persecution, inquisition and bigotry which forms an undeniable part of that history, knows what Dewey was opposing when he spoke disparagingly of 'organized religion' and anyone who takes religion seriously must join with Dewey in that opposition. On the other hand, it is quite naïve to ignore the social character of religion and to suppose that it is found in pristine form only in the depths of the individual soul without dependence on enduring institutions and their structures. All institutions are subject to corruption, not because they are institutions, but because they are controlled by fallible and corruptible men; the irony is that, in principle at least, this truth is best known to the religious traditions themselves, both East and West, but it is not often self-applied due to the inveterate tendency of leaders in church and synagogue to pass judgement more readily on other institutions than on their own. The fact is that no spiritual or cultural form can avoid 'organization' and while it is always necessary to judge religious institutions in terms of their concern to engender and sustain authentic individual piety, it is absurd to suppose that religious institutions can be discarded as if they performed no distinctive functions of their own. That would be like proposing to abandon all political machinery because it is 'corrupt' in order to establish government on 'good citizens' alone. Dewey's wholesale rejection of organized religion led critics to believe that he was underestimating the force and complexity of a very difficult problem and this had the effect on many of weakening the impact of his positive contribution to the reintepretation of religious faith.

The second issue is more complex and its implications are far-reaching as regards the connection between religion and naturalistic metaphysics. One of Dewey's major concerns was to free 'the religious' in experience from institutional authority and at the same time to banish the supernatural. Objectionable, however, as simple conceptions of the supernatural may be, on theological no less than naturalistic grounds, Dewey does not convince us, as James and Peirce do, that he was aware of the subtlety and difficulty of the problem he was addressing. The concept of the supernatural in the sense of God as an object over and above the total system of things and powers denoted by the term 'nature' developed in modern thought against the background of Newtonian mechanics and the conception of nature as a mechanical system. In accordance with the widespread doctrine known as the 'chain of being', nature stood as an identifiable reality distinct both from man and God. Since God could not be identified as one object among others 'in nature', a place outside of nature seemed to be the only other possibility and the result was a simple form of supernaturalism. It is important to notice, however, that this conception makes no sense without the presupposition of a precisely defined nature, whether the definition be given in terms of *substance* or in terms of the *method* by which natural events are known. For if nature has no bounds, it is futile to speak of a reality which is 'above' or 'beyond' it. The difficulty, however, is that the idea of a closed, mechanical system was precisely the conception of nature which Dewey was attacking. Nature, for Dewey, is nothing of the kind, and in fact it is in his view not an exclusively physical affair at all. He was using the term in a distinctly philosophical sense to mean something similar to the classical term 'being' – taken in a distributive sense – or to substance. In the end, nature was, for Dewey, whatever can be disclosed in experience or be grasped through empirical method. The question which naturally arose was: How, on this revised concept of Nature, can any problem of the supernatural even be posed, or, if it does arise, has the problem not been resolved merely by changing the meaning of words? The point here is not to pursue this extensive question as such, but to see how its appearance engendered both confusion and conflict between Dewey and his critics. To many it seemed that he was trading on a fundamental ambiguity; against supernaturalism, he availed himself of the classical conception of nature and declared the exhaustiveness of nature in this sense to the obvious exclusion of any being or power beyond it. Yet, on the other hand, it did not seem consistent for Dewey to invoke for critical purposes a conception of nature which is explicitly rejected by the rest of his thought. It was asked, moreover, why the term designating fundamental reality – what there is – should have a differential, even controversial, connotation, especially within an avowedly pluralistic and non-reductive philosophical scheme. In short, there was considerable uneasiness about the character and precise scope of Dewey's 'naturalism'; there was also a lingering sense that he was trying to avoid the religious problem of transcendence first by identifying it with a crude supernaturalism, and then by resolving it negatively by declaring that whatever is, is nature.[55]

There are, to be sure, genuine issues involved both for Dewey's naturalism and the philosophy of religion generally. As was indicated previously, however, it was controversy over these points which diverted attention from his constructive interpretation aimed at elucidating a view of religion consistent with his philosophy of experience. This consequence was unfortunate because it is clear that in the present climate of opinion the suggestive insights expressed in *A Common Faith* are far more significant for understanding religion than the controversies provoked by the book years ago.

Three topics are central: first, Dewey's conception of 'the religious' in contrast to 'religion' and 'religion'; second, the significance of the object of faith and of the term 'God'; and finally, the function or role of faith in human affairs. The first topic introduces an original conception: Dewey gave priority to the adjective 'religious' over the noun in order to identify his primary subject matter as a *quality* or dimension of experience which is present and open to analysis. To begin with, Dewey, like many others, took seriously the fact that it is as difficult to find 'religion' in the singular as it is to find 'science' or 'art'. Consequently, he took the term 'religion' to be a collective name for a quite heterogeneous set of individual religions each of which is identified through a body of beliefs, rituals, practices usually associated with a form of organization. His main contention is that there does indeed exist 'a religious quality of experience' which needs to be emancipated from the burden of beliefs and institutional practices which tend to obscure it and make it next to impossible for this quality to emerge clearly in consciousness and to be understood. In short, many people, according to Dewey, including those who are negatively disposed towards institutional religion, have within themselves attitudes and impulses which are essentially 'religious' in character. The question then arises: What is the nature of the religious, and how does it make its presence felt?

'The adjective "religious",' Dewey wrote, 'denotes nothing in the way of a specifiable entity, either institutional or as a system of beliefs.'[56] Nor does the term point to anything which can exist by itself or be brought into existence by the imposition of order or form. The 'religious', in Dewey's view, must be understood as 'attitudes that may be taken toward every object and every proposed end or ideal',[57] and it is this emphasis on disposition and orientation which makes it inappropriate to think of the religious in terms of substantial entities, institutions or traditions. At an earlier stage in the discussion mention was made of Dewey's lack of sympathy with the concept of 'religious experience' and especially with the role it was made to play some decades ago in the development of 'empirical' theologies aimed at being 'scientific'. It is highly significant that at the outset of his presentation of the religious Dewey thought it necessary to distinguish his own view quite sharply from similar-sounding positions which he regarded as mistaken. Superficially, at least, the issue is clearly drawn, but there are problems concerning the relation between experience and religion which are scarcely touched in Dewey's discussion.[58] His main concern was to distinguish his view from any attempt to use 'religious experience' as evidence for the existence of God in much the same way that experiential evidence is cited as the ground for laws and theories in the sciences. The basis of his rejection is found in the theory of experience; for Dewey, there was no 'religious experience' which is 'specific' with respect to its content and marked off from experience designated as 'moral', 'aesthetic', 'scientific', etc., because the adjective 'religious' could apply to all these experiences. And, in so far as the term denotes a quality in experience, the point Dewey wished to make is clear enough. His sentence, however, ends with a further distinction the force of which is not at once obvious. First, it was said that there is no specific religious experience to be contrasted with generic types or modes of experience such as the moral and aesthetic, but that is followed by the same denial in relation to 'experience as companionship and friendship'. The latter two are not modes of experience in the sense represented by the moral and aesthetic, but are individual relational experiences. It is not clear whether Dewey meant to single out 'companionship' and 'friendship' as having some special relation to the 'religious', or whether he was simply offering examples of individual experiences along with the modes of experience cited in order to point out that there is no specific 'religious experience' to be set in contrast to either.

Quite apart, however, from this ambiguity Dewey clearly wished to deny that there are special experiences to be used as evidence for belief in 'some special kind of object' such as the God of the Judaeo-Christian tradition. His opposition was based in part on his disapproval of attempts by theologians to ride on the coat-tails of science, but, more importantly, Dewey was concerned to identify the religious aspect of experience and keep it from being tied exclusively to the doctrinal framework of some one historical tradition. He was, of course, correct in pointing out that anyone undergoing the sorts of experience which form the substance of James' *Varieties* will inevitably interpret them in terms of the dominant religious tradition of the culture to which they belong. Dewey cites what he takes to be the typical case of the harassed person on the edge of despair who seeks through quiet meditation to relate himself to the source of his life and in so doing overcomes despair and finds a new direction in life. But here, to a greater extent than anywhere else in his thought, Dewey insisted on a clear distinction between a 'complex of conditions that have operated to effect an adjustment in life, an orientation that brings with it a sense of security and peace'[59] and the 'interpretation' placed on that experience. According to Dewey the latter is not inherent in the experience, but belongs instead to the culture and is merely superimposed. One is tempted to say that, for Dewey, there is no variety in *religious* experience, only variety in cultures (embracing, of course, specific religious traditions), while 'the religious' remains underneath in the form of a universal quality of experience quite independent of the cultural frameworks through which it is expressed. It is possible that this is not a view which Dewey would have wanted to hold, but it follows consistently from his disjunction between conditions existing in the make-up of the person and his situation, and the interpretation of that situation. The curious fact is that, for all his pluralism, Dewey had a somewhat monolithic conception of 'the religious', better suited for the expression of 'a common faith' than for an accurate representation of the actual differences in feeling, practice, outlook and experience to be found in the literature of the world religions. This line of argument cannot be pursued further, but it is necessary to point out that the actual plurality of major religions poses problems not to be resolved by a ready-made dichotomy between existent conditions on the one hand, and their interpretation on the other.

The foregoing discussion, however, does not mean an attempt at reductionism on Dewey's part. In saying that in the case of the person whose despair was overcome nothing was 'proved' but the existence of a set of conditions which resulted in a new orientation and a sense of security, Dewey claimed that he had no intention of denying either the genuineness or the importance of the result, but only to show the undesirable consequences of declaring religious experience to be *sui generis*. The principal reason that reductionism is not involved appears in the first clue Dewey offered as to the specific nature of the 'religious' – the religious quality in experience is an *effect* which he described as 'better adjustment in life and its conditions' and, since the value of the religious is in the function, it is not necessary to be concerned with the mode or cause of its production. If one is especially interested in what is distinctively 'pragmatic' about this interpretation, one has but to attend to the fact that the emphasis falls on 'fruits' and not on 'roots'. The consequence and the result have first priority because on this view the religious ultimately concerns changes and transformations of the self as a whole which manifest themselves as results taking the form of a new attitude and orientation. It is, moreover, no more than a preconception belonging to the mythology that has grown up around Pragmatism to think of these consequences and results as 'actions' which issue from 'thought'. For here the results in question go far beyond individual deeds or acts of will; they concern nothing less than the being of the individual, the quality and direction of life as a whole.

The religious is primarily an attitude which, in company with imagination, embraces loyalty to an ideal. This attitude is mobile in the sense that it can be exhibited in such diverse situations and activities as 'art, science and good citizenship'. On this account Dewey could say that faith in the continued discovery of truth through the efforts of human intelligence and the cooperation of nature is 'more religious' than faith in an authoritative body of revealed truth. Any activity engaged in by an individual dedicated to an ideal which is believed to have enduring value is, according to Dewey, 'religious in quality'. One must be careful here not to overlook what is in fact the central point of Dewey's theory, namely, the *effect* of displaying the religious attitude on the life pattern of the individual. It is not the external 'success' of the endeavour which is central but rather what Dewey described in citing the devoted work of scientists, artists, philanthropists, as the 'unification of themselves and of their relations to the conditions of existence'[60] which results from their labour. The truly distinguishing feature of the religious for Dewey, as will become more clear in connection with his discussion of faith, is focused on the unification of the self and its becoming harmonized with its surroundings. To achieve and realize a *whole* self is the chief concern of the religious in experience. The intimate connection which exists between the religious and the underlying problem posed by the human self and its quest for fulfilment must not become obscured by the polemical context of the entire discussion. Dewey's conception of the religious is positive in its own right and something more than a weapon with which to subdue the supernatural. And this remains true even if, as many have felt, his attack on the supernatural is at once too simple and not a little overdrawn.

In the interest of elucidating Dewey's conception of faith and its object or orientation, it would be wise not to focus exclusively on the account he gave of the science–religion controversy. For to join issue with him on the question of intellectual content or knowledge in religion would involve a long discussion which might in the end serve only to force into the background what is most important, namely, his conception of what answers to the word 'God'. Since, however, that conception is heavily dependent on his view of the impact which modern science has had upon traditional religious thought, it is necessary to summarize his account of the matter.[61] His first point is that all religions insist upon intellectual beliefs, including the belief that there is a special access to the truths on which the religion is based. Dewey's contention was that the scepticism, agnosticism and indifference to religion characteristic of modern life are all direct results of the fact that these intellectual claims have been nullified by the findings of geology, biology, anthropology, psychology and the 'higher criticism' of the Bible. More important, however, than the discovery of the untruth of some particular item of religious belief is the revolution that has taken place in what Dewey liked to call the 'seat of intellectual authority'. 'New methods of inquiry,' he wrote, 'and reflection have become for the educated man today the final arbiter of all questions of fact, existence and intellectual assent.'[62] Therefore the educated person finds intellectual assent to traditional doctrines increasingly onerous and the more these doctrines are insisted upon as the justification of a religion the more it becomes assailed by doubt. Dewey's proposal for resolving the problem here presented was to free the religious function in experience from any dependence whatever on items of intellectual assent, including belief in the existence of God understood in the theistic sense. If, moreover, the method of the sciences is accepted as the one method for attaining truth and fact, no discovery in any branch of inquiry could possibly prove inimical to religious faith. This consequence follows not only from the fact that the religious does not involve intellectual acceptance of a creed, but also from Dewey's further definition of faith as 'the unification of the self through allegiance to inclusive ideal ends'.[63] There is presumably no truth to be discovered about any region of existence which could conflict with the religious in Dewey's sense.

In order to consolidate his position *vis à vis* other religious views, Dewey singled out for criticism two claims which he regarded as central. He would not accept a division of the field into a domain of nature where science rules and a domain of grace under the aegis of religious experience. This solution runs counter to his belief that there is but one method for attaining knowledge throughout the whole of existence. Moreover, he contended, the two-territories approach invariably leads religious thinkers to locate religion in the gaps existent in our knowledge or, as Dewey said, in those aspects of our experience which have not yet been 'invaded' by science. James, it will be recalled, made the same point when he said that to locate the divine in the domain of man's ignorance leads only to the gradual erosion of religion as human knowledge advances. Dewey's second criticism touches something far more fundamental, namely, his attack on the view which regards mystical experience as religion *par excellence,* and thus as a 'special reserve' beyond explanation. There are two distinct features in his criticism: one is an emphasis upon the difference between mystical experience and the interpretation placed upon it, and the other concerns the claims to private and immediate knowledge of a religious object which mystics have frequently advanced.

With respect to the first feature, Dewey invoked a sharper distinction than usual between experience and interpretation,[64] and it is not clear whether he wanted to identify 'interpreting' experience with 'explaining' it. What is clear is that he saw great variety among the forms of mysticism and very little in common between types which range from Neo-Platonic contemplation to Yoga to inner personal communion with God. His conclusion was that all 'interpretations' of mystical experience are derivative from the *culture* in which the experience takes place, and he suggested that the concepts prevailing in a given culture serve to 'explain' that experience. Dewey's concern was not to deny that there are experiences to be called mystical, but rather to reject the claim that these experiences represent the occasion for an immediate knowledge of the presence of God. This is the second feature of his criticism and it is crucial; it cannot, however, be passed by without comment because there is a curious shift of ground in Dewey's argument which is bound up with his previous passing from 'interpretation' to 'explanation' as if the two terms were synonymous. 'As with every empirical phenomenon,' he wrote, 'the occurrence of the state called mystical is simply an occasion for inquiry into *its mode of causation.*'[65] Surely it is one thing to 'interpret' mystical experience in terms of the concepts prevalent in a culture, and quite another to suggest that such experience is 'explained' with respect to its causes by invoking that same cultural system. Perhaps, however, Dewey wanted to claim that the prevalent cultural system 'produces' the experiences in question. The reference, moreover, to causation is peculiar and not consistent with Dewey's previous claim that the religious quality in experience is to be understood in terms of the effect it has on a person's life and not through 'the manner and cause of its production'.[66] Dewey could reply by saying that he was prompted to focus on the cause of these experiences because those who have them claim that the presence of God is their cause. On the other hand, mystics have rarely turned their basically experiential approach into a strict, causal argument of the sort represented by the traditional cosmological proofs, for, as was pointed out previously in the discussion of Peirce, that would make the experiences themselves superfluous. There is, moreover, a difference well known to mystical writers between thinking of God as 'presence' *in* experience and as 'cause' *of* experience, and therefore the issue is rather more complicated than Dewey seems to have thought. In any case that issue cannot be resolved here; the important consideration is to understand Dewey's main view, which was that science or the method of intelligence is 'open and public', whereas the method of mysticism as a special mode of 'religious' experience is 'limited and private', so that if the religious in experience (including the mystical) is to be maintained and freed from the supernatural, it must be understood through its function in life and not as entailing immediate knowledge of transcendent reality.

Having thus cleared the ground of stumbling blocks which, in Dewey's view, prevent the modern man from appreciating the religious in experience, Dewey could go on to his positive view which is that the objects of religion are *ideal* in relation to our present situation, and that their claim upon our conduct is authoritative just because they are ideal. Thoroughly in accord with his repeated rejection of 'antecedent being' in favour of 'eventual functioning', Dewey insisted that to think of the objects of religion as already real is to add nothing to their force and at the same time to weaken their claim on our allegiance by involving us in what is 'intellectually dubious'. We come here to the heart of the matter and Dewey was most explicit in his posing of the central question. 'Are the ideals that move us,' he asked, 'genuinely ideal or are they ideal only in contrast with our present estate?'[67] This question is central because Dewey's answer to it indicates what is to be meant by the term 'God' and how the religious is decisively distinguished from a religion. On the assumption that the word 'God' is not to mean a particular Being, but rather the unity of all ideal ends which are to have authority over human will and feeling, Dewey argued that this authoritativeness derives not from the unity as already existent and non-ideal, but from its own inherent value as an ideal. The line dividing the religious and the historical religions is clearly drawn: the religions envisage God as having prior and therefore non-ideal existence, whereas those who adhere to the religious as a function of experience understand 'God' to be a unification through the medium of imagination of ideal values. Here again Dewey laid emphasis on the advantages gained for the religious when it is no longer tied to an antecedent existence which has become extremely dubious. Apologetics, for example, are no longer needed because the force exerted by an *ideal* on human behaviour is a fact which need not be argued for.[68] In addition, the aim of promoting ideal values induces men to develop their powers to the utmost, whereas dependence on an external power means no more than the 'surrender of human endeavour'.

In refusing to identify the ideal with a particular Being, Dewey was at pains to point out that the ideal nevertheless has *roots* in natural existence and is far from being a 'mere' ideal without operative force in the world. In fact, for him, ideals have their force precisely in the form of *operative purposes* which shape human life and institutions. In denying the claim that the ideal is already embodied or existent, Dewey was denying that this embodiment is necessary for its authority over us. That authority is instead a function of the intrinsic worth of the ideal and the force of imagination whereby human beings work for its realization. This point is of the utmost importance because it helps to define further what Dewey meant by the name 'God' – the '*active* relation between ideal and actual'.[69] If the divine is understood, as Dewey intended it, to mean *ideal* possibilities unified in imagination, and these possibilities have roots in existence, it follows that the actual situation must be one of tension. We are confronted neither by completely embodied ideals nor by ideals wholly disconnected from existence. What is needed is an *active union* of clearly perceived ideals and the actual conditions which support their realization. Thus God is the *function* which this active union of ideal and actual performs in human experience as it develops against the background of a natural environment. That background is of fundamental importance because it focuses attention on the cooperation of man and nature. It is significant that Dewey regarded supernaturalism and 'aggressive atheism' as coming together in upholding the isolation of man from nature; in the case of supernaturalism nature is subordinated to the isolated soul of man, while militant atheism sees nature merely as the hostile or indifferent enemy which man confronts in defiance.

The remaining task is to come to some understanding of the religious function as it is embodied in the fabric of social life. Here Dewey rightly pointed out that in his exposition he reversed the proper order; consideration of the intellectual content of religion should not precede the description of religion as it exists immediately in the form of social rites and ceremonies. Actual religion is to be found first and foremost in the form of a community which structures life in accordance with the sacred times, places and powers that form the substance of faith. The interpreting word of myths of theogony and cosmogony represents a subsequent development aimed at expressing the meaning and value of the more primordial ritual and ceremony. Dewey's first point centres on the fundamental difference between being born into a religious community where the religious permeates the whole of life, and joining a church which has become a special institution within a secular community.[70] The religious situation in America and in many European countries is predominantly of the latter type where the church as an organization is incorporated under the laws of the secular society in which it exists. As a result of the latter development which Dewey called a shift in the 'social center of gravity', numerous associations formed for educational, philanthropic, political and scientific purposes have grown up outside the aegis of any particular religion. These associations have come more and more to dominate the interests, thought and activity of all members of society, including church members. Dewey's point is that the direct effect of science and technology on society took the form of a profound change in the conditions under which human beings associate with each other. The multiplication of secular interests plus radical social changes resulting from the new technological society place a far greater burden on the religiously oriented than any intellectual crisis precipitated by the incongruity between science and religious doctrines. In Dewey's view, creeds can be accommodated to change, even if the process is slow and uncertain, but the day-to-day life in which all participate has been so radically altered by the application of new knowledge that non-religious interests and considerations have taken command and the traditional concerns of religion have been thrust into the background. 'The essential point,' said Dewey, 'is not just that secular organizations and actions are legally or externally severed from the control of the church, but that interests and values unrelated to the offices of any church now so largely sway the desires and aims of even believers.'[71] It would be difficult to find a more truly prophetic comment than this statement of almost four decades ago pointing to the development on the American scene of the 'secular city' and the 'death of God'. Dewey, moreover, was correct in pointing out that even if an individual attempts to carry his religious motivation over into the other pursuits in which he is engaged, two unescapable facts confront him. His action is, first, a matter of personal choice and does not stem from a social organization, and, second, he must accept the fact that, quite apart from any role played by the church in the growth of new secular interests, they *are* secular interests presenting themselves as independent and autonomous. As W. E. Hocking put the point in connection with the relation between religion and culture, religion was once mother of the arts, but time and again the offspring have joined themselves together for the express purpose not only of denying their origin, but of taking her place as well.

Against the background of secularization, Dewey's conception of the religious function takes on new force and significance. The decline of religion in the sense of *a religion* which proclaims a clear distinction between the sacred and the secular, need not mean loss of *the religious* understood as an attitude and outlook which can figure in all human activity and in every aspect of life. The religious is not confined to a special sphere nor is it indissolubly tied to any single organization. Dewey's contention was that if all significant values, ends and purposes in human life can be seen and appreciated as having arisen in the matrix of human relations and apart from the supernatural, their power will be greatly enhanced. The relations he had in mind and which he believed perform a religious function in society are, as he said, 'natural relations' and they embrace those of 'husband and wife, of parent and child, friend and friend, neighbor and neighbor, of fellow workers in industry, science, and art'.[72] The developing of these relations should be our main concern and the responsibility to do so is ours alone; we are not to suppose, following traditional religious thought, that human relations are so debased that our only recourse is to 'supernatural aid'. On the contrary, our task is to work for stability and peace in society with the aid of the method of intelligence. In short, our task is to build the 'secular city' whose maker and founder is man.

In developing the meaning of the religious in experience as contrasted with a religion based on a particular conception of the supernatural, Dewey connected the religious with the problem of unifying the self as a whole. That problem does not figure prominently in Dewey's discussion of how faith functions in the social matrix within which all experience takes place. Perhaps the reason is that he was struggling so desperately to free the religious from the supernatural and to recover the meaning and authority of purely natural social relations, that the predicament of the individual self fell from sight. There is, however, every reason to believe that the unification and self-realization of the person as a whole remained for Dewey a central value. If this is so, it is to be regretted that he did not describe more clearly how the development of the human relations – parent and child, friend and friend, etc. – he thought so valuable contribute to that unification of the self which was previously described as the focal point of the religious function in experience. Fortunately, Dewey gave us two clues as to the

G

essential connection between the religious function and the social matrix of human life. One is his conception of the 'community of causes and consequences' in which *all* human beings exist in virtue of the fact that all exist in nature and confront the same problems of precarious existence in a world where the success of man is not guaranteed in advance. All men are brothers in the sense that, as Dewey said, 'we are at least all in the same boat traversing the same turbulent ocean'. This community enmeshes all men in 'the widest and deepest symbol of the mysterious totality of being the imagination calls the universe'. It is the ultimate matrix within which all human values, purposes, ends are realized. The second clue concerns the special quality of life which this human community should have: it is the quality of democracy, of human equality, dignity and freedom. Only under the aegis of 'the democratic ideal as a vital moral and spiritual ideal in human affairs'[73] can there grow those relations between persons which can ultimately bring about the unification of the self which is the religious function in experience. It is not difficult to see that, for Dewey, democracy ultimately assumed *religious* proportions if it did not actually supplant religion in his total view of things. Democracy, which he repeatedly characterized as a total way of life and much more than a form of government, becomes a sort of final spiritual community. It is less like a church which, under present conditions, is one institution among others, and more like the ancient symbol of the Kingdom of God or the Heavenly City which contains no church precisely because all the religious values are already realized there among men.

By comparison with Peirce and James, Dewey's view of religion is by far the most consistently secular and naturalistic. Peirce was inspired by the speculative dimension in Christian theology and was adventurous enough to envisage the power of love as a cosmic force. James, sensitive to the religious problems of the sick soul and the divided self, looked for a source of power beyond the human will as the means of resolving the human predicament. Dewey, by contrast, was earthbound and thoroughly convinced of the sufficiency of the gospel of intelligence and of man's capacity to control his own destiny. No matter how sympathetic one may be in attempting to do justice to Dewey's interpretation of religion, one keeps coming back in the end to the sobering judgement of Santayana in assessing Dewey's *A Common Faith* – 'a very common faith indeed!'

Appendix: Note on the origins of Pragmatism

I cite here first the relevant historical and philosophical studies and, secondly, a number of significant references in the writings of Peirce, James and Dewey containing comment on the origins and background of the movement. Anyone acquainted with this literature will very soon come to the conclusion that the 'origin' of Pragmatism is a very tangled affair. For light on the 'Metaphysical Club' in Cambridge and the earliest use of the term 'Pragmatism' see Philip P. Wiener, *Evolution and the Founders of Pragmatism*, Cambridge Mass., 1949; Max H. Fisch, 'Alexander Bain and the Genealogy of Pragmatism', *Journal of the History of Ideas*, vol. 15 (1954), pp. 413–44; Max H. Fisch, 'Justice Holmes, The Prediction Theory of the Law and Pragmatism', *Journal of Philosophy*, vol. 39 (1942), pp. 85–97. See also Fisch's essays 'Was there a Metaphysical Club in Cambridge?' in Morse and Robin (eds), *Studies in the Philosophy of C. S. Peirce*, second series, Amherst, 1964, pp. 3–32, and 'A Chronicle of Pragmatism, 1865–1897', *The Monist*, vol. 48 (1964), pp. 441–66. A reader would be well advised to start with this chronicle; it provides not only a helpful chronological orientation, but introduces the main puzzles to be solved if we are to have a comprehensive account of the 'origins' of Pragmatism. H. S. Thayer, *Meaning and Action. A Critical History of Pragmatism*, Indianapolis, 1968, is an extremely valuable study and it contains extensive bibliography; see especially sections 19 and 27 for information on the beginnings of Pragmatism and the initial use of the term. Thayer is quite right in calling attention to the difference between Peirce and James. With regard to the meaning of 'Pragmatism', Peirce took it to connote a close connection between purpose and cognition, while James emphasised action, practice and the practical. Since Peirce had Kant's distinction in mind, he could not call the new doctrine 'practicalism' because Kant's *praktisch* points to the moral sphere, the realm of freedom; it is Kant's term *pragmatisch* which brings in the reference to human purpose that Peirce wanted to stress. Peirce therefore spoke of 'pragmatism' and not 'practicalism'.

Extremely valuable for the placing of Pragmatism in historical perspective is Herbert W. Schneider, *A History of American Philosophy*, New York, 1946, 2nd ed., 1963.

Among references in the writings of the pragmatists themselves concerning the origins of the movement we must reckon with the following: in his paper 'Philosophical Conceptions and Practical Results' (*University of California Chronicle*, Berkeley, Sept. 1898, repr. in *Collected Essays and Reviews*, ed. Ralph Barton Perry, New York and London, 1920, pp. 406–37; a modified version also appeared in *Journal of Philosophy*, vol. 1 (1904)). James referred to Peirce's paper 'How to Make Our Ideas Clear' (*Popular Science Monthly*, vol. 12 (Jan. 1878), pp. 286–302, repr. in Hartshorne and Weiss (eds), *Collected Papers*, Cambridge, Mass., 5 (1934), paras 388–410, as the introduction of 'Peirce's principle' – 'the principle of practicalism – or pragmatism, as he called it, when I first heard him enunciate it at Cambridge in the early '70s'. (See P. R. Anderson and Max H. Fisch (eds), *Philosophy in America*, New York, 1939, p. 526.) It has been generally supposed that James was referring to discussions held at meetings of the 'Metaphysical Club' which both he and Peirce were supposed to have attended. Peirce was thus established as the 'father' of Pragmatism, although it was he who pointed out later that Kant was the first to distinguish between *praktisch* and *pragmatisch* (using the latter term in the full title of his *Anthropologie*). See Thayer, *Meaning and Action*, pp. 499 ff for Peirce's description, in a letter of 1903 to James, of Berkeley as the one who has 'more right to be considered the introducer of pragmatism into philosophy than any other one man'. James reinforced the point later in *Pragmatism* (New York and London, 1907) when he referred to Peirce's paper of 1878 declaring that the term 'pragmatism' was 'first introduced into philosophy' by Mr Charles Peirce in that year (p. 46). And James went on to call attention to the fact that Peirce's principle 'lay entirely unnoticed by anyone for twenty years until I, in an address before Professor Howison's philosophical union at the University of California, brought it forward again and made a special application of it to religion' (p. 47). For Peirce's account of how Pragmatism was started, and especially his invention of the 'barbarous' term 'Pragmaticism' as the name for his own position, see *Collected Papers*, 5, 1–13, 14–19, 411–37, 438–63, 464–9 (this latter piece should be read following section 13), 497–501. Special attention must be called to the notes attached to section 402; these serve greatly to clarify Peirce's position as expressed in 'How to Make Our Ideas Clear'. Particularly important is his insistence that it is 'conceived action' to which thought ultimately applies. If we couple this point with his denial that any act – Peirce regarded acts as the most *singular* items there are – is ever identical with the 'intellectual purport' of any symbol, it becomes evident why it is utterly false to say that Peirce believed all thought is for the sake of action or that thought is to be translated into or reduced without remainder to some form of action.

Among Dewey's voluminous writings, several items may be cited as having special bearing on the history of the pragmatic movement; see especially 'The Development of American Pragmatism' in Department of Philosophy of Columbia University (ed.)), *Studies in the History of Ideas*, vol. 2, New York, 1935, pp. 353–77; 'What Pragmatism Means by Practical',

Journal of Philosophy, vol. 5 (1908), pp. 85–99, repr. in Dewey's *Essays in Experimental Logic*, Chicago, 1916, repr. New York, 1954, pp. 303–29; 'The Pragmatism of Peirce', *Journal of Philosophy*, vol. 13 (1916), pp. 709–15.

Notes and references

Introduction

1. A. J. Ayer, *The Origins of Pragmatism,* San Francisco, 1968, p. 3. Russell expresses a similar idea in *A History of Western Philosophy,* New York, 1945, p. 151.
2. See *Collected Papers of Charles Sanders Peirce* (8 vols: vols. 1-6, ed. Charles Hartshorne and Paul Weiss, vols. 7-8, ed. A. W. Burks, Cambridge, Mass., 1932-58 – all references are to volume and section, *not* to pages), 5.402 and the later notes which are of the greatest importance.
3. Since Dewey believed in a market place of ideas and in the constructive role of philosophical discussion, much of his writing was directed by response to criticism; one has to follow him through changes both in doctrine and terminology resulting from his attempts to meet objections advanced by critics.
4. See especially John Dewey, 'An Empirical Survey of Empiricisms', repr. in Richard J. Bernstein (ed.), *John Dewey on Experience, Nature and Freedom,* New York, 1960, pp. 70–87; 'The Need for a Recovery of Philosophy' in John Dewey *et al., Creative Intelligence: Essays in the Pragmatic Attitude,* New York, 1917.
5. Ayer, for example, in *The Origins of Pragmatism,* seems to ignore the fact that the pragmatists were strenuously attacking the empiricism of his own tradition, and therefore he discusses Peirce and James as if they were seeking to answer all the epistemological questions which have become the stock-in-trade of British philosophy.

1 The Pragmatic approach to meaning, belief and action

1. *Collected Papers of Charles Sanders Peirce* (8 vols: vols. 1-6, ed. Charles Hartshorne and Paul Weiss, vols. 7-8, ed. A. W. Burks, Cambridge, Mass., 1932-58), 5.3.
2. See Max H. Fisch, 'Peirce and Leibniz', *Journal of the History of Ideas,* vol. 33, no. 3 (1972), p. 495. See also *Collected Papers,* 8.218 for Peirce's revised opinion to the effect that the third grade of clearness does not supersede the other two. For the meaning of 'concrete reasonableness'

see *Collected Papers*, 5.433 from 'What Pragmatism Is' (1905); this section also contains a definite rejection of the thesis that the *summum bonum* consists in action.

3. *Collected Papers*, 5.3 Peirce made the same point repeatedly: an action or reaction is above all individual and nothing individual can be the meaning of an intellectual concept.

4. *Collected Papers*, 5.400.

5. *Collected Papers*, 5.402. The italics were not in the original but I have added them in order to call attention to what Peirce's note of 1906 pointed out about the significance of his having repeated 'conceive', 'conceivable' and 'conception'. See n. 3 to *Collected Papers*, 5.402. In the decade following 1900 Peirce was engaged in revising the original version of his Pragmatism; these revisions are to be found in *Collected Papers*, 5.411-501.

6. *Collected Papers*, 5.402, n. 3.

7. *Ibid.* Since Peirce clearly connected the meaning of a concept with the behaviour of an object, and in turn connected thinking with the development of habits or resolutions to act, what he said here about acts may seem puzzling. The difficulty is cleared up if it is kept in mind that when Peirce identified the conception of an object with the conception of its effects or behaviour, he meant the conception of what the object *would do* under a multiplicity of conditions; the 'would do' with respect both to objects and human behaviour is, for Peirce, *not* identical with the perceptual report of some actual occasion of behaviour nor with any finite number of such occasions. And the reason is clear: a conception, for Peirce, always involves the 'general', whereas all acts and all occasions when the effects of an object are manifested are singular. Therefore there is no concept the meaning of which is identical with an act.

8. *Collected Papers*, 5.403.

9. *Ibid.*

10. *Ibid.*

11. See especially *Collected Papers*, 8.216 (*c.* 1910) for his own specific criticism of what he had written earlier in 5.409.

12. *Collected Papers*, 8.217.

13. For the central role played by the concept of the 'would be' in Peirce's theory of reality, see my 'Community and Reality' in R. J. Bernstein (ed.), *Perspectives on Peirce*, New Haven, 1965, pp. 92–119.

14. In his paper 'The Fixation of Belief' (*Collected Papers*, 5.358-87) the methods of tenacity, authority and *a priori* reasoning, though not without important functions in experience, are compared unfavourably with the method of science on the ground that the latter alone initiates critical discussion of an issue and is, in principle, self-correcting in the sense of continually reviewing previous conclusions. The other methods,

by contrast, are self-terminating and thus fall under Peirce's ban on anything that 'blocks the road to inquiry'.

15. *Collected Papers,* 5.405.
16. *Collected Papers,* 5.406.
17. *Ibid.*
18. *Collected Papers,* 5.407.
19. The choice of this term has been called into question and Peirce himself had a note in which he said, 'Fate means merely that which is sure to come true, and can nohow be avoided.' (*Collected Papers,* 5.407, n. 1.) The term expresses Peirce's dramatic flair and his belief that scientific inquiry represents an objective order of discovery under the constraint of the subject matter unless the investigator wilfully allows his own interests to subvert the process.
20. *Ibid.*
21. See John E. Smith, 'Community and Reality' in Bernstein (ed.) *Perspectives on Peirce.* It is important to notice that in his discussion of thirdness and abduction (*Collected Papers,* 5.195 ff) Peirce made a distinction between holding that 'truth consists in a conformity to something *independent of his thinking it to be so,* or of any man's opinion on that subject' and holding that 'the only reality there could be, would be conformity to the ultimate result of inquiry' (*Collected Papers,* 5.211). This suggests that conformity to the ultimate result of inquiry is not *sufficient* for defining truth and reality. Peirce, in fact, asserted that the person maintaining the second view quoted is forced to conclude that there is no reality at all 'except that he now at this instant finds a certain way of thinking easier than any other' (*ibid.*). I believe it is clear from the above that Peirce was not satisfied with any view of truth and reality which does not place inquiry under the constraint of the independent reals that he regarded as the presupposition of science. And yet because Peirce developed his ideas on so many different occasions for different purposes, discrepancies were bound to arise. In an article written for Baldwin's *Dictionary* (1901), Peirce made a rather sharp distinction between truth and reality. See *Collected Papers,* 5.565 ff.
22. As it turned out, this feature of Pragmatism as expressed by James as well as Peirce became such an issue that Dewey was finally led to attempt to set the record straight in a paper published as 'What Pragmatism Means by Practical' in his *Essays in Experimental Logic,* Chicago, 1916, repr. New Pork, 1954, pp. 303–29.
23. *Collected Papers,* 5.400.
24. *Collected Papers,* 5.589.
25. *Ibid.*
26. *Ibid.*
27. *Ibid.*

28. *Collected Papers*, 5.411 ff. The article appeared originally in *The Monist,* vol. 15 (1905).
29. The difference is partially expressed as the difference between the 'verified' and the 'verifiable', a distinction of long standing within the confines of positivism. In putting the matter thus, however, one must not overlook the fact that no positivism can make consistent sense of the 'verifi*able*' because of its nominalism and the identification of 'what's what' with the present, sensible singular; Peirce, on the other hand, could consistently allow for both real possibility and potentiality because he understood the real not in terms of the sensible singular, occupying a present, but as the 'would be' of an open future.
30. *Collected Papers,* 5.412.
31. *Collected Papers,* 5.27. This passage is from the *Lectures on Pragmatism* of 1903, twenty-five years later than the initial formulation of the famous pragmatic maxim. These lectures belong to the extensive re-thinking of Pragmatism which Peirce was carrying on just after the turn of the century.
32. *Collected Papers,* 5.32.
33. *Ibid.* Further light is shed on this point by Peirce's discussion in 'Reason's Rules' (*Collected Papers,* 5.538 ff) where a distinction is drawn between theoretical and practical beliefs. The substance of the distinction is that a practical belief, such as that anthracite is a convenient fuel, is 'a habit of deliberate behaviour' which invariably involves the use of something for some purpose in self-controlled behaviour, whereas in a theoretical belief, such as that the pole of the earth describes an oval of a few rods' diameter, no such habit is called forth. Theoretical beliefs about the behaviour of some object used will always be involved in practical belief and Peirce's question was: Given the fact that 'every theoretical belief is, at least indirectly, a practical belief', does it follow that the practical belief is the *whole* meaning of the theoretical belief? His answer was no, but it is clear that he was still troubled by the distinction between the commensurable and the incommensurable; on the one hand, as he said, it is difficult to see what 'experiential difference' there can be between these two types of magnitudes, and on the other he was reluctant to deny that one may exist. He concluded that there is at least the 'practical' consequence that it is useless to try to find the exact expression of the diagonal as a rational fraction of the side. The basic point, however, remains: the practical function of a theoretical belief does not exhaust the meaning of that belief, and, although the entire discussion is somewhat confusing (because Peirce could not decide whether *all* belief involves expectation), there are passages in which theoretical belief is defined in terms of expectation and contrasted with practical belief on that account. Unfortunately, we are then told (540) that practical

belief is expectant of muscular sensation, whereas theoretical belief is expectant of sensation not muscular.

34. *Collected Papers,* 5.33.
35. *Ibid.*
36. *Ibid.*
37. William James, *Pragmatism,* New York and London, 1907; repr. New York, 1943, p. 114.
38. *Pragmatism* (1943 ed.), pp. 118–19.
39. *Collected Papers,* 5.358–87.
40. *Collected Papers,* 5.396.
41. *Ibid.*
42. *Collected Papers,* 5.397.
43. *Ibid.*
44. *Collected Papers,* 5.398.
45. *Collected Papers,* 5.397; cf. 5.547.
46. *Collected Papers,* 5.399.
47. See Fisch, 'Peirce and Leibniz', p. 486, n. 5.
48. *Collected Papers,* 5.339.
49. *Ibid.*
50. See Fisch, 'Peirce and Leibniz', p. 495 for a quotation from Ms 137, p. 19 where Peirce claimed that he had originally derived his Pragmatism 'from a logical and non-psychological study of the essential nature of signs'.
51. *Collected Papers,* 5.13, n. 1.
52. *Collected Papers,* 5.371. In the note of 1893 appended to this passage Peirce criticised his earlier 'nominalism' and claimed that consciousness of a *habit* implies consciousness of what is *general* and therefore of what is not in all respects determinate. The point is that believing is not identical with an act because believing is consciousness of what is general and all acts are singular for Peirce.
53. Once again the notes added in 1893 are instructive. In the note to *Collected Papers,* 5.373 Peirce indicated that for him doubt does not imply hesitancy 'about what is to be done then and there'. The reason is that he wanted to allow for 'anticipated' or 'feigned' hesitancy wherein we can consider fictitious or make-believe dilemmas and possibly arrive at decisions which will be effective 'in a real emergency'. The duality between actual or real hesitancy and that which is feigned reflects a tension running throughout Peirce's conception of doubt. On the one hand, he opposed Cartesian doubt because it is 'paper doubt' and, as a programme for doubting, it abstracts from the actual situation – 'do not pretend to doubt, what in your heart you do not.' On the other hand, Peirce allowed not only for feigned doubt but also spoke of developing a method of doubting and, in addition, fully appreciated the extent to which scientific inquiry requires hypothetical doubt.

54. *Collected Papers*, 5.375.
55. Peirce identified 'A believes that *x*' and 'A believes that *x* is true'. (*Collected Papers*, 5.375, cf. 376, n. 3.)
56. *Collected Papers*, 5.383.
57. *Collected Papers*, 5.384.
58. *Ibid.* Peirce made numerous changes in this section in 1903; one of the central issues concerns whether he wished to identify the 'true' and the 'real'. This problem will be considered later; let it suffice to say that, despite his several statements about the matter, a consistent view emerges. By 'reals' or 'realities' he meant whatever affects the senses or influences thought and thus puts us under an external constraint. The aim of inquiry is to reach opinions that are 'true' in the sense of representing the convergent result of inquiry carried on by a community of investigators committed to following the same logical and experimental procedures. It is this opinion which is said to be true and the object of that opinion is the real.
59. *Collected Papers*, 5.384, n. 1.
60. *Ibid.*
61. It is important to notice that here Peirce disposed of any suggestion that truth is conventionally determined by the scientific community or any other.
62. *Collected Papers*, 5.384, n. 1.
63. *Ibid.*
64. Peirce discussed the circularity problem in his attack on 'foundationalism' in 'Grounds of the Validity of the Laws of Logic'; see especially *Collected Papers*, 5.351 ff. and 405 ff.
65. W. P. Montague, *The Ways of Knowing*, London, 1925, ch. 5.
66. *Collected Papers*, 5.385.
67. *Collected Papers*, 5.382, n. 1.
68. *Collected Papers*, 5.385. The entire passage suggests that Peirce saw a parallel between his own method of experience for dealing with the hypotheses of science and Hegel's 'trying out' of the viability and adequacy of philosophical standpoints by determining how much of reality a given standpoint can consistently comprehend.
69. *Ibid.*
70. See *Collected Papers*, 5.497 ff for a brief discussion of the connection between Pragmatism and critical commonsensism.
71. 'Philosophical Conceptions and Practical Results', *The University of California Chronicle*, Berkeley, 1898, repr. in William James, *Collected Essays and Reviews*, ed. Ralph Barton Perry, New York and London, 1920, p. 413.
72. 'Philosophical Conceptions', p. 414.
73. It is not clear that James was aware of the fact that the reactions to the alternatives, whenever they are considered, are 'prospective' in

the sense that they represent the way someone *would* feel were he to accept one or the other as the truth about the world, even a finished world. James would no doubt have regarded this as a purely 'theoretical' consideration in so far as it makes no reference to an individual's *interest in* and *engagement with* a real *future* of ongoing experience.

74. From a logical standpoint the relevance in question need not be of cosmic proportions since, as was noted earlier, there are many quite ordinary situations where objective differences of fact 'make no difference' to the achievement of the purpose at hand. The size of the Flicker's egg, for example, is different from that of the Robin, but that difference 'makes no difference' if I wish to identify a Flicker in the field and not confuse it with a Robin. I refer above to a person's life and destiny because James was most often considering metaphysical and religious questions bearing on life as a whole.

75. See *The Meaning of Truth, A Sequel to 'Pragmatism'*, New York and London, 1909, repr. Ann Arbor, 1970, pp. 189–90, note.

76. 'Philosophical Conceptions', p. 416.

77. 'Philosophical Conceptions', p. 417.

78. *Ibid.* Here James meant that 'God' and 'matter' would be merely different names for the 'power' that has produced precisely the world just finished as specified in the original supposition of a last moment.

79. *Ibid.*

80. 'Philosophical Conceptions', p. 418.

81. At many points James seems willing to follow without question the lead of classical empiricism and even positivism in reducing all meaning to denotation so that if the materialist and the theist are denoting the same past 'facts' their respective theses, whatever they assert, *mean* the same, i.e. those facts. It is difficult, however, to see precisely on his view how it can happen that two alternatives in a metaphysical debate differ in their meaning as regards facts yet to be actualized, when these same alternatives did not differ with respect to past facts. It would appear that the differences cannot be in the facts, past or yet to come, but only in our *response* to them.

82. 'Philosophical Conceptions', pp. 420–1.

83. 'Philosophical Conceptions', p. 423.

84. I do not claim that there is nowhere in James' confusion between the consequences (implications) of a doctrine, and the consequences of believing that doctrine. What I do claim is that the consequences of believing enter only when *action* is called for and the actual believing is a factor leading to that action.

85. 'Philosophical Conceptions', p. 424.

86. 'Philosophical Conceptions', pp. 424–5.

87. *Ibid.* The suggestion seems to be that one must begin with some conception of the experiences which represent the 'meaning' of the term

'God'; whether, however, God is 'real' for the individual depends on his actually having these experiences.

88. See 'The Perception of Reality', *Principles of Psychology*, New York, 1890, vol. 1, ch. 21, pp. 283 ff.

89. 'Philosophical Conceptions', p. 428.

90. *Ibid.*

91. For James' most comprehensive account of concepts and their functions see *Some Problems of Philosophy*, New York, 1911, ch. 4–6.

92. 'Philosophical Conceptions', p. 434.

93. 'Philosophical Conceptions', p. 435. James made this point on numerous occasions; part at least of what he had in mind was Hume's tendency to treat the distinct and separable ('other than') as more primordial than the continuous and the connected ('with'). James regarded this tendency as a non-empirical bias, holding that the transitions and connections in experience are as well founded as the distinctions, although he put this doctrine down to his 'radical empiricism' which he sometimes described as independent of his Pragmatism. See John E. Smith, 'Radical Empiricism', *Proceedings of the Aristotelian Society*, vol. 65 (1965), pp. 205–18.

94. In the end James was appealing to practical consequences not solely for determining meaning, but for endowing a proposed belief with a here-and-now relevance which might be lost if the belief became a purely 'theoretical' affair. For, when the issues were posed on theoretical grounds, James did not believe that any metaphysical dilemmas could be resolved. His appeal to practice, therefore, has a decided scepticism for a background.

95. *Pragmatism*, p. 45.

96. *Pragmatism*, p. 44.

97. *Pragmatism*, p. 45.

98. *Ibid.*

99. *Ibid.*

100. *Pragmatism*, p. 50.

101. One has to bear in mind that a special version of this problem was in the centre of discussion at the beginnng of this century because of the monistic tendency in the early Royce and the emphasis placed on the Absolute by the British idealists. James, Howison and others were equally determined to defend the rights of the many.

102. *Pragmatism*, p. 51.

103. *Pragmatism*, p. 67.

104. *Ibid.*

105. Royce's critique of James' theory reflects this way of thinking and it is summed up in his witty proposal of the pragmatist oath for a witness about to take the stand: 'I promise to tell what is expedient and only what is expedient, so help me future experience.'

106. *Pragmatism,* p. 60.
107. *Pragmatism,* p. 61.
108. *Pragmatism,* p. 63.
109. Though included as ch. 12 of *Essays in Experimental Logic,* this essay was originally written as a review of James' *Pragmatism.*
110. It is important not to confuse changes dictated by a theory in an experimental situation where the ultimate purpose is *knowing* with changes in the world at large such as building a bridge in accordance with an engineer's plans where the purpose is that of *making.* The confusion might not have arisen were it not for the tendency of the pragmatists to view knowing as a doing, and even as a making.
111. At many points James gave the impression that he did not believe, as Royce did, in the possibility of showing the logical or rational superiority of one formula over another, but only of estimating the values stemming from belief in a formula. Despite his own studies and the evidence he cited against the truth of determinism in such papers as 'Are We Automata?' and 'Great Men and Their Environ- ment', James still approached the same problem in 'The Dilemma of Determinism' by arguing *ad hominem,* forcing the determinist into the uncomfortable position of having to accept undesirable alternatives in order to remain consistent.
112. One can cite in this connection A. J. Ayer's *The Origins of Pragma- tism.* He simply assumed without notice and without question that the pragmatists were asking the same questions about perception and about knowledge that have occupied British philosophers since Hume's time. Consequently, he failed to notice their rejection of the primacy of epistemology, or their thoroughgoing critique of the empiricism and theory of experience which he took for granted. Much that is both important and distinctive in Pragmatism will be missed if it is sup- posed that the movement can be understood simply as 'empiricism' combined with a measure of American 'practicality'. James was closest to classical empiricism, although even he called it into question in the formulation of his radical empiricism. Peirce and Dewey, however, were most critical of just about everything that the Hume–Russell position represents.

2 The theory of truth

1. For example, W. P. Montague, *The Ways of Knowing,* New York, 1925, ch. 5; Brand Blanshard, *The Nature of Thought,* London, 1939, vol. 1, ch. 10.
2. The principal reason for the difficulty one encounters in trying to present the doctrines of the pragmatists in neat formulae is that their ideas were continually developing. They believed in philosophy as

discussion and communication and that involved attempts to answer criticism, to meet demands for clarification, and to improve their theories on the basis of shared reflection. It is this philosophical interaction that helps explain why they made many statements and restatements of their positions. It would be fair to say that their own thinking exhibited the experimental spirit so fully defended in their respective philosophies. This open-ended approach was bound to result in loose ends and even incoherencies. Dewey, especially, seems to have believed that every critic could be answered on the spot, as it were, and in the attempt to do so he often stretched his position to the breaking point.

3. Numerous passages could be cited; one of the most appropriate is *Collected Papers* (for publication details, see above), 7.659, where Peirce claimed unambiguously that were there not a reality independent of what it is thought to be, there would be no truth.

4. *Collected Papers,* 5.565.

5. *Ibid.*

6. *Collected Papers,* 5.549 ff.

7. *Collected Papers,* 4.536; cf. 5.564.

8. *Collected Papers,* 5.581; cf. especially 1.175, 325.

9. See A. P. Ushenko, *Power and Events,* Princeton, 1946, pp. 2 ff for an illuminating contrast between what the author calls a 'conform' conception of truth and a 'transform' conception. The view of Peirce, and that of James but to a lesser extent, represents the conform position, while Dewey's conception of knowledge places him clearly in the transform camp.

10. *Collected Papers,* 1.578.

11. *Collected Papers,* 1.44. In the light of all that has been said about Pragmatism's having reduced truth to success, practical advantage, etc., such an 'intellectualist' conception of truth must certainly come as a surprise. Cf. *Collected Papers,* 8.143 for Peirce's rejection of a conception of truth which appeals to whether some truth is 'conducive to the interests of society or not'. Also in this connection attention should be called to Peirce's discussion of the nature of problems in logic and their relation to needs and fulfilments. In discussing Schröder's views Peirce insisted on an 'intellectual' need to answer questions, on the need for 'generalization' implicit in the intellectual need and on the need for 'theory' which is a synthesis of a multitude of predicates. See especially *Collected Papers,* 3.516.

12. *Collected Papers,* 8.126.

13. Sometimes called 'retroduction', although it is not clear that the two terms were always used by him synonymously. One should remember that Peirce often characterized Pragmatism as a maxim for the admissibility of hypotheses and hence as a matter of the 'logic of abduction'.

Consideration of the point at this juncture would interfere with the discussion in the text. A brief summary of the connection, however, will prove helpful. An hypothesis is to be understood as a proposed explanation of phenomena considered as a suggestion that is expected to be true. The pragmatic maxim, Peirce argued, is sufficient to determine the admissibility of any hypothesis as hypothesis because the appeal to 'possibly practical considerations' would exclude any rule of abduction that would prohibit on 'formalistic grounds' any inquiry into how we ought to shape our conduct. Hence the hypotheses it admits are such as all would admit, and, on the other hand, the maxim cannot exclude any hypotheses that ought to be admitted because the appeal to difference in practical consequences indicates the testability of the hypothesis, at least in principle. Among other notions, Peirce aimed at rejecting the classical positivist thesis that no hypothesis is to be admitted, even as an hypothesis, unless its truth or falsity can be directly perceived. Peirce saw this abductive principle itself as passing beyond what is directly perceived. See *Collected Papers,* 5. 195 ff.

14. E.g. *Collected Papers,* 5.171 ff.
15. *Collected Papers,* 1.74.
16. *Collected Papers,* 8.209.
17. *Ibid.*
18. *Collected Papers,* 7.183 ff (*c.* 1902).
19. *Collected Papers,* 7.187.
20. Peirce did not always reiterate the normative constraints under which, in his view, the process of inquiry is to be conducted in the scientific community. There are the constraints which the *inquirers impose on themselves* in the form of the elimination of self-interest in a given outcome, fidelity to truth-seeking and perseverance with respect to following logical and experimental canons. There is, in addition, the constraint *imposed upon the inquirers by the real.* If these constraints are not kept constantly in view, two sorts of distortions with respect to the meaning of science are bound to result. On the one hand, if the self-imposed constraints are forgotten, science ceases to be understood as the essentially *human* activity which it is because one loses sight of the fact that science is sustained only as long as flesh-and-blood inquirers continue to abide by normative conditions. If, on the other hand, the constraint of the real is ignored, science may appear as no more than a closed circle of human opinion, which, though largely unanimous, does not penetrate to what's what.
21. *Collected Papers,* 7.335.
22. See my paper 'Community and Reality' in Richard J. Bernstein (ed.). *Perspectives on Peirce,* New Haven, 1965, pp. 94–5.
23. See especially *Collected Papers,* 7.659.

H

24. *Collected Papers,* 7.335.
25. *Collected Papers,* 6.452 ff; 7.220; 1.118, 204, 264, 266, 496, 628, 648.
26. *Collected Papers,* 7.220.
27. *Ibid.*
28. *Collected Papers,* 6.452 ff.
29. *Collected Papers,* 6.476.
30. Philip P. Wiener, *Evolution and the Founders of Pragmatism,* Cambridge, Massachusetts, 1949.
31. The latter point has sometimes been obscured by the tendency to think of 'practice' only in relation to the subsequent application of scientific knowledge in technology. Dewey's claim, however, is that theory and action cannot be divorced because both were required for the *acquisition* of knowledge *in the first instance.*
32. *Collected Papers,* 5.552.
33. *Collected Papers,* 5.558.
34. I think it is essential to point out in view of some recent discussion that James' approach was not basically 'linguistic'; that is to say, he began not with language but with the description and analysis of lived experience and expressed many of his results in quite familiar or ordinary language. Thus he *used* ordinary language in philosophical thinking, something which is quite different from making the analysis of such language – however that may be understood – the basis of philosophy. See what Dewey said about James' use of 'American idioms' in 'The Development of American Pragmatism' in Department of Philosophy of Columbia University (ed.), *Studies in the History of Ideas,* New York, 1935, vol. 2, p. 366, n. 9.
35. See John E. Smith, 'Radical Empiricism', *Proceedings of the Aristotelian Society,* vol. 65 (1965), pp. 205–18.
36. *The Meaning of Truth, A Sequel to 'Pragmatism',* New York and London, 1909; repr. Ann Arbor, 1970, p. xxxix.
37. James' immediate purpose in distinguishing the 'how' and the 'what' of cognition was to avoid having to talk, as he said, about brain events, souls, etc, as the materials of a genetic account, so that he could concentrate on the elements of cognition as the product or outcome. The fact remains, however, that the 'how it comes' reappears within the experimental 'workings' of an idea when it issues in knowledge.
38. *The Meaning of Truth* (1970 ed.), p. xxx. James clearly did *not* say that a knower 'makes' truth; in speaking of an idea 'becoming' true he referred to the process of verifying; it is the events which 'make' the idea true. James might have helped his case by saying not that the idea 'becomes' true on some occasion, but rather that the knowledge that it is so is realized by someone making the test. I do not see any-

thing in James' thought that would stand in the way of his holding that the world was 'round' prior to the discovery by Columbus that 'rotundity' is an idea which holds true of the world.

39. It is important to notice that there are times when James thought of 'copy' as the most obvious sense of agreement and he seems to have assumed that where 'copying' exists agreement exists as well, so that we have a kind of immediate verification. However, where copying fails to obtain, as in the case of the idea of energy in the spring of the watch, he asked what agreement means and proposed in those cases to appeal to the pragmatic maxim – grant an idea to be true, what difference will it make, etc. – as the proper way to determine whether there is 'agreement' in a non-copy sense. See *The Meaning of Truth*, p. xxix.

40. *The Meaning of Truth*, p. 24 (italics in original).

41. *The Meaning of Truth*, p. 25.

42. *The Meaning of Truth*, p. 36.

43. *The Meaning of Truth*, p. 39.

44. James later modified his earlier view in a reference to 'the treatment of percepts as the only reality' (*The Meaning of Truth*, p. 42) and added, 'I now treat concepts as a co-ordinate realm'. James seems to have had in mind at least three distinguishing features of concepts *vis à vis* percepts and it is not easy to say which of them commands the field or whether all must be reckoned with on equal terms. Concepts are sometimes said to be *representational* in contrast to percepts as *immediate* or intuitive, and the concept's function is to bridge the gap between present thought and absent object by showing how we can pass, through the intermediaries of the surrounding universe, from one to the other. At other times concepts are viewed as *abstract* or *partial thoughts,* representing colour, shape, etc., in contrast to a *whole* or *concrete object* that is presumably present as such to the percept. And at still other times the concept is seen as expressing a frozen or static *excerpt* from a *primordial experience* which is all stream or flow. There are thus three sets of contrasts involved: (a) immediate–representative; (b) whole–part; and (c) dynamic–static, and in each case the concept stands subordinate to the percept, since the former is always 'about' the reality grasped in the latter. This picture, however, is incomplete if one omits – as seems generally to be done – the final chapter of *The Principles of Psychology* where James sided with the *a priorists* on the issue of the status to be accorded the 'house-born' concepts or categories and agreed that they cannot be derived from percepts, even if he was dissatisfied with Kant's deduction and proposed instead another explanation in terms of genetic psychology.

45. And they would remain so even if a person had learned how to *use* them correctly in well-formed sentences through the study of grammar

and the use of a dictionary, but still had no acquaintance with the phenomena denoted.

46. *The Meaning of Truth,* pp. 43–50.

47. *The Meaning of Truth,* pp. 44—5.

48. Logic and mathematics would, of course, appear to be exceptions to this thesis, but it is by no means clear that they are. The intuitionist approach to mathematics initiated by Kant excludes its reduction to logical conceptions alone, and the history of logic shows the frequency of the resort to diagrams, schemata and other spatial sorts of devices for the representation of the relations between propositions. One must also recall Plato's divided 'line'.

49. Current analyses of 'perception' such as that offered by Merleau-Ponty, for example, understand perception in a quite broad sense so that it embraces both conceiving and interpreting. One need not object to this extension of meaning as long as 'perception' does not still retain the exclusive meaning it had in the perception–conception dichotomy.

50. *The Principles of Psychology,* New York, 1890, especially vol. 2, ch. 19–21.

51. Perception in the *Principles* is taken as 'the consciousness of particular material things present to sense' (*Principles,* vol. 2, p. 76). This is consonant with the idea of percept as acquaintance, but in the psychological treatment more emphasis is placed on perception as 'supplementing' a sense impression by associations derived from other impressions.

52. *The Meaning of Truth,* pp. 41–2, note.

53. *The Meaning of Truth,* pp. 180–216.

54. Despite the criticism and confusion surrounding past discussions of this pragmatic notion of 'workability', what James wrote about it seems to suggest something quite simple. If I think of or have the idea of an automobile which I have just won in a raffle and therefore with which I am not very familiar, that idea may include the thought 'motor at the front end'; if I 'follow' that thought through the intermediaries which terminate in my attempt to open the hood and expose the motor only to find that 'motor at the rear end' is the 'satisfactory' idea, then the thought I actually followed was *not* 'satisfactorily adapted' to its object and therefore did not 'work'. James' critics at this point invariably insisted that the reason it did not work is to be found in the fact that the facts in the situation were actually arranged in a fashion *other than* that indicated in the idea, without further reference to the satisfaction or dissatisfaction of the *person* who had the idea and followed where it led. James, on the other hand, invariably wanted to keep the person in the picture and especially what he was *doing* with the idea, so that there arises the possibility of confusion between the success or failure of the idea in relation to an actual

state of affairs and the success or failure of the *person's purpose* in using the idea.

55. *The Meaning of Truth*, p. 39.
56. 'The Pragmatist Account of Truth and its Misunderstanders', *The Philosophical Review*, 1908, repr. in *The Meaning of Truth*, pp. 180–216, p. 180.
57. *The Meaning of Truth*, p. 189, n. 1.
58. The meaning of the term 'work' here is not as clear as it might be; it seems to mean that unless a belief fulfils a stated human need, that belief fails to 'work'. Also implied, however, is the very different view that a belief which no one takes seriously is one which, pragmatically, does not 'work'.
59. *The Meaning of Truth*, p. 195.
60. *Ibid.*
61. *The Meaning of Truth*, p. 101.
62. *The Meaning of Truth*, p. 195.
63. *The Meaning of Truth*, p. 196.
64. *The Meaning of Truth*, p. 191.
65. *The Meaning of Truth*, p. 197.
66. *The Meaning of Truth*, p. 184.
67. *The Meaning of Truth*, p. 185.
68. *The Meaning of Truth,* p. 186. The influence of Royce's criticism is evident at this point. In *The World and the Individual* (New York, 1899, Second Series, New York, 1901; repr. New York, 1959) Royce contended, in his examination of realism, that 'being independent of' can be construed as a symmetrical relation, so that when it is said on behalf of realism 'the object is independent of the idea' the converse of this proposition also holds and ideas become coordinate realities.
69. *The Meaning of Truth*, p. 186.
70. *Ibid.*
71. Royce, it is true, invariably presented an unsympathetic account of James' position, relying heavily on the latter's use of the term 'expedient' which Royce took to mean the right to calculate one's advantage. This point comes out clearly in Royce's adaptation, as a test case, of Kant's example about the man who entrusts to another a sum of money which is to be transmitted to a third party, and then dies, so that there is nothing in the realm of evidence, apart from the memory of the man who received the money, pointing to the fact of the transaction. Royce's question does not concern moral obligation but rather what, on James' view, we are to understand as constituting the *truth* about the transaction. The idea behind Royce's question is that only if the person's interest and calculation of what would be 'satisfactory' to him were suppressed in favour of a purely objective concern to disclose exactly what was the case, regardless of the 'difference' it would make to

anyone if the transaction were reported as fact, could it make any sense
to speak about truth. In short, on Royce's view, the appeal to the
'expedient' in the way of thinking as the meaning of truth, puts no
constraint on the person to disclose 'what's what', but allows him instead
to represent the situation through ideas calculated to bring about his own
satisfaction. In view of James' avowed realism, it is clear that he could
meet Royce's objection, but it is equally clear that he could not consistently have done so on the basis of what he had written about truth,
expediency, success, etc., in *Pragmatism* and prior to *The Meaning of
Truth*.

72. *The Meaning of Truth*, p. 198.
73. *The Meaning of Truth*, p. 199.
74. *Ibid*.
75. How is it possible for a theory to remain unformulated? Scepticism
    may be allowed as an attitude or a stance, and one can see, as
    Sextus Empiricus pointed out long ago, why a person determined to
    preserve this attitude inviolate would resort to the device of making
    no claim for its 'truth', 'superiority', etc., of a sort which would involve
    logical inconsistency. But if scepticism need not be a theory to be
    asserted as 'true', it is difficult to see how a theory of truth can fail to
    be a 'theory' which must be asserted as in some sense superior or
    'more satisfactory' than other alternatives. Moreover, if as we have
    seen in other cases, James was ready to construe 'satisfactory' in terms
    of being true or in accord with the external reality, why should he
    not have been willing to do so in the case of the theory of truth itself?
76. See 'Purpose in American Philosophy', *International Philosophical
    Quarterly*, vol. 1, no. 3, repr. in John E. Smith, *Themes in American
    Philosophy*, New York, 1971, pp. 390–406.

3   The new conception of experience

1. See John E. Smith, 'The Reflexive Turn, the Linguistic Turn and the
   Pragmatic Outcome', *The Monist*, vol. 53, no. 4 (1969), pp. 588–605.
2. Thus, for example, A. J. Ayer in his otherwise clear and judicious
   treatment of some doctrines of Pragmatism in *The Origins of Pragmatism* (San Francisco, 1968) concentrates almost exclusively on the
   conceptions of truth and knowledge in Peirce and James, with the suggestion that Peirce's metaphysics is 'a florid decoration'. Because of
   this selective emphasis and his omission of Dewey entirely, Ayer's work
   conveys no impression whatever of the extent to which Pragmatism
   generally represents a critique of classical empiricism. Peirce rejected
   any view which requires thought to start with simple, and therefore
   certain, items of sensible content or of thought; Dewey launched the
   full-scale attack on traditional empiricism set forth in the text,

and even James, who clearly accepted more of classical empiricism than either of his colleagues, criticised Hume for being non-empirical when, for example, he gave to disjunctions a more secure status than conjunctions and togetherness in experience. A similar failure to notice the critique of previous empiricism expressed in Pragmatism is exemplified in Charles Morris' monograph *Logical Positivism, Pragmatism and Scientific Empiricism* (Paris, 1937). Once again the impression is given that Pragmatism is simply one more stage in the development of modern 'empiricism' without any awareness of the extent to which the pragmatists were attempting to break out of the circle of problems established by that empiricism, and to reorient philosophy under the aegis of a new conception of experience. See L. Kolakowski, *The Alienation of Reason,* trans. N. Guterman, New York, 1968, pp. 149 ff.

3. It is important to notice that in one of the papers where Dewey's criticism is expressed, 'An Empirical Survey of Empiricisms' (repr. in R. J. Bernstein (ed.), *John Dewey on Experience, Nature and Freedom,* New York, 1960, pp. 70–87), Locke rather than Hume is taken as typical. I regard the choice as dubious because Locke's emphasis on 'power' and the 'realism' surviving in his thought manifest affinities with Dewey's own position. Hume, on the other hand, having carried phenomenalism to the end point, espouses a doctrine that forms the proper antithesis of Dewey's. The more detailed account offered by Dewey in 'The Need for a Recovery of Philosophy' (repr. in Bernstein (ed.), *Dewey on Experience,* pp. 20–69) more clearly reflects Hume as the archetypal exponent of the classical empiricism Dewey was rejecting.

4. 'The Need for a Recovery of Philosophy' in Bernstein (ed.), *Dewey on Experience,* p. 28.

5. Confusion in interpreting Pragmatism can be avoided if one bears in mind that its proponents did *not* propose to eliminate the theoretical standpoint or to dissolve it into 'practice', but rather to call attention to its character as a *special* standpoint among others and one which is not supervenient. Knowledge is ingredient in all experience, but not every experience is that of theoretical knowing.

6. In English we have but one word, 'experience', to cover the ground; the distinction in German between *Erfahrung* as a strictly cognitive affair as it is in Kant and *Erlebnis* which means living through or undergoing is helpful. The latter is close to what Dewey had in mind when he spoke of sufferings and undergoings in the primordial sense; experience as specifically cognitive is the special affair of inquiry.

7. Paul A. Schilpp (ed.), *The Philosophy of John Dewey,* The Library of Living Philosophers, vol. 1, Evanston and Chicago, 1939, p. 544.

8. Bernstein (ed.), *Dewey on Experience,* pp. 49–50.

9. Bernstein (ed.), *Dewey on Experience*, p. 50.
10. Bernstein (ed.), *Dewey on Experience*, p. 53. To avoid misunderstanding it must be said at once that here 'use' is not meant in a reductive or utilitarian sense, but to indicate that these natural events provide clues as to what is to be expected in similar or changed circumstances.
11. Bernstein (ed.), *Dewey on Experience*, p. 23.
12. George Santayana, 'The Genteel Tradition in American Philosophy' in his *Winds of Doctrine*, London, 1913; repr. in Harper Torchbooks, New York, 1957, p. 207.
13. The ambiguity in Kant's thought on this head has often been pointed out. There are passages in the *Critique* where *Erfahrung* has to be construed as meaning the *sense* component exclusively, despite his defence of the main thesis that *Erfahrung* is impossible except as the joint product of sense *and* understanding.
14. Bernstein (ed.), *Dewey on Experience*, p. 23.
15. Bernstein (ed.), *Dewey on Experience*, p. 33.
16. See John E. Smith, 'Purpose in American Philosophy' in his *Themes in American Philosophy*, New York, 1971, pp. 7–25, for an account of the essential connection between thought and purpose which is at the root of Pragmatism.
17. James was not altogether clear in his own mind about the relation between radical empiricism and Pragmatism. In the Preface to *Pragmatism* (New York and London, 1907; repr. New York, 1943) he declared the two doctrines to be independent. 'One may entirely reject it [radical empiricism] and still be a pragmatist.' But in the Preface to *The Meaning of Truth. A Sequel to 'Pragmatism'* (New York and London, 1909; repr. Ann Arbor, 1970) we are told that establishing the pragmatist theory of truth 'is a step of first-rate importance in making radical empiricism prevail'.
18. Preface to *The Meaning of Truth* (1970 ed.), p. 317.
19. William James, *Essays in Radical Empiricism*, New York and London, 1912, p. 42.
20. David Hume, *Treatise*, ed. L. Selby-Bigge, Oxford, 1896, Appendix, p. 636.
21. *Collected Papers* (publication details above), 5.416 ff.
22. *Collected Papers*, 5.611 ff.
23. It is interesting to note that Peirce was a radical in coining new philosophical terms, but extremely conservative about old ones. Actually this view is quite consistent; the uniqueness of novel terminology becomes clear only when the older expressions retain fixed meanings free from tampering.
24. *Collected Papers*, 5.613.
25. *Collected Papers*, 5.50.
26. *Collected Papers*, 5.53. This is an example of Peirce's 'phenomenology'

or appeal to observation of the phenomena which, as he said, 'each of you must make for himself'.

27. *Collected Papers,* 5.524; cf. 6.454.
28. *Collected Papers,* 1.321. See also 2.784 where experience is connected with cognitions 'forced upon us'.
29. *Collected Papers,* 1.335.
30. *Collected Papers,* 1.336. Here Peirce added, characteristically, 'from a well-understood cause' by which he meant an explanation in terms of acoustics; in company with Dewey, Peirce did not treat the case as one of 'relativity' in perception or of appearance and reality.
31. A significant part of Peirce's thought is summed up in his 'critical commonsensism' which is a revised version of Scottish commonsense philosophy strengthened or made 'critical' by his doctrine of fallibilism and his concept of vagueness.
32. *Collected Papers,* 6.571.

4 Inquiry, science and control

1. *The Quest for Certainty,* London, 1930, p. 120.
2. See *Logic: The Theory of Inquiry,* New York, 1938, pp. 101–19.
3. *Logic,* pp. 3–4.
4. *Logic,* p. 5.
5. *Ibid.* Although Peirce was critical of Dewey's genetic approach to the interpretation of logical forms and felt that he failed to do justice to the autonomy of logic as a formal discipline, it is clear that Peirce's attack on foundationalism in his 'Grounds of the Validity of the Laws of Logic' (*Collected Papers,* 5.318–357) has affinities with Dewey's position. Both were attacking the long tradition according to which knowledge is thought to rest on some ultimate foundations which are certain, necessary and incorrigible. The difference between them is that whereas Dewey was determined to limit the scope of logic to its specific contribution to actual inquiry, Peirce was more concerned for the internal development of exact logic and for the application of formal probability theory to scientific explanations such as the Darwinian hypothesis. In numerous places (see e.g. *Collected Papers,* 6.15) Peirce was prepared to 'generalize' Darwin's principle in the form of a statistical formula for 'possible evolution'. Chapter 4 of Philip P. Wiener's *Evolution and the Founders of Pragmatism* (Cambridge, Mass., 1949) contains most illuminating material about Peirce's conception of logic and the influence of the theory of evolution upon it.
6. Critics have pointed out that Dewey used this term instead of the traditional term 'truth', and that it raises the question as to whether, on his view, we ever really 'know' anything at all. The basic idea behind the use of the term 'warranted assertion' is that it represents

H*

the outcome or terminal judgement of inquiry which must come with certain conditions attached; the warrant is limited because the judgement may be imprecise or one-sided in some respect and, moreover, it stands open to correction. In short, the tentativeness attaching to 'warranted assertions', a tentativeness not generally associated with the term 'truth', is meant to allow for the bearing of temporality and contingency on the knowing process.

7. *Logic,* p. 66.

8. *Logic,* p. 69.

9. Although here Dewey was supposed to be characterizing the nature of a situation as such, he naturally assumed that the 'problematic' situation is a paradigm. The assumption is allowable in so far as the context of inquiry is taken for granted but the conception of pervasive quality is not confined to this context since it figures as well in his theory of art. The ultimate question is whether Dewey did not have but two kinds of situations: problematic situations which call for knowing and subsequent control, and aesthetic situations which are 'had' and which, being terminal, call for nothing beyond themselves.

10. Some confusion has arisen over Dewey's use of the term 'doubtful' with respect to the problematic situation. Russell, particularly, insisted that the situation itself cannot be 'doubtful', because that term can refer only to someone confronting the situation who is in doubt. Even allowing that the use of the intentional term may bring its own problems, the fact is that Dewey meant to attribute the trait to the situation, and if one says that it is the inquirer who is in doubt, this can only mean, assuming that his doubt is focused, that there is something in or about the *situation* that is unsettled or incoherent and is thus the basis of his being in doubt.

11. *Logic,* p. 104. Here again emphasis falls on what has already proved itself effective, apart from 'epistemological' justifications.

12. *Logic,* p. 103.

13. We have here, as in every other part of Dewey's thought, the 'naturalistic suspension' – 'better than' can be determined without the implication of a 'best'.

14. See 'Grounds of the Validity of the Laws of Logic', *Collected Papers,* 5.318 ff.

15. See *Collected Papers,* 8.188–90 for the review, and 8.239–44 for correspondence between them on the nature of logic.

16. *Logic,* pp. 105–6.

17. *Logic,* p. 107.

18. *Logic,* p. 108.

19. If it is said that the accuracy of the measuring device *could* be called into question, that fact would serve to initiate a new inquiry, but in

order to check the instrument other components, for example other instruments, would have to be regarded as trustworthy.

20. *Immanuel Kant's Critique of Pure Reason,* trans. Norman Kemp Smith, London, 1933, B, xiii.
21. *Logic,* p. 113.
22. *Logic,* p. 115.
23. *Logic,* p. 118.
24. *Ibid.*
25. *Collected Papers,* 5.374.
26. Cf. *Collected Papers,* 5.510; 6.485.
27. See *Collected Papers,* 8.60 where Peirce criticized James for speaking of what 'natural science' declines to do, when it is only the students of the science who can 'decline'. This point is typical of Peirce's concern to reflect what actually happens in inquiry, in the fixation of belief, etc., as opposed to an emphasis on abstractions.
28. *Collected Papers,* 5.375.
29. *Collected Papers,* 5.376, n. 3.
30. *Collected Papers,* 5.443.
31. *Collected Papers,* 5.451.
32. *Ibid.* (italics added).
33. *Collected Papers,* 1.135.
34. *Collected Papers,* 1.56.
35. *Ibid.*
36. *Collected Papers,* 1.668.
37. Peirce published a review of *Studies in Logical Theory,* Chicago, 1903, to which Dewey had contributed the lion's share of the essays. This review appeared in *The Nation* (1904) and is found in *Collected Papers,* 8.188–190. During the following year Dewey wrote to Peirce commenting favourably on the latter's paper 'What Pragmatism Is' which was published in *The Monist* (April, 1905) and is found in *Collected Papers,* 5.411 ff. A letter from Peirce to Dewey dated '1904 June 9' is to be found in *Collected Papers,* 8.239–242.
38. *Collected Papers,* 8.241.
39. *Collected Papers,* 8.243.
40. Consider, for example, the following comment: 'All my studies are conducted in full view of actual scientific memoirs and other records of scientific inquiry.' (*Collected Papers,* 8.243.)
41. Consider the following from *The Quest of Certainty* (p. 214): 'Many definitions of mind and the mental have been given; I know of but one that goes to the heart of the matter: – response to the doubtful as such. No inanimate thing reacts to things *as* problematic.'

5 Pragmatism and metaphysics

1. *Essays on Truth and Reality,* Oxford, 1914, p. 67.
2. Berkeley saw this point in connection with his acknowledgement of *activity* or active spirit for which he employed the term 'notion'; he could not use the term 'idea' because it denoted what is passive and absolutely singular.
3. Here it makes no difference whether one refers to James' later 'radical' empiricism or to the general empirical bent of his thought with its focus on finding the cash value of abstract terms. Radical empiricism had the special function of dealing with the dualisms of object and consciousness, body and mind, etc., but it did not differ from his earlier appeal to experience in terms of asking what something is actually 'known as'.
4. William James, *Pragmatism*, New York and London, 1907; repr. New York, 1943, p. 107.
5. Cf. *Pragmatism* (1943 ed.), p. 122: 'Pragmatism, so far from keeping her eyes bent on the immediate practical foreground, as she is accused of doing, dwells just as much upon the world's remotest perspectives.'
6. *Character and Opinion in the United States,* New York, 1955, p. 46.
7. *Immanuel Kant's Critique of Pure Reason,* trans. Norman Kemp Smith, London, 1933, A462=B490 ff.
8. *Critique,* B493.
9. *Ibid.*
10. *Critique,* B494.
11. To mention but one, Kant would have allowed theoretical *meaning,* even if not knowledge, to his theses and antitheses, whereas James would have regarded the ascription of such meaning as a case of taking a doctrine 'intellectualistically' rather than as a prophecy or a promise.
12. It is true that James often used these terms as if they were synonyms, but the reason for distinguishing them will become clear in the context.
13. *Pragmatism,* p. 132.
14. *Pragmatism,* p. 148.
15. It is instructive that in James' best-known discussion of the problem of freedom, 'The Dilemma of Determinism', the use of the dilemma makes the issue turn on the *consistency* with which one can *believe* certain doctrines.
16. *Pragmatism,* p. 12.
17. *Collected Papers,* 1.417 ff.
18. *Collected Papers,* 1.486.
19. *Collected Papers,* 1.487.
20. *Ibid.*

21. Notice that Kant, for example, in discussing the modal categories held, first, that they do not affect the content, and, second, that possibility and necessity can be construed in terms of *existence* plus the time factor logically quantified by 'some' and 'all'.
22. *Collected Papers,* 1.229.
23. *Collected Papers,* 1.129.
24. See *Collected Papers,* 1.487.
25. *Collected Papers,* 1.301.
26. *Collected Papers,* 1.421.
27. *Collected Papers,* 1.560 ff.
28. *Collected Papers,* 1.490; cf. 1.491: 'So far Hegel is quite right.'
29. *Collected Papers,* 1.417.
30. See especially *Collected Papers,* 1.491, 544. It is interesting to note that while Peirce was familiar with the way Hegel had reworked Kant's categorial scheme, he insisted that it was the Kantian and not the Hegelian table which was decisive for him.
31. Peirce's Scotistic realism and his evolutionary metaphysics provide sufficient evidence for the claim that he cannot ultimately be regarded as maintaining a 'transcendental' position in the Kantian sense. This point is not to be confused with the conflict in Peirce's thought, as alleged by some writers, between his 'naturalism' and his 'transcendentalism'; because in the discussion of that conflict, the latter term refers to Peirce's speculative metaphysics which is supposed to be at odds with the evolutionary or 'scientific' elements in his philosophy.
32. *Collected Papers,* 1.301.
33. *Collected Papers,* 1.418; cf. 1.303.
34. *Collected Papers,* 1.422.
35. Since the relation of the concept of possibility to Peirce's doctrine of firstness is one of the topics treated by Dewey in his paper, 'Peirce's Theory of Qyuality' (*Journal of Philosophy,* 32 (1935), pp. 701–8, this juncture is an appropriate one for comment on Dewey's discussion. Dewey's paper was written in response to an earlier one in the same journal by T. A. Goudge in which Goudge identified Peirce's 'firstness' with the 'given' and then went on to claim that Peirce's view is inconsistent because it involves at once both immediate qualities of feeling and possibilities or universals. Dewey came to Peirce's defence by pointing out, as in the text above, that Peirce was referring to material potentiality and not to logical possibility, and that, in addition, it is quite erroneous to equate Peirce's firstness with any of the 'givens' of classical empiricism – Locke's 'ideas', Hume's 'impressions' or the '*sensa*' of later discussion. The ground of the error, and this is the central point in Dewey's paper with which I entirely agree, is that these givens all involve *existence* and hence secondness; whereas firstness has its essential relation to secondness as another

feature of the phenomenon. Firstness has to be understood in itself, which means in abstraction from secondness.

36. *Collected Papers*, 1.306.
37. *Collected Papers*, 1.310.
38. Quality, fact and law in the sense in which Peirce understood them represent quite precisely Kant's modal categories, and if Peirce was reflecting this triad, it would help to explain his characterization of quality as possibility.
39. *Collected Papers*, 1.431.
40. From 'x is other than y' it follows that 'y is other than x' but from 'x is independent of y' it does not follow that 'y is independent of x'.
41. *Collected Papers*, 1.437; cf. 1.434 where the exclusion of reason from what is 'brute' or 'just there' is qualified.
42. *Collected Papers*, 1.433 where Peirce considered different kinds of existence, but characterized them in the same generic way.
43. *Collected Papers*, 1.345.
44. *Collected Papers*, 1.344.
45. *Collected Papers*, 1.545 ff.
46. It is important to notice that one must not confuse the interpre*ter* as one actually performing the sign-reading function, with the interpre*tants* by means of which he performs that function. The interpretant is the interpreter's *reading* of the sign, or, in other words, his assertion that a given sign is equivalent to another sign. The interpre*ter* cannot in any case be omitted because no sign interprets itself.
47. *Collected Papers*, 1.427. The above statement follows on Peirce's question: 'What is *fact*?'
48. *Collected Papers*, 1.420.
49. *Ibid*; cf. 1.475.
50. Cf. *Collected Papers*, 1.480.
51. Peirce was most puristic on this point as can be seen from *Collected Papers*, 1.480, where it is said that while a genuine triad cannot occur within the sweep of the categories of quality or fact, there are 'mere' laws or regularities of both quality and fact – the monadically or dyadically 'degenerate' triads – which are not to be confused with genuine triads. In the place cited, or part of his development of the categories as the 'logic of mathematics', a *thoroughly* genuine triad is said to occur only in the universe of *representation*.
52. In several places, moreover, Peirce expressed his interests in making for his categories the claim of 'these and no others', and it is difficult to see how such a claim could be supported if the categories were entirely independent of each other. See, for example, *Collected Papers*, 1.421.
53. The 'New List' is found in *Collected Papers*, 1.545–567.
54 *Collected Papers*, 1.531.

55. *Collected Papers*, 6.37.
56. A related version of this claim runs as follows: 'If we knew every-thing, then we would see clearly that this total necessitarianism is so.' Apart from the seductiveness of the idea that 'knowing every-thing' would be the same as knowing that all states of affairs had to be as they were and not otherwise, this appeal to total knowledge reduces to a postulate or presupposition not itself supported by evi-dence because it is supposed to be the supreme intellectual condition for obtaining any evidence in the first place.
57. *Collected Papers*, 6.44.
58. *Collected Papers*, 6.63.
59. *Ibid.*
60. *Collected Papers*, 6.60.
61. *Collected Papers*, 6.104; cf. 6.127–130.
62. *Collected Papers*, 6.109.
63. Peirce used the terms 'instant' to mean a 'point of time', and the term 'moment' to mean 'an infinitesimal duration'. It is clear that he was addressing the same problem later focused by Whitehead where he ques-tioned the validity of conceiving a duration solely in terms of 'instants' which are durationless. If one thinks of a finite duration in terms of proper parts, these parts must themselves be finite durations.
64. *Collected Papers*, 6.126.
65. See R. J. Bernstein (ed.), *John Dewey on Experience, Nature and Free-dom*, New York, 1960, p. 211. This collection includes Dewey's paper of 1915, 'The Subject Matter of Metaphysical Inquiry', discussed in the text above. This paper, thoroughly Kantian in its rejection of a certain kind of metaphysics, is a clear forerunner of Dewey's *Experience and Nature* (Chicago and London, 1925; rev. ed. New York, 1929) which is the most comprehensive expression of Dewey's naturalistic philo-sophy. Since the earlier discussion is so clear, especially in its indication of the relations between metaphysics as the search for the 'generic traits of existence' and the special sciences, beginning with it will repay the effort.
66. Bernstein (ed.), *Dewey on Experience*, p. 213.
67. It is a good question whether Dewey is entitled to his negative assertion; if it is 'meaningless' to say that nature has an ultimate origin and an ultimate end, the denial of that same proposition cannot be *ipso facto* meaningful. On this point, Kant was more circumspect than either Dewey or the positivists in holding that certain metaphysical theses are not meaningless, but simply cannot be a matter of knowledge.
68. *Experience and Nature*, p. 8.
69. *Experience and Nature*, pp. 9-10.
70. The latter point is well illustrated by the charge against Hegel's cate-gories as 'bloodless' when viewed apart from the reality they structure.

71. *Experience and Nature*, p. 24.
72. *The Quest for Certainty*, London, 1930, pp. 226 ff.
73. See John E. Smith, 'Purpose in American Philosophy' in his *Themes in American Philosophy*, New York, 1971.
74. *Experience and Nature*, p. 26.
75. *Ibid.*
76. *Experience and Nature*, p. 68.
77. *Experience and Nature*, p. 29.
78. The determination and evaluation of human behaviour may have to be regarded as a special case in view of Dewey's attempt to show that the method of intelligence can be made to function effectively in the sphere of ethics.
79. This issue cannot be considered here but it is important to notice that for all of Dewey's criticism of 'sweeping generalizations', he was himself guilty of this vice especially when he was setting up a problem in historical terms. The fact is that in the Christian 'dualism' cited, 'flesh' means not 'body' but the 'natural' man, and 'spirit' means not 'mind' but the 'redeemed' man. Under the influence of Platonism and Neo-Platonism, Christianity became more 'dualistic' than the classical Hebraic tradition which insisted on the unity of the person, but, even so, the dualism in question is still not that of body and mind, matter and spirit.
80. *Experience and Nature*, p. 207.
81. *Experience and Nature*, p. 208.
82. *Experience and Nature*, p. 214.
83. *Experience and Nature*, p. 232.
84. *Experience and Nature*, p. 334. The passage is far from clear. After asserting that the traits mentioned above are 'common traits of all existence', Dewey continued, 'this fact is source both . . .' and I construe the 'fact' in question to be the universality of the traits. It is not clear why the emphasis should fall on the universality rather than on the traits themselves, especially when in the next paragraph we are told that it is *not* the trait as universal that counts but rather its connection with a concrete life situation.
85. *Ibid.*
86. There are, to be sure, certain logical difficulties raised by talk about man's being 'inside', 'outside', 'continuous with' nature when one considers that, for Dewey, 'nature' is not to be thought of as having boundaries of the sort that would allow for these spatial figures. There is a certain ambiguity in the concept of nature which Dewey in a way exploited. By 'nature' he did *not* mean a cosmic system or order of the sort envisaged by those who adhered to the classical conception of a 'Chain of Being' wherein nature stands as something distinct from man and God. And yet there is no denying that the term 'nature' cannot be

so easily divested of this traditional connotation and made to stand for 'what there is' in some non-differential sense as required by empirical method, while at the same time he actually used it in the classical *differential* sense when opposing idealists, theists and others bent on denying that the cosmic system exhausts what there is. If we take Dewey literally, everyone must be a 'naturalist' precisely because whatever there is belongs to 'nature'.

87. *Experience and Nature*, p. 341.
88. *Experience and Nature*, p. 352.

6 Pragmatism and religion

1. *Collected Papers*, 6.448.
2. McTaggart's discussion of this point is excellent; see *Some Dogmas of Religion*, London, 1930, pp. 24 ff.
3. It needs to be pointed out that religion has been subject to other forms of reduction in modern culture, not only to the moral. Interpreted as 'sentiment', religion coincides with personal feeling, wish, fancy; interpreted solely as ritual, it becomes a form of play; interpreted as a 'force making for social cohesion', it is envisaged as an 'instrument' whereby people are kept in decent order.
4. W. James, *Varieties of Religious Experience*, New York and London, 1902; repr. Modern Library Edition, New York, n.d. See 'Religious Experience', *Encyclopedia Britannica*, 15th ed., pp. 647–52. Although numerous philosophers and theologians before James – Edwards, Schleiermacher, Wesley, Otto, for example – laid emphasis on the intimate connection between religious concepts and experience, I have found no instance of the use of 'religious experience' as a technical term prior to James' Gifford Lectures.
5. *Varieties*, (Modern Library Ed.), p. 489 (italics in original).
6. *Varieties*, p. 498 (italics in original). There can be no question that James, simple as his formula may seem, laid hold of a truly universal pattern exhibited throughout the history of religion. The pervasive idea of 'salvation' or 'redemption' is unintelligible apart from a preceding diagnosis of the human predicament aimed at detecting what is 'wrong about us'. The key to understanding any identifiable religious tradition is found in that diagnosis and in the remedy proposed. The profound and significant differences between the world religions can be fully appreciated only when their divergent conceptions of what salvation means are related to the various diagnoses of what it is that men need to be saved from. See John E. Smith, *Experience and God*, Oxford, 1968, chapter 6.
7. *Varieties*, pp. 498–9.
8. *Varieties*, p. 500.

9. Peirce also spoke of an 'hypothesis' with respect to the reality of God, but his treatment includes both an argument and an argumentation in support of the hypothesis and he did not think of it, as James did, in terms of a 'diminished' claim.

10. *Varieties*, p. 505 (italics in original).

11. *Varieties*, p. 506.

12. *Collected Papers*, 6.443. See especially 6.429: 'But religion cannot reside in its totality in a single individual. Like every species of reality, it is essentially a social, a public affair.'

13. *Collected Papers*, 6.429.

14. *Collected Papers*, 6.616 ff.

15. After having begun by associating philosophy with science and the theoretical spirit which countenances no admixture of morals or any attempt to make men better or more successful, Peirce called attention to the 'hybrid character' of his lectures stemming from a confusion over the topic assigned. According to Peirce (*Collected Papers*, 1.622), he had been asked to prepare lectures on 'My views of philosophy' and he had drawn up outlines for eight lectures on Objective Logic only to receive word upon completion of the first lecture that he was expected instead to talk about 'topics of vital importance' (*ibid.*). Risky as it may be to draw conclusions about motives and intentions, it is difficult to ignore the overtones of irony and even of sarcasm in these lectures. If one reads them in a totally naïve way, Peirce will appear to be saying that matters of vital importance have nothing whatever to do with right reasoning, and that right reasoning cannot possibly be a matter of great concern to those chiefly interested in the practical application of ideas. The point is not that Peirce purposely misrepresented his position, but rather that he *exaggerated* the contrast between instinct and reason in circumstances which clearly annoyed him. As with all exaggerations, it is difficult to estimate the degree of the distortion; suffice it to say that while Peirce did adhere to his view that religion and other vitally important topics find their roots in instinct, it is not characteristic of him to oppose instinct to reasoning or to deny that it is susceptible of rational development. See especially *Collected Papers*, 1.622 and the first sentence of 1.623.

16. *Collected Papers*, 6.439.

17. To avoid confusion, it is necessary to call attention to the differences in meaning between terms which might otherwise be regarded as synonyms. 'Agapasm' is the name for one *mode* of evolution – evolution through creative love. The *doctrines* expressing this and other modes of evolution are named 'agapasticism', 'tychasticism', etc., and the 'mere proposition' that the law of love is operative in the universe is called 'agapism'. See *Collected Papers*, 6.302. It is also well to bear in mind the difference between 'tychism' and 'tychasm'. The former

is the name for Peirce's general doctrine of chance and spontaneity as part of his cosmology and metaphysics; the latter is his name for the theory of evolution by fortuitous variation represented by Darwin.

18. *Collected Papers*, 6.293; see 6.297 where Peirce claimed that one factor leading to the enthusiastic reception accorded Darwin's thought was its fitting in so well with the dominant 'greed philosophy'.

19. *Collected Papers*, 6.297.

20. *Collected Papers*, 6.289.

21. There is some room for uncertainty here; at times it seems Peirce regarded the three modes as distinct, but not absolutely distinct, ways of construing the same process as when he claimed that 'all three modes of evolution are composed of the same general elements' (*Collected Papers*, 6.303). At the same time, however, tychasm and anancasm are said to be 'degenerate cases' of agapasm, where the latter is regarded as the most adequate theory especially for understanding the development of thought. In addition to these statements, Peirce posed as 'the main question' whether 'three radically different evolutionary elements have been operative' and went on to suggest that while agapasm is the best theory, manifestations of the tychastic evolution are not wanting. Peirce, in fact, cited a quite ingenious example of tychasm involving the process by which an outlook and attitude veers around to its opposite (see *Collected Papers*, 6.311). Putting his numerous statements together, one has a right to conclude that he thought all three modes are operative, but that agapasm in some sense embraces the other modes and is not itself embraced by either of them.

22. *Collected Papers*, 6.307.

23. *Ibid.*

24. *Ibid.*

25. *Ibid.*

26. Historical studies of the world religions testify to both the pervasiveness and the temporal priority of religious communities *vis à vis* their members as individuals. The 'we' language is frequently found to be primordial and the 'I' language generally emerges from it at a comparatively late stage of development. The experience of Jeremiah in the development of Hebraic religion furnishes an excellent example. The idea that God can be related to *individuals* no longer living within the unity of sacred space represented by the community at Jerusalem was a truly revolutionary notion.

27. *Collected Papers*, 6.315.

28. See especially *Collected Papers*, 6.316, for examples.

29. *Collected Papers*, 6.307.

30. *Collected Papers*, 6.304.

31. *Ibid.*

32. Historically speaking, Peirce's account is basically sound in view of

the fact that from the biblical standpoint the world is not 'evil'. The Old Testament writers maintained that the Creator surveyed the creation and 'saw that it was good', and the Gospel writers reaffirm that view. There developed, as Peirce pointed out, a tendency to think in the opposite direction and this line of thought resulted in the belief that the 'world' must not only be abandoned but that indeed it is from this 'world' that man needs to be saved. Regardless of whether such a view represents the main drift of Christian belief – in fact it does not – what Peirce said is adequate for his example.

33. See *Collected Papers*, 7.335 where Peirce rejected the idea that external realities *cause* the convergent opinion which is the goal of inquiry.

34. *Collected Papers*, 6.494 ff (*c.* 1906).

35. *Collected Papers*, 6.495.

36. *Ibid.*

37. The problem here is, of course, well known and hovers in the background of all discussions about the existence of God. Peirce, like Tillich and others, was aware that if, as has happened in the development of modern philosophy, 'exist' is to be used primarily for objects of the order of stones and stars, the term cannot also be used in the same sense in speaking about God. The confusion becomes evident when the issue turns on 'necessary' existence where the modal concept does not at all qualify the 'existence' in question, but is regarded instead as a purely external logical determination somehow attached to the only 'existence' allowable, namely, that of stones and stars. Peirce sought to avoid this confusion by speaking of God's *reality*.

38. See *Collected Papers*, 5.448, 505 ff; 6.494.

39. *Collected Papers*, 6.496.

40. One consequence which follows from denying that we have intuitive certainty as regards the content of consciousness and our relation to it is that we cannot be *certain* concerning exactly when and what we doubt. Many will accept without question the thesis that we cannot be certain that we actually believe some proposition while at the same time supposing that, when it comes to doubting, one can be certain. Peirce rejected this claim and insisted that we believe all that we do not explicitly doubt on specific and external grounds.

41. *Collected Papers*, 6.500.

42. *Collected Papers*, 6.501.

43. *Collected Papers*, 5.536.

44. Reprinted in *Collected Papers*, 6.452 ff.

45. John E. Smith, 'Religion and Theology in Peirce', P. Wiener and F. H. Young (eds), *Studies in the Philosophy of Charles Sanders Peirce*, Cambridge, Massachusetts, 1952, pp. 251–67.

46. Confusion can be avoided if one bears in mind that in Peirce's entire discussion there are three 'arguments' for God's reality, the second of

which is *the* Neglected Argument. But, as he pointed out, he used the expression 'the N.A.' to refer to all three as a 'nest'. The third, moreover, looks more like an 'argumentation' than an 'argument'.

47. *Collected Papers*, 6.456.
48. *Collected Papers*, 6.465.
49. Not nearly enough attention has been paid to Peirce's avowed affinity with the appeal to commonsense which he recognized in Berkeley.
50. *Collected Papers*, 6.476.
51. *Collected Papers*, 6.487.
52. *Collected Papers*, 6.488.
53. *Collected Papers*, 6.490.
54. John Dewey, *A Common Faith*, New Haven, 1934. This is not to say that Dewey ignored the subject of religion in earlier writings; that would have been impossible for someone who repeatedly followed an historical pattern of thought and formulated philosophical issues against the background of the development of Western thought since its inception in Greek philosophy. Prior to the pointed analysis set forth in *A Common Faith*, however, most of what Dewey wrote about religion was highly general and very much in the Comtean vein; religion means acquiescence in the face of the ills of the environment and represents no more than a primitive and largely ineffectual means of controlling human life and destiny. Such a view, consistently developed, can only end with the conclusion that science is the successor of religion and religion becomes a relic of the past. *A Common Faith* shows that this was by no means Dewey's final view of the matter and, in fact, the publication of that book set off rounds of discussion wherein his naturalistic cohorts expressed great anxiety over the possibility that Dewey had joined the ranks of the theists! See E. E. Aubrey, H. N. Wieman and John Dewey, 'Is John Dewey a Theist?', *The Christian Century*, vol. 51 (1934), pp. 1550–3. Cf. *The Christian Century*, vol. 50 (1933), pp. 193–6, 299–302.
55. Santayana, for one, forced the issue with his claim that such naturalism should be called by its proper name, 'materialism', and be made either to bear the onus of that position or be branded as 'half-hearted'. This demand is unfair to Dewey, since he was under no obligation to identify nature with some one stuff – 'matter.' On the other hand, Dewey was not without responsibility for making a similar all-or-nothing demand of traditional religion when he identified it with a simple 'supernaturalism' and took no notice whatever of more sophisticated attempts to deal with the religious problem of transcendence.
56. *A Common Faith*, p. 9.
57. *A Common Faith*, p. 10.
58. The entire subject is filled with confusion. The concept of religious experience is a legacy from James who illustrated it with more success than he analysed its meaning. The first problem is that the concept

means little apart from a theory of the general shape of experience, and, given that, the next question concerns what there is in or about experience which answers to the 'religious'. The answer to that question calls for another theory. Everything depends on whether it is thought that all experience is 'of' something (i.e. that the one who has the experience encounters another of some sort) and whether it is legitimate to characterize an experience as having 'moral', 'aesthetic' or 'religious' import solely on the basis of the presumed nature of what is encountered. In short, are these characteristics a function of *content* or are they to be taken exclusively as defining *contexts?* A different approach to the problem would involve not concentrating on the 'object' involved, but rather on the attitudes, interests and concerns of the person who experiences so that one comes to speak of qualities, aspects or dimensions of experience which are distinguished on the basis of the different attitudes, interests, etc., involved. In the first case 'religious experience' would imply experience of a religious 'object', whereas in the second it would not; reference would be made instead to the religious 'quality' of an experience. It might appear that one has simply to choose between these two approaches but, unfortunately, the problem is not so easily resolved because an adequate account of experience requires both. Experiencing embraces *both* content *and* qualities or modes as can readily be seen from the fact that the same tree, for example, can be experienced as a botanical specimen, an estimated number of board feet of lumber, a wondrous creation, a lonely sentinel guarding the graves of those who gave their lives in a great cause, etc. Both James and Dewey were well aware of this double-barrelled character of experience, and both insisted on its importance. The problem, however, is to say precisely how the two features are related in the religious situation. As regards content, it is clearly difficult to find a consensus of experience that would support belief in the presence of an identifiable religious 'object', and consequently the tendency has been to follow the path chosen by Dewey which is to abandon search for a content in this sense and locate the religious in a quality of experience. On the other hand, unless the reality of God is either ruled out at the outset or the term is redefined to denote some fact among other facts in familiar experience, the problem of determining the content cannot be avoided since, if God's reality is to be more than a mere idea, that reality must be ingredient at some point in experience.

59. *A Common Faith,* p. 13.
60. *A Common Faith,* p. 27.
61. I find myself at variance with some, but not all, of Dewey's views here, but for the reason indicated above, I shall not join issue with him; I shall attempt instead to set forth his position as objectively as possible. My principal doubts concern his over-simplification of some complex

issues, and his tendency towards a scientism of *method* which alolws him too much freedom from responsibility for the *conclusions* of science and their philosophical implications.

62. *A Common Faith,* p. 31.
63. *A Common Faith,* p. 33. Dewey seems not to have noticed that this characterization of faith also has affinities with a 'two-territory' approach in that the 'unification' in question is a wholly *practical* affair, while *knowing* is reserved for science alone.
64. When, for example, Dewey attacked the 'given' and 'brute facts' in his *Logic: The Theory of Inquiry* (New York, 1938), no such sharp dichotomy between fact and theory is allowed.
65. *A Common Faith,* p. 37 (italics added).
66. *A Common Faith,* p. 14.
67. *A Common Faith,* p. 42.
68. That Dewey was somewhat too optimistic on this head can be seen by making a sober appraisal of his own faith as expressed in the following sentence: 'The validity of justice, affection, and that intellectual correspondence of our ideas with realities that we call truth, is so assured in its hold upon humanity that it is unnecesary for the religious attitude to encumber itself with the apparatus of dogma and doctrine.' *A Common Faith,* p. 44.
69. *A Common Faith,* p. 51.
70. Dewey is more interested here in the social impact of this difference than in explaining how it came to be. The main point is that under the influence of confessional Protestantism, it was no longer thought sufficient to be 'born into' the church; instead, upon coming of age, a 'decision' to join the church was called for and this decision signalized the individual's confession of faith and desire to accept the responsibilities of church membership.
71. *A Common Faith,* p. 65.
72. *A Common Faith,* p. 71.
73. *A Common Faith,* p. 84.

Index